THE COURSE
OF CHRISTIAN HISTORY

THE MACMILLAN COMPANY
NEW YORK · BOSTON · CHICAGO · DALLAS
ATLANTA · SAN FRANCISCO

MACMILLAN & CO., Limited
LONDON · BOMBAY · CALCUTTA
MELBOURNE

THE MACMILLAN CO. OF CANADA, Ltd.
TORONTO

THE COURSE
OF CHRISTIAN HISTORY

BY

W. J. McGLOTHLIN, Ph.D., D.D.

Professor of Church History in the Southern
Baptist Theological Seminary

New York
THE MACMILLAN COMPANY
1918

PREFACE

Christianity is now nearly nineteen centuries old. During this long period it has steadily increased in power, determining the beliefs and hopes and ideals of individuals and more and more of whole nations. Judged from any standpoint it must be recognized as one of the master forces of mediæval and modern history and of the present day. Intelligent men ought, it would seem, to be acquainted with the course of its history, at least in outline, through these centuries.

And yet this history has been comparatively little studied, and when studied emphasis has been laid upon the darker phases of the history, its polemical and political sides. It would seem that the time has come for an effort to secure a wider and more sympathetic knowledge of what Christianity as a whole has done in the midst of the weakness and wickedness of mankind. In a Christian land should not Christian history be regularly and sympathetically taught in all institutions of higher learning? Should not laymen as well as ministers be acquainted in some degree at least with the history of the mightiest single force operative in the life of our day and nation? As the study of history, turning away from the exclusive consideration of politics and government, penetrates more and more into the social and moral life of the people whence the great national characteristics and motives spring, Christianity must become a subject of more intense and sympathetic study.

It is the hope of the author that this little volume may contribute something in this direction. Church history has not been written for college students. It will be years before the many excellent college text-books on general history can be paralleled by similar ones on church history. But this work is intended primarily for college students. The effort has been made to keep to the main important phases of Christian history, showing the course of development, the effects upon social life, etc. The continuity of Christian history has been constantly in mind. At the end of the volume will be found a brief bibliography, followed by *questions* on the text and *topics* for further study. It is hoped that these will be suggestive and helpful to students and instructors in the course of their work.

While the volume has been prepared primarily with the needs of students in mind it is also hoped that it will be used in adult Bible classes, mission study classes, and by individual men and women who desire some better knowledge of the history of their religion. For this reason the text has been kept free from interruptions by notes of any kind, all such matter being relegated to the end of the book. If the volume contributes in any measure to the popularizing of Christian history as a source of religious inspiration and cultural impulse the author will be satisfied.

W. J. M.

Louisville, June, 1918.

TABLE OF CONTENTS

THE COURSE OF CHRISTIAN HISTORY

INTRODUCTION

§ 1

THE PROPER CONCEPTION OF CHRISTIAN HISTORY

THE history of Christianity is the story of the origin, progress and development of the Christian religion, and of its influence upon the world. Almost nineteen centuries have passed since Jesus Christ began his public ministry for the establishment of the religion which bears his name. During this long period Christianity has been more and more dominating the lives of men, illuminating their minds, strengthening them in their moral struggles, irradiating their hopes, making earth more tolerable and heaven more inviting and certain. The story of this growing and spreading influence is the external history of Christianity.

But as Christianity has expanded there has come constant inner change. From the unity and simplicity of original Christianity have developed the multiplicity of Christian sects with their varied forms of organization and worship, their divergent views of theology and the ordinances, their various types of Christian thought and life, as we see them to-day. The story of these changes is the inner history of Christianity.

There has been no break in this history. The stream has broadened and often grown muddy, but it has never ceased to flow. To-day it is the mightiest force operative in the human race. In its singular growth and life-giving power it has been like the stream in Ezekiel's vision (Ch. 47) or like the stone cut out without hands in the vision of Daniel (2: 31–5). It has ever flowed on and brought blessing, ever increased in might, until to-day it is mightier than all kingdoms.

§ 2

THE WORLD INTO WHICH JESUS CAME

When Jesus came into it the world was already old. Around the Mediterranean Sea civilizations had risen, flourished, decayed and fallen. Egypt, Babylonia, Assyria and Persia had played their parts on the world's stage and passed on. Greece and Rome were the great world powers at the beginning of our religion. All the civilized peoples of southern Europe, western Asia and northern Africa were under the political sway of Rome who was then the mistress of the western half of the civilized world. Outside the Roman empire there were various barbarous and savage peoples who were to play a large part in the future history of civilization, but who at that time were negligible. India, China and Japan, lying far to the east, and little known in the West, constituted the eastern half of the civilized world.

Christianity was born near the heart of the ROMAN EMPIRE and remained within its boundaries for some five centuries. This empire contained from fifty to seventy-five millions of people of various nationalities, speaking different languages and possessing unequal degrees of culture. The ruling race was the Roman. Their home was in Italy, but they had conquered all the lands around the Mediterranean Sea and throughout the whole of this vast territory they were the civil and military officials. Their language, the Latin, was the language of Italy, north Africa, Spain and Gaul. They established peace and order throughout the empire, built good roads, fostered trade and travel, made intercourse easy and safe, often protected the missionaries from the fury of mobs. Beyond doubt the empire was a providential preparation for the spread of the gospel in the early centuries; Latins furnished the missionaries who carried the gospel to the western half of the empire, the Latin language became the vehicle of theology and worship for this half of the world and ultimately for the whole Roman Catholic church; the empire furnished the molds into which Christianity was poured to form the Roman Catholic church which in its government is but a reproduction of the imperial government.

THE GREEKS had their home in Greece and the Islands of the Ægean Sea, but they had spread through trade, conquest and colonization over Asia Minor, Syria, northern Palestine, lower Egypt, southern Italy, Sicily and some were found in southern Gaul. They were the most cultivated people of the time. Their beautiful and flexible language, rich in literature and the power of expression, was so widely distributed as to form a sort of universal language in the eastern part of the empire. Apparently all the apostles and early missionaries spoke this language and the New Testament was written in Greek. For two and a half centuries all the important Christian literature was produced in this language. The earliest Christian scholars and schools were Greek and the Greek genius gave tone to Christianity in the East for many centuries. Early theology was all written in Greek.

THE JEWS were the third important race of the Roman empire. They had their home in Palestine, but had been dispersed through trade and captivity until they constituted an important element in all the principal cities of the empire. They were preëminently a city folk, devoted to trade and banking. They lived apart from Gentile society, feared and despised by their neighbors, haughtily preserving their social and religious exclusiveness. The synagogue was the center of worship and instruction, where the Old Testament Scriptures were read every Sabbath and a pure religious and moral life was set forth and emphasized. Living among

polytheists and idolaters they held forth a pure monotheism
— belief in a righteous and almighty God who made and
rules the world and demands hcliness in men.   The majority
of them expected a Messiah who would reign at Jerusalem
and would usher in the Messianic age of peace and happiness, power and glory, for the Jewish people.   Many of the
heathen had been deeply affected by their synagogue worship and some had become converts to the Jewish religion.
They were known as " proselytes " or " devout men " and
furnished many converts to early Christianity.   Paul and
probably other missionaries first went to the synagogue on
beginning work in a new city, and turned to the Gentiles
only when hostility developed so as to make further work
among the Jews difficult or impossible.

§ 3

ECONOMIC AND CULTURAL CONDITIONS

The masses of the people throughout the empire were
distressingly poor ; beggars were everywhere.   On the other
hand, many of the Romans were enormously wealthy, made
so by conquest, graft and extortion.   Slaves were very numerous, constituting the chief element of productive labor
among the Romans.   They were white captives, taken in
war, and their descendants, and were often highly cultivated
people.   Not infrequently they were used as tutors and
teachers by their masters.   This slave population furnished
a large element of the early Christians, not seldom officers
of the church.

The golden age of *Greek literature* was past.   Homer,
Sophocles, Euripides, Plato, Aristotle, Demosthenes were
long since dead.   Their works were eagerly studied, but no
other writers of equal ability appeared.   *The Jews* produced but one or two writers of any note after the birth of
Christ.   *The Latins,* on the other hand, were still in their
productive period.   Cæsar, Cicero and Virgil had been dead

but a few years and important writers of the Latin language were yet to arise.

While there were many men of broad culture the masses of the people were generally illiterate. Books were few and costly. There was no system of public schools; private teachers and tutors furnished all the instruction that was offered. There were a few great libraries as at Alexandria and some institutions that might justly be called universities as at Athens, Tarsus and Alexandria. The Greeks were the great schoolmasters of the world. The Jews instructed their children at home and in the synagogue in the Old Testament Scriptures and in some trade. The courses of study offered in the heathen schools affected them very little if at all.

§ 4

MORAL AND RELIGIOUS CONDITIONS

Morals were bad enough. Poverty and war, political graft and the abuse of power, slavery, ignorance, bad housing, a hot climate, debasing amusements and other things combined to weaken the moral sensibilities that men ordinarily have. Vice, drunkenness, gambling, dishonesty, robbery and cruelty were frightfully prevalent. Abortion and the exposure or murder of unwelcome children were so common as to cause little comment. The theater, the gladiatorial shows and the races were as demoralizing as amusements can well be. The marriage vow was lightly regarded and divorce was frequent.

Every people, tribe and city had its religion, but there was little moral tonic in any of them. Moral and religious ideas were in utter confusion and the hope of immortality was exceedingly vague and the future unattractive. There were lords many and gods many, male and female divinities, great gods of the nation and little gods for the household and the common affairs of daily life. The worshipers erected magnificent temples, chiseled beautiful and impressive images, supported numerous priesthoods, observed with painful care the ornate ritual and impressive ceremonies of public worship, pried into the future through divination and soothsaying, offered multitudes of sacrifices to appease the gods whose help they implored in all the affairs of life, both public and private. Religion entered into every detail of life; but the gods were themselves believed to be immoral and religion made slight demands upon the ethical sense of the people. There was little social worship or religious instruction except by a few wandering philosophers, no sacred books as among the Jews and other Oriental peoples, no inculcation of the lessons of love and right living with which we are so familiar in Christianity. The gods were feared rather than loved and hostile and dangerous spirits were felt to be everywhere; the world was thought to be full of demons. The Jews of course held aloof from all this pagan religion and in general lived on a higher moral plane than their heathen neighbors whom they usually heartily despised.

§ 5

PHILOSOPHY

Philosophy was the religion of the more cultivated heathen of that day. Very many of them had lost all belief in the popular religions with their superstitions, absurd myths and low moral ideals. They found a higher faith and a stronger support for the moral life in the speculations of philosophy. One of the early Christian fathers declared that philosophy was a schoolmaster to bring the Greek to Christ even as the law brought the Jew. All forms of philosophy rejected more or less openly the trivialities and puerilities of the popular faiths, and sought to find a higher view of God and the universe. Plato probably gave the world the most spiritual and satisfying view of the universe that the human mind, unaided by divine revelation, ever attained. Some of his arguments for immortality are still advanced by the Christian thinkers of the present time.

But philosophy was for the gifted and cultured; the common man saw only that it destroyed his faith without giving him anything in return. Its intellectualism was beyond him. And so the masses were growing skeptical and more immoral. The world was religiously and morally bankrupt, the deity himself must intervene. The fullness of the times had come.

FIRST PERIOD — 1 TO 100 A.D.

THE PLANTING OF CHRISTIANITY

§6

THE CHARACTER OF THIS CENTURY

THE political and social life of the first century of the
Christian era was fairly stable. The Roman republic was
rapidly transformed into an empire with the emperor
supreme in power and deified after death, but this change
did not greatly affect the condition of the people. Several
of the emperors were monsters of wickedness, notably
Nero under whose reign Paul did most of his work and
at whose hands he suffered death. There was comparatively little war in this century. The rebellion of the
Jews in A. D. 70 brought upon them a terrible punishment.
Jerusalem was burned and the temple was finally destroyed
never to be rebuilt. Those who survived were banished
from the country. This brought to an end all semblance
of Jewish national life which has never been reëstablished.
Since that date the Jew has been a " man without a country." Rome was burned in A. D. 64 and splendidly rebuilt by
Nero. Responsibility for the great catastrophe was laid
by him at the door of the Christians of Rome upon whom he
inflicted terrible persecutions. But on the whole the century was not unfavorable for the prosecution of successful Christian work.

§7

CHRISTIANITY PLANTED

It was into this wonderful world that the new leaven of
Christianity was thrust. What was it? As a historic

force it was a new religion brought to the world by a Jew, Jesus of Nazareth. He was of lowly origin, a carpenter by trade till he was about thirty years of age, a countryman of the hills of Galilee, and the beginnings of his movement were among the working people of that region.

He was preceded by a young man of the hill country of Judea, a strange character who had spent many years away from the haunts of men in the desert of Judea. About the year twenty-six this forerunner appeared on the borders of civilization and began to preach what was virtually a new religion. Though he was a priest by birth he ignored the temple and the national ceremonial religion of his people altogether, and began to proclaim repentance by the individual as the basis of acceptance with God. Descent from Abraham, that is Jewish blood, was altogether insufficient. The kingdom of God was at hand and men must repent in order to enter in, and repentance must bring forth fruit in holy living.

Still further he declared that the Messiah, long expected, was about to appear with his fan in his hand to cleanse his threshing floor, gathering the wheat into his garner and burning up the chaff with unquenchable fire. He baptized in the Jordan and declared that the Messiah would baptize in the Holy Spirit and in fire. Finally he baptized Jesus and forty days afterwards declared to his own disciples that this Jesus was the Messiah, " the lamb of God that taketh away the sin of the world." Soon afterwards he was thrown into prison for criticizing the marriage of the governor and after a few months imprisonment he was beheaded.

John's views were not new. They are found in the spiritual teachings of the Old Testament, especially in the prophets and the Psalms. But they were new in their negation of the racial and ceremonial basis of religion, and in their emphasis upon the inner preparation of the heart. To him religion was personal and spiritual. He used as his only ceremony baptism which at the command of God he had either adopted from the Jews or instituted anew. The basis of his baptism was not racial descent from Abraham, as was the case with circumcision, but repentance toward God attested by righteous living.

Jesus allied himself with John and his movement by requesting and accepting baptism at his hands. He was then about thirty years of age, having spent these years in the quiet life of the village of Nazareth whose reputation was apparently none too good. Jesus linked his work directly on to that of John by taking up identically the same message, that is a call to repentance on the basis of the nearness of the kingdom. His early message, " Repent ye, for the kingdom of heaven is at hand," sounds like an echo of John's cry in the wilderness. He came because of the world's sin, to seek and to save the lost, to revolutionize and remake the world. He came as a Jew among the Jews, confining his earthly ministry to " the lost sheep of the house of Israel." He assumed the divine origin and truth of the spiritual teachings of the Old Testament, building upon the foundation of Moses and the prophets. He said nothing directly for or against the ceremonial law, but actually gave expression to principles that must in the course of time nullify it. During the three years of his public activities he lived a spotless and winsome life among men, calling them to repentance and higher living, inculcating faith in God and in himself, helping men in every possible way. He taught as one having authority, enlarging and spiritualizing men's conception of God and his worship, elevating and sanctifying all human relations; he wrought miracles, denounced the self-righteous Pharisees, but showed pity and compassion to the penitent outcasts of society. He taught much concerning himself, declaring that he was the son of God, the son of man, the Messiah, the fulfillment of prophecy; he foretold his death and the manner of it, foretold his resurrection and ascension and declared that he would come again to judge the living and the dead. His goal was the kingdom of God as a living reality among men.

Opposition to him began early and increased in bitterness till at last it brought him to death on a Roman cross. The third day the sealed and guarded tomb was found empty. During the next forty days those who had known him best in life became convinced that he had risen from the dead with a new and wonderful body; they saw him repeatedly, heard him teach, examined his wounds, saw him appear and disappear. Above five hundred brethren had seen him at one time; there could be no doubt as to his identity. And yet how greatly he was changed! At last they saw him rise from the earth and disappear in the heavens. So ended his earthly career. He had confined his ministry to the Jews, to the northern part of the little country of Palestine, to the comparatively poor and uneducated; he had written nothing nor commanded any one else to write; he had erected no buildings or schools, enlisted no wealth or worldly influence. He had merely created a new life in a few ordinary human beings and had commanded them to go and make the rest of the world into disciples like themselves, promising at the same time to be with them all the days. "All authority hath been given unto me in heaven and on earth. Go ye therefore, and make disciples of all the nations."

§ 8

CHRISTIANITY AS A HISTORIC FORCE

What then was this new and mighty force now let loose in the world? In a word it was a new type of life, based upon a new faith and inspired by a new hope, all mediated to the world by Jesus of Nazareth. It is not meant that all the elements of Christianity were entirely new to the world. Perhaps none of them were absolutely new, for the world had long been feeling after God and he had wonderfully revealed himself to the law-givers and prophets and psalmists of old. But the grand total was new. Jesus Christ "brought life and immortality to light through the gospel," that is he illuminated them and made them definite, clear and attractive.

Christianity as a force was primarily a new type of life — a life of holiness, love and service. Its first demand was personal holiness and right relations with one's fellows; this holiness was irradiated with love to God and to men and the love expressed itself by bountiful service to all men. All men were recognized as the handiwork of the same loving Creator and hence as essentially brothers, whatever their race, color or present condition. Christians constituted a great fraternal body bound together by a like-mindedness in spiritual things. So distinctly did the Christians manifest a new type of life that they were often called "the third race."

This new type of life was based upon a fuller and clearer faith in God, in his love toward all men, than the world had ever before possessed. It was also illuminated by a clearer and more rational and attractive hope of immortality than they had ever before had. For the first time heaven and the future world became really luminous and alluring. All of life was glorified and made bearable by this hope.

But possibly the most distinctive thing about Christianity was the fact that all these spiritual riches in their fullness and relations were mediated to men by Jesus Christ. It was this that made it *Christianity*. It was Jesus that set these truths forth and gave to men the power, first to accept them as the ideal of life and then in some measure to attain to their ideal. And on down to the present the world is dependent on him for these views and hopes. They do not exist where he is not known. What we are spiritually we owe to him.

§9

SPREAD OF CHRISTIANITY — MISSIONS

Jesus had confined his ministry with slight exceptions to the Jews of northern Palestine. But he had spent much of the latter part of his life in training a few men to carry forward the work when he was gone. His very last injunction was that they should wait in Jerusalem till they were endued with sufficient power by the Holy Spirit and should then go forth to make disciples of the whole world. Ten days after his ascension the power came on the group at Jerusalem by such unmistakable signs as to eliminate all doubt that Jesus was at the right hand of the Father. Three thousand were added that day. Following this great initial impulse their numbers increased rapidly and soon there were five thousand *men* in the Jerusalem church, and doubtless many women (Acts 4:4). Soon afterwards we learn that "a great company of the priests were obedient to the faith" (Acts 6:7). Persecution broke out but did not retard the growth seriously for some time. Finally the zeal and ability of Stephen, a Grecian Jew who was one of seven men chosen by the church to superintend the distribution of its alms, provoked a general and very bitter persecution. Stephen and possibly others lost their lives, and the church was scattered. The vigor of this persecution was probably due to an aristocratic young Pharisee of Tarsus named Saul. He was born a Roman citizen and was educated at the feet of Gamaliel in Jerusalem. This young man was "exceedingly mad" against them and "made havoc" of the church.

The hour had now come when the Christians, who were still tarrying in Jerusalem, were compelled to set forth into the world. Philip went down to Samaria where he was marvelously successful in this first attempt to preach the gospel beyond the Jewish fold. It aroused so much apprehension at Jerusalem that Peter and John were sent down to investigate (Acts 8:4–24). They approved the work and what was more important they themselves "preached the gospel to many of the villages of the Samaritans."

Shortly afterwards Peter, who had at last gotten out into the country as far as Joppa, was led by the invitation of a centurion, supported by a vision vouchsafed to himself, to preach the gospel to some Roman officers and soldiers at Cæsarea the civil and military capital of the country. To the amazement of himself and the Christian brethren who were with him the Holy Spirit fell on these Gentiles, and they spake with tongues as the Jewish Christians had done at Pentecost. This manifestation of divine approval led Peter to propose baptism for them and as nobody had the courage to object he instructed them to be baptized (Acts Ch. 10). It was a clear case of divine leading, but it occasioned acute concern at Jerusalem. When Peter returned they "contended with him saying, Thou wentest in to men uncircumcised and didst eat with them"; but when Peter explained all the circumstances they "held their peace, and glorified God, saying, Then to the Gentiles also hath God granted repentance unto life" (Acts 11:1–18). Here for the first time the gospel was preached to out and out Gentiles (Samaritans were half Jews), a proceeding which had only the reluctant approval of the Jerusalem church. This experience, clearly providential as it was, led to no effort at regular work among the Gentiles.

Sometime after this incident a more consistent attempt was made towards the evangelization of the Gentiles, this time among the Greeks. Some of those who were driven away from Jerusalem by the persecution that arose at the death of Stephen were natives of Cyprus and Cyrene. Having lived among Gentiles they probably had less prejudice than those who lived at Jerusalem. At any rate when they arrived at Antioch in their flight they began to preach to the Greeks; these responded readily, so that "a great number that believed turned unto the Lord." This was evidently a sustained and consistent effort to bring Greeks to a saving knowledge of the gospel. Again it created anxiety in Jerusalem and Barnabas was sent forth to investigate; "who when he was come, and had seen the grace of God, was glad; and he exhorted them all, that with purpose of heart they would cleave unto the Lord." He threw himself into the effort, apparently without even returning to Jerusalem to report, and soon a great work was in progress (Acts 11 : 19–24).

§ 10

SAUL'S CONVERSION AND WORK

In the meantime the persecutor Saul had himself been wonderfully converted and had at once given himself to preaching, first at Damascus, then in Arabia, at Damascus again, then in Jerusalem. On account of dangerous opposition at this point he had been sent back to Tarsus his old home where he disappeared from view for some years, but doubtless he was actively engaged in evangelizing.

Barnabas, finding the work at Antioch too heavy for him, goes over to Tarsus and fetches Saul. For a year they wrought together in the great Syrian metropolis, making such a profound impression that the disciples now began to be called Christians. They also manifested that broad spirit of helpfulness that has so graciously marked the course of Christian history, by sending a contribution to the suffering saints at Jerusalem, the first instance of such Christian charity.

Up to this time the spread of Christianity had not been planned by the disciples, as far as we can see, but had been forced upon them by leadings of Providence. We have now reached the point where there seems to be definite planning of the work. While the leaders of the church at Antioch "ministered to the Lord and fasted," probably seeking divine direction in the prosecution of the work, "the Holy Spirit said, Separate me Barnabas and Saul for the work whereunto I have called them" (Acts 13 : 2). It is

probable that Saul was the moving spirit in this new ad-
venture. In obedience to this divine call the two set forth
on the first missionary journey, probably guided in the
choice of direction by the location of the homes and ac-
quaintances of the two missionaries themselves, Barnabas
being from the island of Cyprus and Saul from Tarsus
with a possible acquaintance with the towns of Derbe,
Lystra and Iconium. The experiences of the journey are
related in such detail in Acts 13 and 14 that they need not
be repeated here. Both Jews and Greeks were converted
in large numbers, but the Jewish authorities were quick and
determined in their opposition. At Antioch in Pisidia the
missionaries turned definitely to the Gentiles. Jews and
Gentiles were treated alike in the ordinances and organization of the churches. Elders were appointed for every
church, so as to conserve the work and lay a foundation for
its further spread.

Paul made two other long missionary journeys through
Asia Minor and into southeastern Europe traversing
Macedonia and Greece as far south as Athens and Corinth
and probably reaching the shores of the Adriatic. At the
end of the third journey he was mobbed at Jerusalem where
he had gone with a large collection which he had gathered
for the poor from the churches of Asia Minor and Greece
(Acts 16:1 to 21:30). He was rescued by the Romans
from the fury of the Jews who would have murdered him,
but was held prisoner at Cæsarea by the venal governor
Felix. On the accession of a new governor Festus the
Jews renewed their efforts to get their hands on Paul who
saved himself by appealing to Rome to be tried before the
emperor. At Rome he was held prisoner at least two years
longer, but had considerable freedom and was able to do
much preaching. After this he seems to have been released,
to have returned to the East, to have been rearrested, and
finally executed near Rome where a great church bearing his
name stands over the spot which is supposed to be his grave.

About the work of the twelve apostles other than Peter,

we know almost nothing. Later tradition has undertaken to fill out our knowledge by assigning extensive mission work to most of them.   These traditions are utterly worthless as history though there may be some grains of truth in some of them.   Peter is said to have made his way to the West and to have been executed by crucifixion with his head downward at Rome where the greatest church building in the world is named for him.   John is said to have lived almost to the end of the first century and to have died finally at Ephesus.

What is certain is that by the end of the first century Christianity was firmly established in most if not all the great cities of the empire, that it had spread into many of the smaller towns and even into the country districts.   In some sections Christians constituted a large and influential element in society.

§ II

THE CHURCHES

Organization is necessary to success in any great task and so we very early find the Christians organized into bodies which they called *ecclesiae,* a word which is translated into English by the word *churches.*   The basis of organization was fraternal equality.   " Call no man your father, for one is your Master and all ye are brethren."   This is fundamental democracy, and these early churches were undoubtedly democracies in principle and as far as possible in practice.   Paul *appointed* elders for the churches, but it must have been in consultation with the brethren in whose hands the ultimate authority rested.   The churches were bodies of regenerated people, brought together by spiritual likemindedness, for the fulfillment of the purposes of the kingdom of God.   All the Christians of a city constituted the church of that city, as the church at Jerusalem, Ephesus or Corinth, and must have had several places of worship and often thousands of members.

Apparently all the churches had two classes of officers: *Elders* (also called *bishops* or *ministers* or *pastors*) and *deacons.* These officers attended to all the affairs of the church, not to the exclusion of the laity nor in the way of lording it over the church, but as brethren chosen by their equals to perform certain duties on behalf of the church. They had no priestly functions and were answerable to the congregation. *Apostles, prophets* and *evangelists* apparently exercised their functions by direct divine appointment and were not answerable to the churches or sent forth by them. They seem to have traveled most of the time.

The worship was very simple and democratic. There was singing and prayer, reading from the Old Testament and the books of the New as they appeared, with exhortation. The formal sermon did not appear till later. These services were much like our modern prayer-meetings with some enthusiasm injected into them. The services often if not usually took place at night, on the first day of the week called the " Lord's day " because of the resurrection and appearances of our Lord on that day. Some of the Jewish Christians continued to worship on the seventh day or Jewish sabbath.

The Lord's supper was celebrated with bread and wine as the memorial of the Lord's death. At Corinth and possibly elsewhere there was a meal in connection with the supper. Baptism was administered to believers only, by immersion in water, in the name of Jesus or the Trinity. It was a pictorial confession of faith, setting forth the essentials of Christian belief, symbolizing the burial and resurrection of Christ, the great spiritual change of death to the old life and resurrection to a new life in the individual, and doubtless looked forward to the resurrection of our own bodies. There is no evidence that anybody was admitted to fellowship in the churches without first accepting baptism as a bond of fellowship and a badge of unity.

§ 12

DIFFICULTIES AND DANGERS

The first great danger arose over the relation of the Gentile Christians to the Jewish system. The Jewish Christians naturally regarded Christianity as the continuation of the Jewish religion. Jesus had never formally abolished the law, and they naturally regarded its observance as still binding. They accepted Jesus as the Messiah and believed that Jews were to be saved by the law plus Jesus while Gentiles were to be saved by Jesus plus the law. The work of Barnabas and Paul on their first missionary journey had raised the question in an acute form. They had baptized Gentiles and received them into Christian fellowship without requiring circumcision or the observance of any other part of the Jewish law. This proceeding was unsatisfactory to many of the Jewish Christians. Some of them came down to Antioch and insisted that the missionaries had preached a defective gospel, " saying, Except ye be circumcised after the custom of Moses, ye cannot be saved." After much futile discussion at Antioch it was decided to carry the question to Jerusalem. Paul and Barnabas with others were sent down to consider the matter with the Apostles and brethren. After mature deliberation it was decided that the Jewish system was not to be imposed upon the Gentiles, that salvation was by faith alone. Neither circumcision nor the distinction in foods nor the sacred seasons (Sabbath, new moon, annual festivals) nor the sacrifices were incumbent on the Gentile Christians. This conclusion was fully approved by James and the other leaders at Jerusalem, but did not command the assent of all Jewish Christians; much of Paul's later life was spent in the struggle with these " Judaizers." The effort to " Judaize " Christianity failed in this form, but the same tendency to add to grace some kind of works as necessary to salvation continued and ultimately produced the Catholic church

in the course of the following centuries. Paul with his
great doctrine of justification by faith actually went down
in defeat in the Christian body as a whole, and to this day
a comparatively small minority of the nominal Christians
of the world are faithful to the gospel of the grace of God
as he set it forth in his letters to the Galatians and Romans.

There were other serious doctrinal dangers among the
churches of the first century. The divinity of Christ, the
humanity of Christ, the resurrection of the body, were denied; apparently the worship of angels had begun and various philosophical and theosophical speculations were detract-
ing from the dignity and glory of Christ. Theology as well
as church order was in its formative period, the new
Christian ferment was working. These heretics were few.

But there was a well defined body of truths which were
held and propagated by the great mass of Christians.
Some of these were the unity, holiness and love of God
the Father, the creator, sustainer and ruler of all things;
Jesus Christ as his only begotten son, the only Savior and
Lord of men, who suffered, died and rose again, and ascended on high whence he will come again to judge the living and the dead at the last day; the immortality of the
soul, the eternal sufferings of the wicked and the everlasting
bliss of the righteous. These were not yet wrought into a
system but they were the great facts out of which later
systems of theology were built.

§ 13

CHRISTIAN LIFE

The *Christians* (usually called *disciples* and *brothers*),
came chiefly from the plain working people who were the
more accessible element of society. There were, however,
some from the higher social and political classes. In Cyprus a governor had been converted, in Rome members of
" Cæsar's household " were Christians, at various places

men and women " of honorable estate " had given in their adhesion to the gospel. " Not many rich, not many mighty, but some," would describe the social standing of the Christians of the first century.

Racially they were chiefly Jews and Greeks, but many other nationalities were represented. Greek was the prevalent language of worship and Christian correspondence, but Aramaic, Syriac and some other dialects were also used.

Christian life was by no means ideal. Coming from the less cultured classes of heathen society, as the great majority did, it was not to be expected perhaps that Christians would escape entirely and at once from the pollutions of their earlier heathen life. The churches were afflicted with faction, strife, schism, racial antagonisms, drunkenness, unchastity, pride, vanity; on the other hand they manifested many beautiful traits of character such as charity, love and service, in sharp contrast with the heathen about them. Gross sins were punished by exclusion from Christian communion and ostracism from Christian society. Heroic efforts were made to maintain honesty and chastity.

In the midst of persecution the Christians showed a calm and confident fortitude that made them unconquerable. Some fell away and caused the churches much sorrow and trouble, but many suffered fines, imprisonment, banishment and mutilation while not a few perished at the stake.

There was nothing like monasticism in this early Christianity nor even asceticism. They abstained largely from eating meats offered to idols and from all employments and amusements that gave any sanction to idolatry. They avoided as far as possible the entanglements of public office, both military and civil. They were a quiet, peaceable folk, zealous to do good works and live a quiet and peaceable life.

SECOND PERIOD — 100 TO 323 A.D.

CONVERSION OF THE EMPIRE AND RISE OF THE CATHOLIC CHURCH

§ 14

CONDITIONS FOR WORK

CONDITIONS in this period were not unfavorable for the advancement of Christianity. It was still confined to the bounds of the empire, scarcely going outside at any point. Life in the empire was fairly safe and stable. Rome's chief enemies on her borders were the barbarous German tribes on her northern frontier and the Parthians and the newly established Persian empire on the east. Her wealth and ordered life were a constant attraction to these marauders, but by hard fighting she was able to hold them at bay. At points she materially extended her territory. She was able to incorporate a considerable area on the north side of the lower Danube. This region, then called Dacia but now known as Roumania, still shows in its language the effects of this Latin occupation, the Roumanian language being a modification of the Latin. The emperor who succeeded in this task was Trajan who celebrated his great victory by a column which is still standing in Rome. He also was victorious in a war with the Parthians and for a time Armenia, Mesopotamia and Assyria were incorporated into the empire.

During most of the third century the empire was afflicted with serious internal disorders. The emperors were made and murdered by the various divisions of the army almost at will. Taking advantage of this internal weakness the various German tribes pressed into the empire again, invading and wasting such provinces as Gaul, Spain, Northern Italy, the Balkan region and Asia Minor. About 270 A. D. the empire appeared to be on the eve of dissolution. Fortunately some very able men appeared as emperors and succeeded in expelling these foreign enemies and restoring internal order. The most important of these were Aurelian, the "Restorer of the Empire," Diocletian who transformed it into an absolute monarchy, and Constantine the Great.

The earlier part of this period was one of material prosperity. Trajan and Hadrian were great builders and some of the most magnificent remains of Roman architecture still extant date from their reigns. Roman citizenship was granted to all free men in the provinces in 212 and the capital was moved from Rome by Diocletian never to return. Increasing poverty and a decreasing birth rate told the story of decay which in the next period would bring down the empire in ruins.

§ 15

EDUCATIONAL AND RELIGIOUS CONDITIONS

During most of this period education was more generally diffused than ever before. The provinces were largely Latinized and Roman education was extended to them, largely supported by the state. North Africa and Spain were producing much of the Latin literature of the time.

The old disposition to skepticism was passing away, the grosser elements of idolatry were being eliminated and emperor worship was made obligatory, becoming a sort of test of political loyalty. The old religion of the Romans was being supplanted by warmer cults from the East, such as the worship of Mithra, a god of Persian origin particularly popular with the soldiers, Cybele the Great Mother from Phrygia, and Isis from Egypt. A wide spread disposition to mix all the religions was manifest. The age was growing more religious, more superstitious, and seemed to be ready to accept any religion that might come.

§ 16

CHRISTIAN MISSIONS

As would be expected under these conditions Christianity made great progress in this period. There were no boards to support the missionaries, no schools adequate to Christian needs, no Christian governments to protect and foster Christianity, no wealth or social influence to weigh in its favor. And yet by the end of the period perhaps as much as one-tenth of the population of the empire was Christian. At places, as in Asia Minor, half of the people were Christian and Christians were found in all parts of the wide spread territory. Very little of the details of the work is known. The very names of most of the missionaries have perished. In the earlier part of the period the work was done by the Greeks using the Greek language, but before the end of the period the gospel was being preached in several other tongues and the Scriptures had been translated into Latin for the Romans, into Syriac for the people of Syria and Mesopotamia and into Coptic for the native populations of Egypt. The Latin proved to be one of the most important versions in all the annals of Bible translation since it became for centuries the only Bible of western Christendom and is still the only authentic Roman Catholic Bible.

As in the preceding period the great majority of the Christians belonged to the masses, but it was reaching up more and more to include the wealthy, cultured and prominent. About 200 A. D. Abgar, king of Edessa, became a Christian, the first crowned head to bow at the feet of Jesus of Nazareth. The Armenians claim him as one of their kings, the first Christian king. In 311 the great Constantine, one of the contestants for the imperial crown, declared that he had seen a flaming cross in the skies having beneath it the words " With this Conquer." He now accepted Christianity in principle, threw himself on the Christians for support in his struggle for the crown, and was completely successful. In 313 he gave the Christians complete liberty of conscience and thenceforward to his death used his great personal and official influence to further the interests of Christianity in both public and private life. Finally just before his death in 337 he himself accepted baptism.

§ 17

OPPOSITION TO CHRISTIANITY

As in the preceding period there was determined opposition to Christianity in this. It endangered too many vested interests, violated too many religious convictions and transgressed too many social and political conventions to succeed unopposed. The masses of the people saw their own religious convictions and practices going down before its resistless advance; the government saw that it was disintegrating and recasting society and no one could foresee the outcome; its powerful semi-secret organization could easily endanger the supremacy of the state; the purveyors of amusements, the idol makers, the priests, the temple keepers all saw their callings threatened. These and other motives led to almost continuous persecution in one or another part of the empire during the whole of the period. No statistics are available, but beyond a doubt thousands of Christians perished by horrible deaths. For the most part persecution was sporadic, that is it was not general but occurred at one place and then another. But twice the empire put forth all its utmost resources for the suppression of Christianity root and branch. From 250 to 260 and again from 303 to 311 all the machinery of the imperial government was enlisted in the effort to eradicate it from the earth. The suffering was terrible. Christians were fined, imprisoned, banished, forced to work in the mines, executed by burning or being thrown to the lions. The churches were laid in ruins, the buildings destroyed or confiscated, the Bible burned.

In addition to this violent opposition many literary opponents rose in this period. Both Jews and heathen attacked Christianity in oral discussions and written works. They argued against the Christian conception of God and the world, the Christian view of the person and work of Jesus Christ, the Christian ideal of life and religion. They raised practically every objection to Christianity that ever has been raised or is likely to be raised, but as far as we can see did not succeed in retarding its progress in the least. In fact most of their work has perished except as it was quoted by some Christian writer in an effort to refute it. The most notable of these opponents was Celsus who studied Christianity and wrote a book about 177 which he entitled "The True Discourse." It was so powerful that Origen, the ablest Christian scholar of the time, felt constrained to answer it seventy-five years after its publication. And yet so slight was the permanent effects of this book that it has perished absolutely except those portions that Origen quoted. Had Origen not written we should not know a single line of the book.

The only response which the Christians made to this opposition and persecution was heroic suffering and earnest oral and written argument. There is no evidence of any attempt at violent resistance during all these long years of terrible suffering. Both Greek and Latin Christians wrote defenses of themselves and their views which were usually addressed, in the most respectful manner, to the emperor and other civil authorities. In these "Apologies," as they were termed, the writers denied all charges of immoral conduct or dangerous designs on the part of Christians, demanded that they be tried on criminal charges before the courts and not condemned simply because they were Christians, explained and defended their beliefs and

practices and exposed the absurdities and immoralities of
the various heathen religious beliefs and practices. Constantine put an end to persecution, as we have seen, in 311.

§ 18

BEGINNINGS OF THE CATHOLIC CHURCH

We have now followed the rapid spread of Christianity
over the empire during the second and third centuries, and
have seen it finally conquer the emperor and achieve its
freedom. But Christianity itself had been in process of
transformation as it progressed and at the close of the
period was in many respects quite different from the apostolic Christianity of A.D. 100. At every step it had been
changing and these changes were making the Catholic
church.

The whole conception of the church had been transformed. At the beginning of the period the church was
a local body of saved people, democratic in government, independent of all other churches and without organic relations with the state. At the end the local churches had been
amalgamated into one great body spread over the empire and
called the Catholic or Universal church. This church was
regarded as a saving institution outside of which there was
no salvation, all the means of grace having been committed
to its keeping. Its unity was thought to be in the bishops
who were supposed to be successors of the apostles and in
perfect harmony with each other. This universal church
was believed to be infallibly guided by the Holy Spirit,
so that it was kept from all error. It was the body of
Christ, a holy entity, to rend it was the worst possible sin.

§ 19

CHURCH OFFICIALS

The general officers of the first period (apostles, prophets, evangelists), disappear in this, while the number of local officers is increased and their character changed. The two officers of the apostolic churches develop into three for each church — one bishop, a plurality of elders or presbyters, and a plurality of deacons. Moreover the one bishop gradually extends his authority, through missions and other methods, over a large section of country which was known as a diocese. Then the bishops of a few of the largest and most important dioceses came to exercise a supervision over the bishops of less important ones and hence were called archbishops or metropolitans. A little later five of these archbishops, those of Alexandria, Jerusalem, Antioch, Constantinople and Rome, increased their authority still further and came to be known as patriarchs. The very essence of the church was thought to reside in the bishops, who had thus grown into officials of great authority.

The laity gradually lost their significance and the whole management of the church's work and worship passed into the hands of the clergy. The property and finances of the church came into the hands of the bishop, and soon he began to select the lower clergy allowing to the people only an advisory power. Thus power passed from laity to clergy and from the clergy as a whole to the bishop.

Moreover the presbyters and bishops came to be regarded as priests, that is they became mediators between God and man, ministering grace through the ceremonies of the church. Without them there was no access to God and no certainty of the forgiveness of sin. This was one of the most fateful changes that ever came over any part of Christian thought, closing the door of heaven against men except as the priest should open it, shutting out God from any direct access to his creatures and confining the blessing of his grace to the ministrations of frail men. The divine power of the priesthood was supposed to be conferred by the laying on of the hands of the bishop in ordination. This view of the ministry first appears in Tertullian about 200.

Many lower officers were developed such as subdeacons, readers, acolytes, etc., as the churches increased in size, thus multiplying the officers and further burdening the church with officialism.

§ 20

THE ORDINANCES BECOME SACRAMENTS

Baptism and the supper were greatly changed in this period, being gradually transformed into sacraments or oaths of loyalty to the church, having ascribed to them power to work marvelous spiritual changes in the soul. They became vehicles of grace necessary to the forgiveness of sins, and the ceremonies connected with their administration were multiplied into an elaborate ritual.

Baptism was still usually administered by immersion, but where sufficient water for baptism was wanting and in cases of supposed fatal illness, pouring was allowed in lieu of baptism. The latter, called clinic (reclining) baptism, was regarded as defective and in case the patient recovered was completed by additional ceremonies. Novatian of Rome about 250 was the first to be baptized in that way, so far as we know. Baptism was preceded by a period of instruction extending over two or three years in which Christian doctrines were taught and Christian ideals of life instilled. At baptism the candidate renounced the devil, his pomp and his angels and accepted the creed by repeating it; after baptism white was worn for several days as a symbol of purity. Baptism was supposed to remove all guilt and punishment due to both original and actual sin and to leave the soul perfectly pure, afflicted only with a certain inclination to sin. It was believed that salvation was ordinarily

impossible apart from baptism.   The belief in the necessity
of baptism appeared in the first half of the second century
and rapidly became general.   Baptism was ordinarily administered by the bishop or a presbyter, but in cases of
necessity could be administered by others.

Infant baptism is first seen in Tertullian at the end of
the second century, but it did not become the general practice until the sixth.   Its rise was due to the belief that baptism was necessary to salvation.   Parents insisted on the
baptism of sickly children, and from this small beginning it
grew to be the general practice of the Catholic church, enforced by both church and state.

The Supper could be celebrated only by the bishop or
priest.   It consisted of bread, and wine (mingled with
water), taken from the offerings brought by the congregation and consecrated by prayer.   None but the baptized
participated in the ceremonies or eating.   The meal (love
feast), which had accompanied the Supper in the earlier
period, gradually disappears in this, doubtless owing to
abuses connected with it.   From the beginning the Supper
had been looked upon as one of the most sacred parts of
worship.   This feeling grew rapidly during this period.
Early in the period the bread and the wine were called the
body and blood of Christ, and before its close some writers
seem to think that Christ was in some sense actually present in these elements.   Before 200 it was called an offering
or sacrifice, important for the nourishing and support of the
spiritual life, though the full Catholic doctrine had not yet
developed.

§ 21

DEVELOPMENTS IN WORSHIP

Worship steadily grows more liturgical, complex and
ornate throughout the period.   This tendency was doubtless
due to the taste of the people, the comparative ignorance

and incompetence of the lower clergy and the growing feeling that the very words of the service were sacred. Christian worship was transferred entirely from the Jewish Sabbath to the "Lord's day." On account of persecution it was often if not usually before day and after nightfall. The service was full of joy and thanksgiving, in sharp contrast to the services and religious atmosphere of the Jewish Sabbath. Certain annual seasons were also kept as religious festivals in this period, such as the Passover, Pentecost, Epiphany and possibly others. The first two were continuations of Jewish festivals but with Christian meaning. The Passover was the festival of the resurrection and Pentecost that of the descent of the Holy Spirit. Paul and the other apostles continued to observe the Jewish festivals after they became Christians, and it is probable that the whole Christian body continued them without interruption, though it was formally decided at the Jerusalem conference that they were not to be imposed on Christians as in any sense necessary to salvation.

In the earlier part of the period the Christians continued to worship in private houses and in such other safe places as they could find; but in the freedom which they enjoyed toward the close of the period they began to erect separate buildings designed especially for Christian worship and work. These they called "churches," "houses of God," "houses of prayer," etc. None of these earliest buildings have survived to the present, but they are known to have been parallelograms with vestibule in front and a raised platform at the rear for the seats of the clergy who were already beginning to raise themselves above the people.

Worship consisted of singing, Scripture reading, prayers and informal preaching. The instruction was given in classes and men were won to Christ in private so that preaching was much less important than at a later time. However toward the end of the period preaching was, under the influence of the Greek and Latin orators, becoming more elaborate and formal. The bishops were the preach-

ers and some of them were beginning to show considerable
ability as pulpit orators.

The Supper was at first a part of the general worship, but
as the feeling of its sacredness grew the unbaptized part
of the congregation was dismissed before its celebration.
The Latin term *missa* with which they were dismissed then
gradually came to be the designation of the following communion service.   As a result of this practice the communion
service of the Catholic church, or at least that part of it
in which the elements are consecrated, is called the *missa*
or in English *mass*.

§ 22

CHRISTIAN LIFE AND DISCIPLINE

Candidates were prepared for baptism by a long period
of instruction as we saw above.   Repentance and faith were
presupposed.   All that care could suggest was done to preserve the purity of the church members, and yet there can
be no doubt that the tone of Christian life was declining.
In fact society in general was decaying and Christianity but
felt the general world-wide tendency.

Discipline for moral lapses in the church was certain
and severe.   For very heinous sins such as apostasy, excommunication was the penalty and as much as twenty years of
penance was imposed before readmission to the communion.
Excommunication involved ostracism from Christian society.   Christians sought to mitigate the divorce evil, to
abolish the practice of exposing children, to elevate the
character of the marriage relation and home life, to al-
leviate the conditions of slavery, and in these respects they
made an appreciable impression.

Some earnest souls despairing of saving society and rest-
ive under the increasing and oppressive ecclesiasticism of
the church began to live the ascetic life.   At first they only
renounced marriage and property and the eating of flesh

and the drinking of wine, and continued their place in society. Later they began to leave the world and withdraw into the desert and other places of retirement. The first man of note to adopt this anchorite life was Anthony of Thebes in Egypt who withdrew into the desert where he lived for many years. From his place of retirement he exerted an immense influence on the Christian life of Egypt. Later his biography was written, possibly by the great theologian Athanasius, and became one of the most popular books of devotion of that period. Great numbers of likeminded men gradually gathered round him and in order to bring some order out of the chaos Pachomius drew up a rule about 322 which was the first of the long list of monastic rules. It was the beginning of the ordered monasticism which has played so large a part in the history of Christianity.

Marriage began to be discredited in this period. The clergy were still married but second marriages were forbidden to them and there was a distinct tendency to regard the unmarried life as moving on a higher plane than the married.

Christians rather shunned public life because it frequently involved the recognition of idolatry, put them into danger both in the army and civil positions, and often led to the taking of human life. Most of the early Christians opposed capital punishment. They withdrew from the pollutions of heathen society, from degrading amusements such as the circus and the theater.

Christians buried their dead rather than cremated them as the Romans did. On account of persecution and the high cost of ground in the neighborhood of the great cities like Rome they buried in extensive underground galleries often miles in length and containing tens of thousands of bodies. These galleries are known as *catacombs* and when first discovered in modern times contained many most interesting and important memorials of the life and faith of the early Christians. The earliest Christian art is found here in the form of symbolic pictures and figures such as the dove, the anchor, the lamb, the palm branch, crown, harp and fish. The last, a sort of Christian cryptogram, served as a password among Christians by which they could recognize each other in times of danger. The letters of the Greek word for fish are the initial letters of the words "*Jesus Christ God's Son Savior.*" The fish therefore served as a means of recognition and a confession of Christian faith.

Most of the Christians continued to be uneducated. They established no schools of their own except a few catechetical schools for the training of Christian workers, and they patronized the heathen schools very little. This was undoubtedly one of their greatest mistakes.

§ 23

THE DEVELOPMENT OF DOCTRINE

Some phases of Christian truth began to be gathered into what may be called a system in this period. The most important work in this direction was the collection and canonizing of the books of the New Testament. About twenty years after the death of Jesus the Christians, some apostles and others, began to write brief pamphlets for the practical needs of the churches. These were letters dealing with the practical and doctrinal difficulties of churches and individuals, brief accounts of the life and teachings of Jesus, short history of the early labors of some of the missionaries and books called apocalypses expressing the glowing hopes and expectations of the Christians for the future triumph of the kingdom of God. There was a great mass of this Christian literature, some of it of the highest value and some of it of comparatively little value. These writings at first circulated separately among the churches and were read in their public services as each thought best. Under the test of practical service, and as we believe guided by the Holy Spirit, the great majority of the churches found themselves in substantial agreement as to what writings

ought to be considered a rule for the faith and practice
of the churches.   These they called a *Canon* or rule.   They
were then gathered together and eventually put along with
the Old Testament.   Thus our Bible was finished.

The earliest creed was the so-called " Apostles' Creed."
It was not drawn up by the apostles as its name might indicate, nor was it the work of a council as was the case with
later creeds.   It rather grew up in the process of missionary
activities as a brief comprehensive statement of Christian
faith which candidates were required to accept before baptism.   Traces of it occur before 200, but the exact words
were not fixed until the fourth or fifth century.   It is a confession of facts rather than of doctrines and is the oldest
and most widely used statement of Christian faith in existence.   Millions of Christians in all parts of the world still
repeat it every Sunday as the expression of their faith.   On
account of its history and wide use it is here given in full:
" I believe in God the Father Almighty, Maker of heaven
and earth; and in Jesus Christ His only begotten Son
our Lord; who was conceived by the Holy Ghost, born of
the Virgin Mary; suffered under Pontius Pilate, was cruci-
fied, dead, and buried; he descended into hell; the third day
he rose from the dead; he ascended into heaven; and sitteth
at the right hand of God the Father Almighty; from thence
He shall come to judge the quick and the dead.

" I believe in the Holy Ghost; the holy catholic Church;
the communion of saints; the forgiveness of sins; the resurrection of the body; and the life everlasting.   Amen."

There were a few unitarians in this period but the great
body of Christians accepted Jesus as the Messiah of the
Old Testament, the divine Son of God, the son of man,
truly God and truly man, through whose teachings, sufferings, death, resurrection and endless life we have our redemption.   In this regard the Christians of that day did not
differ materially from the great body of the Christians of
the present.

§ 24

SECTS AND HERESIES OF THIS PERIOD

As we saw in dealing with the preceding period the Christians were never entirely in agreement about all questions of faith.   These and other differences led in this period to serious schisms in the Christian body, and the formation of several parties more or less hostile to each other.   The great body of the Christians were called Catholics and they were fairly harmonious in their beliefs and practices; but by no means all the Christians agreed with them.   The great stream of Christian history flowed along the channel indicated above, caught in the process of evolution and rapid change without knowing that they were drifting away from the ancient apostolic moorings.   They were in the midst of heathenism and absorbing from it, they were illiterate and the Scriptures were little circulated, they had very few trained leaders, the churches being compelled to use such leaders as they could find among their own members, and there were very few Christian schools.   Consequently the Christian propaganda was lacking in those elements which were necessary to hold it true to the New Testament.   The dominant characteristic of the period is *drift*.

The most important of the sects were the Montanists, Novatians and Donatists.   They were all bitterly hostile to the Catholic church, all were efforts to realize the ideal of a pure church on earth.   The Montanists were founded by Montanus, a presbyter of Phrygia, about the middle of the second century.   He protested against the growing laxness of the churches in the matter of discipline and insisted on the continuation of the prophetic presence and activity of the Holy Spirit.   He was assisted by two prophetesses Priscilla and Maximilla.   The movement developed wonderful enthusiasm and power, spreading over most of the empire, dividing churches and founding new ones on a stricter basis.

Novatianism was founded at Rome about a century later by a presbyter by the name of Novatian. He was the leader of the party that believed in strict discipline and when Cornelius, the leader of the lax party, was elected bishop, Novatian revolted and had himself elected an opposing bishop, thus causing a schism in the Roman church. He did not differ materially from the position of the church in doctrine, but he was a man of great moral earnestness and believed that those who had lapsed in persecution should not be so easily restored to fellowship. The schism spread over the entire empire and continued to the sixth century.

The third important schism took place in north Africa in the midst of the Diocletian persecution about 311. It was led by Donatus and was a protest against the acceptance of the lapsed back into church fellowship as in the case of the Novatians. The Donatists rebaptized all who came to them from other Christian bodies, insisting that the *character* of the administrator must be considered as one of his qualifications. This sect was also a protest of moral earnestness against laxness and ran much the same course as the other two.

All three of these schisms were protests against the growing laxness of the great church and were more nearly biblical than the church. But we come now to study two that were less scriptural and were really serious heresies, endangering the very essence of Christianity itself. They were Gnosticism and Manichæism. They were much alike and both arose from an effort to amalgamate Christianity with certain heathen philosophies and religions.

Gnosticism arose in Asia Minor and Egypt and was an effort to unite Christianity and the religious beliefs of these regions into a new religion composed of the two. God was believed to be wholly good and incapable of any relations with this evil world; matter was regarded as eternal and the abode of evil; God and matter came into relations by a descending series of spiritual beings known as æons, who emanated from God; one of the lowest of these formed the universe as we see it; man is a mixture of the good and the evil of the universe. Christ who was one of the lower æons redeems men by *knowledge* (*gnosis,* hence *gnosticism*) not by *faith.* Some men are entirely material and incapable of redemption; others can be only partially redeemed and only the gnostics are fully saved. Christ had no real body and there is no resurrection of the bodies of men. The Old Testament and much of the New was rejected. Thus it will be seen that they attacked nearly every important Christian truth. The Christian writers and preachers of the second and third centuries laid themselves out to disprove and overthrow this dangerous heresy and after a long and hard struggle they succeeded in gradually eliminating it.

Manichæism was founded by Mani of Persia and was an attempted combination of Christianity with the Persian religions. It was much like Gnosticism which it followed by half a century. It spread all over the Christian world, organizing churches and continuing for several centuries.

Thus at the end of this period we see Christianity already being torn by schism and heresy. On the one side men were trying to keep the churches pure and as true as possible to the New Testament model, and on the other they were trying to corrupt them by combining Christianity with something else. We shall see these efforts continuing through the centuries.

During this period the production of literature was gradually passing over to the Christians. The heathen still wrote, but their literary output was decreasing in quantity and degenerating in quality. On the other hand the stream of Christian literature was steadily increasing in quantity and improving in quality. It was still chiefly in the Greek and Latin languages, and consisted of missionary tracts, defenses of Christianity and the Christians, attacks upon the heathen systems and ideals, and polemics against various heresies and schisms. The world was compelled to wait many centuries for the production of a " polite literature " which could be called Christian.

THIRD PERIOD — 323 TO 600 A.D.

THE UNDIVIDED CATHOLIC CHURCH

§ 25

OUTWARD CONDITIONS AFFECTING CHRISTIAN WORK

THE history of this period is marked by one of the profoundest upheavals that ever affected the political and social life of Europe, namely the expansion of the Germans and the fall of the Roman empire. We have already had glimpses of the Germanic tribes in their forest home on the north side of the Danube and the east side of the Rhine. For some years it had been difficult for Rome to hold them behind these natural barriers and more than one Roman army had been practically destroyed by their valor. They had only reached the higher stages of barbarism in their culture; they had no literature, not even a written language, there was little agriculture and no manufacturing. But they were brave and ruthless, and had looked for centuries with hungry eyes across the borders into the fair fields and wonderful cities of the empire. The settled life and accumulated riches of these imperial lands were a constant lure.

As long as the empire was strong and possessed abundance of men it had little to fear. But it was now declining. Constant wars and crushing taxes were depopulating the lands and impoverishing the people. Germans were allowed to move in and settle; they were obtaining positions in the army and civil service, thus effecting a peaceable penetration of the country. Moreover they were themselves hard pressed from behind by other tribes more barbarous than themselves, moving westward from Asia.

39

Meantime the government of the empire itself had been split into an eastern and a western division. Constantine before his death in 337 had divided it among his sons, and it had never been reunited except for brief periods. He had removed the capital to Byzantium on the Bosphorus which was renamed Constantinople, Constantine's city. The western capital was removed to Ravenna on the Adriatic and the city of Rome was left to the rule of the bishop. This western half of the empire rapidly grew weaker and about 375 the German tribes began to break into it over the Rhine and the Danube. It was now no longer able to withstand them. They crushed its armies, overthrew its government, looted its wealth and appropriated its lands. The whole political and social life from the Adriatic Sea westward was pulverized in a century, the last vestige of Roman government ceasing in 476 with the overthrow of Romulus Augustulus. Much of the fruits of centuries of Roman civilization was utterly destroyed. When the storm was over and the various German tribes had settled down they began to build up smaller national governments on the ruins of the old imperial government. The Franks took over Gaul and ultimately gave their name to the country of France. The West Goths set up an extensive kingdom in Spain, the Vandals in north Africa and the islands of the western Mediterranean, the Lombards in northern Italy and less important tribes in other sections.

The first effects of this great invasion seemed to be disastrous, but the German masters soon began to accept from their conquered subjects both civilization and religion. The subjects conquered their masters in an intellectual and spiritual way, and a process of assimilation soon began which ultimately formed a new basis for the life of all western Europe.

§ 26

MISSIONS

Amid the shock of such mighty movements and transformations it could hardly be expected that Christian missions would make much progress. But as a matter of fact there was decided progress during the two hundred and seventy-five years of this period.

In the first place the evangelization of the Roman empire was completed. With the beginning of this period governmental opposition and persecution ceased and the period of governmental favor began. Constantine and all subsequent emperors except Julian (361–3) exerted their influence actively in behalf of Christianity. Property confiscated during persecution was restored, churches were erected at governmental expense, laws were revised in the interest of Christian ideals, the church was rapidly endowed. Julian was brought up a Christian but apostatized and sought ineffectually to restore heathenism. After his death in 363 all the emperors were Christians and before the end of the fourth century Christianity was virtually made the established religion of the empire. The government now began to use repressive measures against the old heathenism and eventually the temples were destroyed or forcibly transformed into Christian churches, heathen worship was suppressed, heathen priesthoods dissolved and heathen schools were closed. The closing of the great school at Athens in 527 may be called the end of heathen culture in the empire. With governmental favor gradually arose governmental control over the church with all its varied evils.

Of course under these circumstances conversions were not thorough and by the end of the period the church was at places but little better than baptized heathenism. But such Christianity as it was the empire was Christian by the year 600. The Greco-Roman world had been incorporated into the church.

The second great phase of mission work in this period was the conversion of the German hordes that had poured into the western part of the empire. A few had been converted before they entered, but the great majority were trophies of the Christianity in the midst of which they settled. It was a stupendous piece of home mission work. Here again hosts of them became Christians *en masse* under the influence of their princes or other worldly considerations and were little changed in character. But henceforth they will look to the church for culture and religious light. Many of them, like the Visigoths, Vandals and others, were first converted to Arianism and then later to the orthodox Catholic church; others, like the Franks, were converted directly to orthodox Christianity. Clovis, the king of the Franks, had a Catholic wife. Doubtless owing in part to her influence he became a Catholic Christian and was baptized on Christmas day, 496. This led to the rapid conversion of all the Franks and threw the whole of their influence with Catholic Christianity. As a consequence orthodoxy was completely triumphant throughout the territory of the empire by the end of the period.

Christianity also began to spread beyond the borders of the empire in this period. *In the West* Ireland was converted, chiefly by the labors of Patrick, a Briton who had as a heathen been a slave in Ireland. Escaping from his Irish masters he fled to his native land, where he was converted to Christianity; he then returned to Ireland and in 432 began work for the conversion of his former masters. He was wonderfully successful and before long Ireland could justly be called the "Isle of Saints." The type of Christianity was much more evangelical than that of Rome, with which it had no connection for several centuries.

Irish Christians were filled with the missionary spirit and in the next century they carried the gospel to the Scotch, who were of the same racial stock. A company of Irish missionaries led by Columban settled on the Island of Iona in southwest Scotland in the year 563, and made it a famous center of missionary effort. Christianity had already been planted in Scotland but it had not flourished. Under the inspiration of these Irish the whole country was soon Christianized and became a model of holy living and missionary zeal, sending missionaries to the continent. It too was much more evangelical than the Romans.

In the East Christianity was firmly planted in Persia, Armenia and Georgia, and in Abyssinia in Africa. All these churches suffered more or less persecution and before the end of this period for one reason or another had split off from the Catholic church. Christianity even reached India and China in this period and started promising missions, but the work in these lands was not permanent.

Northward Ulfilas, a Visigoth, had carried Christianity across the Danube to his own people about 341, before they entered the empire. He reduced their language to writing and began a German literature by translating parts of the Bible into their language. His work was markedly successful, but the Visigoths crossed the Rhine soon after their conversion and then moved westward, so that this work had little effect on the later evangelization of Germany. This brief survey will serve to show that the period was one of great activity and efficiency in missionary endeavor.

§ 27

THE CHURCH AND ITS OFFICERS

This was also a period of further and rapid development in organization. The centralizing tendencies of the preceding period were accelerated and strengthened in this. The laity lose all share in the control of the churches, and the clergy become a close self-perpetuating corporation in whose hands all ecclesiastical authority rests. They were freed from the burdens of civil life and largely from civil control. A system of church courts and church law, composed of the decisions of councils and leading bishops and known as *canon law,* grew up as a rival to the courts and laws of the state.   Church law was administered in *church courts,* by *church lawyers* and *judges.*   Ultimately these church courts obtained a recognized jurisdiction over most of the affairs of clergymen and over laymen in such matters as marriage and divorce, inheritance of property, etc. Church property, rapidly increasing in quantity, was held entirely by the clergy.

As the power of the great bishops increased the state felt compelled to interfere in their selection.   As a consequence the civil authorities began to influence the elections and ultimately to make the appointments to these important positions.   The church's increasing power thus led to friction with the civil authorities and ultimately to its enslavement to the state.

Among all the churches of the world that of Rome had been the most influential almost from its foundation.   This was due to its location in the capital city of the world as well as to its intrinsic worth and high character.   As we see in the Epistle to the Romans it had been active and efficient from the beginning of its history.   Later it was believed to have been founded by Peter and Paul and, as reverence for these apostles deepened, their supposed authority, especially that ascribed to Peter, was gradually transferred to the bishop of Rome, now widely regarded as Peter's successor. During the chaotic conditions which accompanied the fall of the empire the church seemed to be about the only stable and enduring institution, and the bishop of Rome became an actual ruler of great power.   Thus he gradually grew into the pope, coming to exercise extensive civil powers over central Italy and an ever widening ecclesiastical influence over western Europe.   He was the only great bishop in this part of the world; consequently his authority was acknowledged by others, while in the East there were several other great bishops and so his authority was never acknowledged there.

The need of mutual counsel and advice amid the difficulties of Christian work led to the organization of various grades of *Councils*. There was the *local council* or *synod* composed of the bishop and clergy of a diocese; then the *provincial council* composed of the clergy of a larger section of country; and finally the so-called *Ecumenical Council* composed of the bishops of the whole world. This last council was supposed to be the church's mouthpiece of infallibility; its doctrinal decisions were regarded as inspired and final; they were called dogmas and could not be changed. It was convoked by the emperor and its decisions were published as the laws of the empire. Several of these world councils were held during this period and their doctrinal decisions are still regarded by the Catholics as final, and by other Christians as of the utmost importance. That of Nicea in 325 defined the doctrine of the *Trinity* as orthodox Christians still receive it, and that of Chalcedon in 451 stated the doctrine of the *person of Christ* as it is usually held.

§ 28

HISTORY OF THEOLOGY IN THIS PERIOD

This was a great theological age. All classes of Christians were deeply interested in theology and the profoundest doctrines were discussed and defined. The world was torn by continuous and bitter controversies for centuries; sometimes the empire was shaken to its center by theological struggles. Bloodshed was not infrequent, bishops were banished by imperial authority, mobs raided now this side and now that, emperors supported first one side and then the other, in the varying fortunes of battle. Probably the greatest of these controversies was that known as the *Arian controversy,* in which the divinity of Christ was involved. Arius had denied the essential divinity of Christ declaring that he was created. So popular were his views at one time that Athanasius, the great bishop of Alexandria, was the only prominent man who was brave enough to stand for the divinity of our Lord. Hence the saying, "Athanasius against the world." He was banished again and again for his faithfulness and all the power of a heretical emperor was exerted to crush the truth. But the truth would not down and the first world council decided that Jesus was real God. Their decision was as follows: "We believe in one Lord Jesus Christ, the only begotten Son of God, begotten of the Father before all worlds, God of God, Light of Light, very God of very God, begotten, not made, being of one substance with the Father; by whom all things were made; who, for us men and for our salvation, came down from heaven, and was incarnate by the Holy Ghost of the Virgin Mary, and was made man," etc.

This then was the age when standards of orthodoxy concerning God and Christ were fixed. In the main the decisions of these centuries have held to the present time, though criticism and denial of the divinity of Christ have never been entirely silenced. This was a marvelous intellectual and spiritual feat. Whatever else one may say about Unitarian views of Christ one must admit that those who have held these views have borne few of the burdens and done little of the work of Christian history. Unitarianism has had no power.

These great controversies caused many serious schisms in the Christian body, some of which still remain. The Nestorians split off from the Catholic church and fled to Persia where they flourished for several centuries and of whom a feeble remnant still survive.

The Armenians and several smaller bodies also split off during this period and still remain apart from the Catholic church. All these schismatic churches have suffered fearful persecutions through the centuries, but they still maintain an independent existence. They differ considerably from the Catholics in doctrines, organization and worship. They are neither Catholic nor Protestant.

§ 29

THE CHURCH'S ORDINANCES

During this period the development of the Catholic view of baptism and the supper was well-nigh finished. These ordinances gradually cease to be beautiful and simple ceremonies, setting forth in pictorial fashion the great facts of redemption and the fundamental realities of Christian experience, and become sacraments with mysterious powers effecting in some magical way the regeneration and sanctification of the soul.

Baptism was still administered almost exclusively by immersion, often three-fold, in the name of the Trinity. But infant-baptism was becoming more and more common in lands where Christianity was well established. Baptism was believed to wash away all previous sin, both original and actual, and to effect regeneration. In ordinary circumstances there was no salvation without it; it was the one thing absolutely essential. In view of its tremendous importance any one was permitted to administer it and often it was postponed till near death so that the soul could depart this life in the spotless purity of a new baptism.

The evolution in the view of the Lord's supper was not yet complete. It was now firmly believed that Christ was actually present in the elements, but it had not been determined just how. Moreover the belief that there was in some sense a real sacrifice of Jesus in connection with the ceremony of consecration was also rapidly developing, but was neither clear nor complete.

§ 30

CHRISTIAN WORSHIP

This was a period of great Christian preaching. In the earlier centuries preaching was comparatively simple and informal, the services being much like our modern prayer-meetings. But as the church absorbed the culture of the Greek and Roman worlds the preaching tended to conform to classic models and rose in quality until it equaled the oratory of Greece in her palmiest days. Thousands hung on the lips of the pulpit orators in rapt attention, often expressing their approval in wild applause. Dr. Broadus used to say that John Chrysostom, John the golden-mouthed patriarch of Constantinople, was probably the greatest preacher that Christianity has produced. His sermons deserve to rank along side the oratory of Demosthenes.

Along with great preaching the churches continued their careful instruction of the young. The course of instruction preceding baptism and church membership usually continued over three years or more. All the fundamental principles and duties of the Christian religion and life were diligently taught, and an earnest effort was made to have a thoroughly intelligent church membership. This instruction was all the more necessary because of the absence of Christian schools and general education. The majority of the Christians continued to be illiterate and whatever of instruction they received was given orally.

The few church buildings of the preceding period were destroyed during the terrible persecutions with which it closed. With the peace and governmental favor that came with the conversion of Constantine an era of rapid church building began. The destroyed property of the Christians was restored by imperial edict. Constantine and his mother Helena set a worthy example by contributing largely to the erection of noble church buildings at various important places. Other princes did likewise and by the end of the period there were beautiful church buildings in many parts of the empire. The greatest church of the world was St. Sophia in Constantinople, built by the emperor Justinian in the sixth century. It was one of the most splendid edifices in all human history and still stands, though it is now a Mohammedan mosque.

By the year 600 the services were not uniform, but in all

the great centers they were much like the Catholic services at the present time. The priests wore special vestments, candles were burning, smoking censers were swinging, there was chanting and responsive singing, pictures and images were freely used. Much of this had been absorbed from heathenism and Judaism. The whole service was written and the very words of it had become sacred. In the East it was in the Greek language and in the West usually in Latin. Compared with the simplicity of the apostolic worship it was all very strange and complex. Doubtless the simplicity and fervor of the apostolic churches remained in outlying districts, but there had been a wonderful change in the great cities. Paul and the other laborers of early days would not have recognized the churches of their planting.

The principal festivals of the so-called "Christian Year" were now complete. They gathered into three cycles around the birth of our Lord, his passion and resurrection, and the gift of the Holy Spirit, that is, around Christmas, Easter (then still called passover) and Pentecost. These festivals were intended to bring annually and in a striking way before the Christians the great facts of redemption. They constituted a sort of "chronological confession of faith."

§ 31

CHRISTIAN LIFE

As the churches absorbed more and more of the unregenerated heathenism around them the standard of Christian living declined. Morals were not so pure, superstition increased, the Christian body was torn by frightful discord and strife. Unable to keep these evils out of the churches the earnest Christians began to form a special class within the church devoted to what was believed to be higher standards of Christian living. Ascetic tendencies existed, as we have seen, in the preceding period. These were emphasized and intensified until about the beginning of the present period men began to withdraw from society in great numbers and live alone in the solitudes of deserts and caves. They went apart to fight out the battle with sin in themselves and to escape from a corrupt world and an oppressive church; they were intent on the saving of their own souls. The thought of serving others practically disappeared. The movement first appeared in Egypt, where the temperament of the people and the conditions of climate were favorable. Thousands betook themselves to the deserts, where they lived an idle and useless life devoted to contemplation and prayer.

Under these conditions some organization became absolutely necessary. The necessity for feeding and controlling these hordes and giving them something worthy to do created the strict rule under which the monks have ever since lived. As we have seen, the first important organizer was a man named Pachomius in Egypt. His form of organization was quickly carried to other lands, both east and west, becoming the basis for the organization of Eastern monasticism.

One further step was taken in the West. At Monte Cassino in southern Italy Benedict of Nursia began the creation of the first *order,* the Benedictine, in 529, and his rule became the model for all subsequent orders. By this plan many separate monasteries located in different parts of the world, live under the same rule and are controlled and directed by a common central government, now usually located at Rome. This was the beginning of a tremendous movement which has deeply affected all subsequent Christian history. The early monasteries were filled with earnest men, but the life is so artificial and unnatural that they have frequently degenerated into the basest corruption. However much good they may have done during the Middle Ages, and undoubtedly they did much, still one feels sure that more could have been done had the inmates remained in society and borne their share in Christian work.

The founding of monasteries for the men was followed

by convents for women and throughout the Middle Ages the women vied with the men in their devotion to the monastic ideal. Every detail of life was carefully and strictly regulated, and the service rendered within the monastic walls was often large. The monks and nuns became teachers, missionaries, copyists, musicians, and servants of the people. While we recognize their earnestness and devotion, we deplore the misguided zeal which has wrought so much evil in Christian history. They took the threefold vow of poverty, chastity and obedience, and this vow was irrevocable.

While these changes were taking place in the church it must not be forgotten that the church was slowly but steadily elevating the general public life. Laws became more humane, many of the worst vices of the ancient world were either eliminated or ameliorated. Gladiatorial games were brought to an end, bloody sacrifices ceased, crucifying and branding criminals were forbidden, Sunday was made a legal holiday, and many other similar improvements were made. Evidently the church was gradually leavening the world as the world corrupted the church.

FOURTH PERIOD — 600 TO 1050

BEGINNING OF THE MIDDLE AGES

§ 32

As we turn into the Middle Ages we are conscious of passing rapidly into a new and strange atmosphere. There is an air of decline and decay over the whole world. Darkness seems to be settling down on the face of the earth and for some centuries civilization and Christianity appear to be about to perish, especially in the West. This darkness grows deeper till about 900 A. D., when we can begin to see the faint dawning of a better day. This period is preëminently the heart of the "Dark Ages." The civilization of the Roman world was perishing before the Teutonic world had become civilized and cultured.

RISE OF MOHAMMEDANISM

Perhaps the most tremendous event of the period is the rise of a new religion in Arabia, the last of the great religions to appear. It was founded by an Arabian camel-driver named Mohammed. Its official name is Islam and its devotees are called Moslems. Mohammed was born a heathen at Mecca in 571, but about middle life came to the conviction that there is but one God and that he himself was the prophet of God. He was a deeply religious and meditative man, but was probably led to his monotheistic conviction by contact with Jews and Christians whom he met in his travels. He was subject to epilepsy and believed

52

himself to be the organ of divine revelations. He began to preach his new doctrines about 611 and eventually succeeded in winning the support of his wife and a few relatives; but so bitter was the persecution directed against him by his neighbors that he fled to Medina in 622 A. D. This flight is called the *Hegira* and is the year from which Mohammedans date their era. Gradually he succeeded in winning enough adherents to return to Mecca in 630 and compel his former adversaries by force of arms to accept his claims. Soon, through preaching and the exercise of force, all Arabia was united under the new religious banner. By the history of these early years Islam was made a political as well as a religious movement.

Mohammed died in 634, but he left a religiously and politically united people, fanatical, ruthless, with their eyes turned hungrily outward on the fair fields and rich cities of their neighbors. All things were ripe for a mighty religious and racial movement.

Moreover, world conditions favored the success of such a movement. The empire and Persia had been at war with each other for several years and both were exhausted. They had neither armies nor money to resist the onslaught. The result was an easy victory for the Arabs or Saracens during the first century of their wonderful career. They attacked Palestine and Syria first and in five years had conquered the whole of this region. Jerusalem was taken in 638. Then turning westward they rapidly subdued Egypt and North Africa and by 711 had reached the Atlantic and crossed into Spain. In a few years they had conquered most of Spain and had penetrated to the heart of France. Here they were defeated in the great battle of Tours in 732 and turned back. This was the high-water mark of their conquests in the West.

In the meantime, in the East, they had completely destroyed the government of Persia and had advanced to India. Northward they had penetrated Asia Minor and were hammering at the gates of Constantinople. All this

was the work of but one century by a people who had
hitherto played no part in the world's affairs.

All their expansion westward and northward had been in
Christian territory and it constitutes the greatest setback
Christianity has ever suffered. Christians were oppressed
and persecuted, their church buildings were appropriated
for mosques, their missions stopped, their civilization well-
nigh overthrown and destroyed in the lands that were conquered. To escape their sufferings many Christians joined
the Mohammedans. After a century or so the unified government of the Mohammedans broke up and their expansion ceased; but they have continued to dominate the territory won at that time and have always been intellectually
and spiritually a blight. Christianity has never flourished
under Mohammedan rule.

What do the Mohammedans believe? The principal
article in their creed is monotheism, belief that there is but
one God. "There is no god but God and Mohammed is
his prophet." Mohammed is God's final prophet, conclud-
ing all revelation to men. Jesus was a man, born of a
virgin, divinely endowed, ascended on high, whence he will
return to judge the world at the last day. Their bible is
the Koran, all of it produced by Mohammed; their chief
religious duties are the recital of their creed, reading the
Koran, the spread of their faith, the reciting of five daily
prayers with face toward Mecca, fasting in the month
Ramadan, the giving of legal alms, a pilgrimage to Mecca.
Their only social worship is on Friday. Mohammed sanc-
tioned polygamy, which is practiced in all Mohammedan
countries, and looked forward to a sensual heaven. The
use of intoxicating beverages and swine's flesh are entirely
forbidden, likewise the use of images or relics in worship.
Predestination was so emphasized as to make it practically
fatalism, causing ultimate social stagnation and being one
of the greatest possible clogs on progress. Mohammedanism benefitted the heathen up to a certain point, and beyond
that became an effectual bar to further progress.

§ 33

MISSIONS IN THE EAST

Unlike the Germans who came into the western part of the empire in the preceding period, these Mohammedans were not converted by the Christians. On the contrary, many of the Christians were perverted to Mohammedanism and those who continued faithful were permanently depressed and shorn of their power. That part of the Christian world which remained under Mohammedan rule sent forth no more missionaries.

On the other hand that part of the empire which was not overrun still showed some missionary activity. As the Slavs, Bulgars and other barbarous tribes pressed into the Balkan region from the heart of Asia they were Christianized and to some extent civilized. In particular two brothers, Cyril and Methodius, were notable missionaries in these regions. They went out from Constantinople and evangelized wide stretches of eastern Europe. They reduced the Slavic language to writing and began a Christian literature in that tongue. They worked about the middle of the ninth century and succeeded in Christianizing the Moravians, Bohemians and Bulgars. In the next century the Servians received Christianity and a beginning was made among the Russians, who were rapidly converted when the Princess Olga was baptized in 955 and Prince Vladimir in 988. No people accepted Christianity more readily or devotedly.

All these tribes received the Eastern or (as we now call it) Greek Catholic Christianity. Henceforth, all the missions in this part of the world were of this type.

§ 34

MISSIONS IN THE WEST

As we have seen, the Mohammedans swept away all the Christianity there was in North Africa and overwhelmed but did not destroy the Christians in Spain. Most of the islands in the Mediterranean also fell into their hands and the coasts of Italy were harried and wasted. In all this conquered territory except Spain and Italy Christianity was quite stifled.

On the other hand this is the period in which most of the Germans, who had now settled down in their new homes, accepted Christianity and began to acquire culture. Britain had once been largely Christianized, but the invasion by the Germans (Angles, Saxons, Jutes, etc.) had destroyed Christianity outside of Wales and Cornwall. Missionary work now began among these Germans in England. In 597 Pope Gregory, who had years before been greatly impressed by the beauty of some Anglo-Saxon slaves in the market at Rome and had determined himself to go as a missionary to them, now that he was pope, sent a band of missionaries to England. They were led by a monk, Augustine, who carried letters of introduction and commendation from some of the Frankish princes to Ethelbert, king of Kent, whose wife, Bertha, was a Frankish princess and a Christian. The king was very soon baptized and was followed by all his subjects. There were at this time seven small kingdoms in England and most of them quickly followed the example of Kent, only Mercia and Sussex remaining heathen as late as 630.

But in the year 633 Mercia led a heathen reaction; the Christian king of Northumbria was overthrown and fled for refuge to the Scotch missionaries at Iona. After a while he regained his throne and then introduced the Scotch type of Christianity into Northumbria through the labors of the famous monk, Aidan. From Northumbria the Scotch type spread over all north England and it looked for a time as if the country was destined to have this type rather than the Roman. However, at the synod of Whitby in 664 the king of Northumbria decided to adopt the Roman type and in the course of the next fifty years the whole of the British Isles followed his example. The Scotch needed only to accept the Easter reckoning and the monastic tonsure of the Romans, and acknowledge the pope. They were allowed to use their own language in worship and the ministers of religion were permitted to marry. The country was not thoroughly Romanized until the Norman conquest in the eleventh century.

The Anglo-Saxons were filled with the missionary spirit from the beginning of their Christian history. Their kindred on the continent east of the Rhine and north of the Danube were still raw heathen, while the Frankish church was in a very low state of morals and life, and was dominated by the government. The Scotch had sent a company of missionaries to eastern France under the leadership of Columban in 590. They had founded the famous monastery of Luxeuil, and had preached repentance and reform throughout this part of the country; but when they were driven away to Switzerland in 610 by the hostility of the Queen Brunhilda, whom they had rebuked, their work fell into ruins.

Christianity had been planted at various points on the east side of the Rhine by Scottish and other missionaries, but it did not flourish until the Anglo-Saxon missionaries began their work. Winifried of York, on a journey to Rome in 677, suffered shipwreck on the coast of Friesland in Holland and devoted himself during the winter to preaching to the Frisians. He returned to England next spring and induced one of his disciples, Willibrod, to enter upon the work. After 690 this remarkable missionary enjoyed the protection and support of Pippin, the great Frankish statesman, and worked with noteworthy success. He was

the first archbishop of Utrecht and earned the title of
" Apostle of the Frisians."

Before his death in 739 he was joined by the greatest of
the Anglo-Saxon missionaries of this period, Boniface the
" Apostle of Germany." Of a good family, naturally gifted
and well educated, he declined attractive positions in England and at about forty years of age devoted himself to the
German mission. Finding the conditions unfavorable for
mission work at the time in Friesland he went to Rome in
718 and secured the support of the pope, at the same
time promising to relate all the work he did to the papal
chair. Returning to Germany he labored ceaselessly for
more than thirty years, reforming and reorganizing the
Frankish church, rendering a similar service to the church
in Thuringia and Bavaria, and himself carrying the gospel
to Hesse and other lands where it had not as yet been
preached. He was made bishop at large and then archbishop of Mainz, and gave ecclesiastical organization to all
these lands. In 752, when an old man, he laid down all
his ecclesiastical dignities and went again to the Frisians
as a missionary, where he was stabbed to death by the
heathen July 5, 754. He was a notable missionary, and a
great ecclesiastical organizer.

The Emperor Charlemagne, for both political and religious reasons, took great interest in Christian missions.
He forced the remnants of the Frisians and the Saxons to
accept Christianity at the point of the sword; he furthered
the mission among the Slavs along the eastern border of
his dominions, and in many ways spread the Christian
religion.

The beginning of mission work in Denmark, Norway and
Sweden took place in the ninth century and the foundations
were laid by German missionaries. The work in Denmark
was begun about 823. Three years later the king was baptized, and there seemed to be much promise of rapid conversion of the whole country. A young monk by the name
of Ansgar, " the apostle of Scandinavia," was earnestly at

work. But about 840 almost the whole Scandinavian mission was destroyed by a heathen reaction and the work had to be begun all over again.

In the next century all three of the kingdoms received Christianity from England, with which they had come into intimate relations through their raids upon that country. Christianity was accepted by the princes and made the state religion. Soon Iceland, Greenland and other northern islands were also Christian. Thus was finished the Christianizing of all western Europe, though it must not be forgotten that the Christianity which these countries received was in every case Catholicism. They knew nothing approaching pure Christianity till the Reformation.

§ 35

DIVISION BETWEEN EASTERN AND WESTERN CHRISTENDOM

For some centuries differences between the eastern and the western parts of the Christian world had been developing and leading steadily towards a schism. First among the causes were differences of race, language, and mental and moral characteristics. The East was Greek in blood, spoke Greek, used Greek in worship and wrote its theology in Greek; the West was Latin and used the Latin language in the same way. On account of these differences of language communication and mutual understanding were difficult, leaving the two parts of the Christian world to drift apart. Racial differences led to religious variations that finally made further communion impossible. In the East, where the Greek language was known and employed, the church continued to administer immersion only as baptism; in the West, where Latin was spoken, other forms were admitted in exceptional cases and finally as general usage; in the East only the bishops were required to abstain from marriage, while in the West marriage was forbidden to all the clergy; in the East leavened and in the West

unleavened bread was used in communion; the East held
that the Holy Spirit proceeds from the Father *through* the
Son, the West that he proceeds from the Father *and* the Son;
the Easter and Christmas reckoning differed in the two
sections, and there was much rivalry between the pope and
the patriarch of Constantinople.

Relations became very strained in the ninth century when
the pope went so far as to excommunicate the patriarch for
several years. Controversy broke out afresh in the eleventh
century and on July 16, 1054, the pope and the patriarch
mutually excommunicated each the other and his followers,
condemning them to everlasting perdition. This condemnation has never been recalled, though there have been numerous attempts at reconciliation. Henceforth, there was an
Eastern and a Western Catholic church, opposing each
other at many points of contact.

§ 36

CONTROVERSY OVER IMAGE WORSHIP

Although many of the early Christians came from
heathenism, where they had been accustomed to the use of
images in worship, these were apparently entirely discarded
in the early churches. But as time passed, feeling among
the Christians gradually changed, due no doubt to the early
disappearance of the Jewish element from the churches.
At any rate we find pictures and images of various kinds
in the catacombs from the second and third centuries. They
were symbolic as we saw in an earlier chapter. Just how
soon they were introduced into worship and into the
churches it is now impossible to determine. It seems probable that they were brought in at first for didactic purposes
rather than as a feature of worship, but we know they were
welcomed and finally called forth the enthusiastic veneration
and support of the worshipers. By the eighth century the
superstitious adoration with which they were regarded was

almost as gross as the idolatry of the heathen themselves. Jews, Mohammedans and a few Christians declared it to be idolatry, charging that the Catholic church had become both polytheistic and idolatrous. Reform was urgently needed.

The attempt at reform was the work of laymen, while the monks and clergy and most of the women passionately supported the use of images. The effort to remove images was led by the emperor and the army. In 726 the Emperor Leo III ordered the images in the churches to be elevated so that the people could not kiss and fondle them, as they were doing. In 730 he ordered them to be taken out of the churches entirely and destroyed. The church authorities resisted the order, but it was carried out forcibly by the army and was accompanied by much rioting and bloodshed.

Images were now kept out of the churches in the East for about fifty years, but in 780 they were restored by the Empress Irene, who was an enthusiastic supporter of them. In 787 she called a council (the last one recognized as ecumenical by both the Eastern and Western churches), which approved the use of images in worship, but declared that worship (*latria*) must be given to God alone, while service (*douleia*) or veneration (*veneratio*) could be rendered to images. This theoretical distinction between the *worship* given to God and the *veneration* given to images is still maintained by both the Catholic churches, and it is on the basis of this distinction that they deny that they are idolaters or Mariolaters.

This council did not, however, bring the controversy to an end. In 813 the Emperor Leo V took up the fight again. For a time he was successful, but in 842 another woman, Theodora, the imperial regent, had images restored to the churches. Since that time they have never been disturbed in the Eastern church, which uses, however, only flat surfaces, rejecting statues entirely.

In the West objection to images had little support. The pope steadily encouraged their use, while Charlemagne ap-

proved them for their didactic value. The controversy led
the pope to excommunicate the Eastern iconoclasts in 731.
The emperor responded by confiscating the papal estates in
the Eastern provinces and annexing the churches of southern Italy, Sicily and Illyria, all of which were under his political control, to the patriarchate of Constantinople. The
controversy grew in bitterness until the pope renounced his
allegiance to the emperor and soon afterward allied himself
with the Franks in the West. Images were not again disturbed in the West until the Reformation in the sixteenth
century. The great controversy had only served to fasten
them more firmly in Christian worship.

§ 37

THE RISE OF THE PAPAL STATE

The beginnings of the Papal State are still shrouded in
obscurity, but the course of development seems to have
been about as follows. Like the bishops of other cities the
bishop of Rome early became a land-owner in the name of
the church. On account of the wealth and influence of the
Roman church its possessions were larger and more widely
distributed than those of any other church. This ownership of land gave to the bishop immense influence, and as
civil government decayed in the West and fell in ruins in
the Germanic invasion, economic ownership was gradually
transformed into a quasi-political control. This was especially true of a large district in the immediate neighborhood of Rome, which was known as the Patrimony of
Peter (*patrimonium Petri*). For two centuries the Lombards had held all of central Italy except this *Patrimonium
Petri,* when about the middle of the eighth century they
began to make encroachments on this territory. The pope
could do no more than protest since he was not strong
enough to resist and had recently broken with the Eastern
emperor, who had long been his protector.

These conditions led the pope to seek alliance with the rising Frankish power, already the most important government in the West. Accordingly Boniface, with the sanction of the pope, assisted in the overthrow of the Merovingian line of Frankish kings and the accession of the Carlovingians by anointing Pippin king of the Franks at Soissons in 751. Three years later the pope himself was driven into exile by the Lombards. He naturally fled to his new allies, and in 754 he crowned and anointed Pippin and his sons as the lawful sovereigns of the Franks. By way of recompense Pippin the next year invaded the Lombard territories, destroyed their power and established the pope's rule over central Italy. This was the beginning of the pope's position as the recognized civil and political ruler of central Italy, which was henceforth known as the papal states. In 773 Charlemagne destroyed the last vestige of the Lombard kingdom, confirmed the pope's authority and considerably enlarged his dominions. From this time on the pope was not only a religious leader, but also a political ruler of influence and the Papal State was a reality. It continued to cut the Italian peninsula in two until the reunion of Italy under one government in 1870.

§ 38

THE REVIVAL OF THE EMPIRE IN THE WEST

As we have seen the western part of the empire was knocked to pieces in the fifth century by the Germans, who set up several independent governments. In the east it continued, with Constantinople as its capital, and was later called the Byzantine empire as it became more and more Oriental, but it was politically a continuation of the old Roman empire.

After a time the Franks began to unite the political fragments of the West again by extending their sway over much of the territory that had once composed the western part of the Roman empire. As their dominions extended dreams of reviving that empire began to haunt the Frankish mind. These ambitions embodied themselves in Charlemagne. To his title as *King of the Franks* he added *King of Italy* in 773 when he overthrew the Lombards and established his own sway over northern Italy as far south as the Papal State. Finally on Christmas day 800 while he was kneeling in worship at the grave of St. Peter in Rome the pope suddenly advanced and placed upon his head the imperial crown, thus restoring the empire in the West and constituting Charlemagne emperor. Irene was then officiating as empress in Constantinople, but the West refused to recognize her or her government and declared the throne to be vacant; hence, they claimed, there was place for Charlemagne to become emperor. There were now two political powers, each claiming to be the only empire and refusing to recognize the claims of the other.

As a matter of fact Charlemagne's act was one of the most fateful in the whole history of Europe. It laid the foundation for the long and exhausting struggle between the emperor and the pope, between Germany and the papal power in Italy, which is to break out in the next period.

After the death of Charlemagne the Frankish imperial power decayed very rapidly, but in the tenth century it was restored by the great emperors, Henry the Fowler and Otto the Great. In 962 Otto again made his way to Rome, where he deposed a very unworthy pope, appointed a worthier one and compelled the Romans to promise never to select a pope in the future without the emperor's approval. He then had himself crowned emperor of *The Holy Roman Empire of the German Nation*. For nearly a century after this time the German emperor dominated the papacy, appointing and deposing popes at will. And it must be admitted that this method of procedure materially improved the character and ability of the popes. For a long while none but Germans were appointed to this high office. The fortunes and the moral condition of the papacy

were never again as low as they had been the first half of
the tenth century.

§ 39

THE GROWING POWER OF THE PAPACY

Many things contributed to the elevation of the pope in
this period. The rise and spread of Mohammedanism
weakened his great rivals in the East, alliance with the
Franks gave him a powerful political support in the West,
the establishment of the Papal State made him a political
ruler over central Italy and secured *entré* into diplomatic
circles, missions extended his sway over all of western
and most of northern Europe, and finally the general decay of society made all elements turn to him for support.
By the middle of the ninth century he began to cherish
ambitions of ruling over the churches of the whole world
and over the princes of the western world. About the middle of this century there was forged, somewhere in Germany or France, a document called the " Donation of Constantine," in which it was declared that the Emperor Constantine had on his conversion withdrawn from Rome and
donated all his imperial dignities and paraphernalia to the
pope, constituting him ruler over all the churches of the
whole world and over all the princes of the West. The
popes, even if they had nothing to do with the fabrication
of this document, eagerly seized and used it through succeeding centuries as a means of realizing its ideas. Henceforth there swayed before their eyes continually the hope of
dominating the whole world.

As missionary effort extended into new heathen territory
bishoprics and archbishoprics were established and the hierarchy was extended in obedience to the Roman See. In
Germany many of the bishops were elevated into the position of civil rulers and were rated as princes. In order to
control them the emperors came to assert their right to

appoint them, insisting that the episcopal power was so great as to render such control necessary, thus laying the foundations for future struggles with the popes.

§ 40

CHRISTIAN LIFE AND WORSHIP

During this period monasticism grew to a position of leadership in the Catholic church — a power which it has never since lost. Monasteries for both men and women were multiplied in the older Christian lands and were rapidly established in the newly Christianized countries. In fact the monks and nuns had before the end of this period come to constitute almost the sole agency for the prosecution of missionary work. Pushing far out into heathen territory they established monasteries and from these institutions by preaching, teaching and service they evangelized the surrounding country. Almost every monastery had a school attached and for a long time these were the only schools among the Germanic peoples. The monks wrote and copied the books, taught the schools, produced the literature, and in general were the principal conservators of the religion and civilization of the time. The monasteries in this and the succeeding periods were the most famous institutions of the Christian world.

As would be expected under the conditions detailed above there was a general decline in Christian life and worship all over the world. The church continued to absorb elements from the heathenism which it was supplanting and thus continued to grow more corrupt. Nearly all the superstitions of the Germanic world soon found place in the German church. The conflict of races, the mingling of various degrees of culture, the breaking down of religious convictions and social customs led to an inevitable decline in morals. High church officials were often chosen for their social position or political influence rather than for any fitness to perform the spiritual functions of the church. Bishops, archbishops and even popes were sometimes notoriously immoral and utterly careless of their duties as shepherds of souls. The lower clergy were usually ignorant and little fitted for their duties. This is the " dark age " of European history from the moral and religious standpoint as well as from the cultural. The church of the West suffered with the general decline.

It was a great misfortune that the church carried the Latin as the language of culture and religion into these Germanic lands. The Bible and the worship were retained in this foreign and dying tongue, thus depriving the great mass of the people of acquaintance with the Bible and adequate understanding of the service. By this means the unity and uniformity of the church was maintained, but at the expense of efficiency in instruction. For several centuries only fragments of the Scriptures were translated into the living languages of the European peoples.

The process of endowing the churches and monasteries proceeded very rapidly, and they were also permitted to collect the tithe or church tax in many parts of the Christian world. Men believed that they could purchase blessings by the gift of money to the church and this belief was a mighty stimulus to liberality.

Private confession began to be common and was occasionally required; the use of the organ in worship was introduced in the West in the eighth century. The church had long been accustomed to impose punishment on its members as a part of its discipline. During this period the custom was established of permitting the commutation of a part of this punishment by the payment of money into the treasury of the church. This commutation was called an *indulgence,* and was destined to play a very important part in the future history of the Catholic church.

§ 41

ANTI-CATHOLIC PARTIES

We have thus far been following the main stream of Christian history, but not all Christians were Catholics. Not only did the Nestorians and other independent bodies in the East maintain their existence; some of them, notably the Nestorians, flourished.

Still other evangelical parties appear. Perhaps the most important of these were the Paulicians, who first come into the view of history about the middle of the seventh century in southeastern Armenia. Their name is said to have been derived from the apostle, Paul, whose teachings they sought to reproduce in their churches. They seem to have preserved democratic church government, to have had only one grade of ministers, to have practiced the baptism of believers only; they rejected saint, image and relic worship, the hierarchy and the doctrine of purgatory; in short they rejected the whole sacramental theory of salvation and believed and practiced a type of Christianity that was almost wholly biblical.

They were bitterly persecuted by the Catholics, but maintained their existence in Armenia and Asia Minor for several centuries, being at one time a very influential part of the body politic. Some of them were transplanted to the Balkan region, where they flourished for several centuries in Bulgaria and neighboring lands.

The Bogomiles or Friends of God were another anti-Catholic party of this period. They appeared in southeastern Europe about the middle of the tenth century and may have been derived from the Paulicians, though they were less evangelical. They rejected the entire Catholic system with all possible decision, but were themselves more or less heretical. They rejected baptism and the supper, were ascetic in morals and dualistic in theology.

FIFTH PERIOD — 1050 TO 1300

A. HISTORY IN THE EAST

§ 42

GENERAL TENDENCIES

THE tendency in the eastern part of the Christian world
was steadily downward. The new menace was the Turks.
These rude and cruel heathen people, coming from the interior of Asia, appeared in eastern Persia about the middle
of the ninth century. Gradually they acquired unity and
power and finally overthrew the Persian government, accepted Mohammedanism and usurped the political authority
of the Caliph at Bagdad, establishing themselves as the political leaders of eastern Mohammedanism. By 1050 they
were the masters of Persia. They then turned westward
against both the empire which was Christian and the Arabs
who were Mohammedan. Nothing could resist them.
They rapidly wrested Armenia and the interior of Asia
Minor from the empire, and Syria and Palestine from the
Fatimate caliphate of Cairo. Jerusalem was captured from
the Arabs in 1075.

§ 42ᵃ

THE CRUSADES

This advance of the Turks occasioned the Crusades.
The Turks were much more ruthless than the Arabs had
been, particularly in their dealings with the stream of Christian pilgrims that now flowed continually from western
Europe to the holy places of Palestine. The hardships and
sufferings of these pilgrims at the hands of these Turkish

conquerors of Palestine gradually aroused all western
Europe to attempt to recover and bring under Christian
control the holy places.   These efforts are called Crusades
or Wars of the Cross, and constitute one of the most ro-
mantic chapters of Christian history.   They began in 1095
and did not end till 1292, almost exactly two centuries.
The first Crusade, consisting almost exclusively of Frankish
and Norman nobles and their followers, succeeded in re-
covering all of Syria and Palestine and much territory on
the uppper Euphrates.   A Kingdom of Jerusalem and some
smaller governments were set up, and the *Roman* Catholic
church was established in the conquered territory.   This
was a tremendous check to the Turkish power enabling the
eastern empire to recover control over most of Asia Minor
and roll back the Turkish flood for a century and more.

But in 1203 the fourth Crusade turned aside to Constantinople to replace on the throne Isaac Angelus, who
had been deposed and blinded by his brother.   Constantinople was captured and Isaac was restored, but in attempt-
ing to raise the indemnity which the Crusaders required for
their services he provoked a revolt in which he lost his
life.   The Crusaders then captured the city again and set
up a Latin Empire over the city and as much of the imperial territory as they could control.   As in Palestine the
Roman Catholic church was established throughout this
territory in the room of the Greek.

But they could not conquer all the imperial territory.   Independent Greek governments were set up where the Crusaders could not control.   Gradually that one which had its
capital at Nicæa gained the upper hand and eventually in
1261 succeeded in recapturing Constantinople and driving
the Crusaders out of the country.   In the struggle the city
was stripped of most of its wealth and was never again able
to recover its former power.   At the end of the period the
governments of both the empire and of the Turks were in
disorder.   This period had been one of general decay in the
East.

FIFTH PERIOD — 1050 TO 1300

B. HISTORY IN THE WEST

§ 43

GENERAL TENDENCIES

In the West the general tendency during this period was steadily and continually upward in almost every respect. This was particularly the case among the Germanic peoples. The Mohammedans continued to hold all of north Africa, most of Spain and the islands of the western Mediterranean. Naturally there was stagnation in these regions as far as Christianity was concerned, though there was a striking culture among the Mohammedan Moors in Spain.

There was revival of intellectual activity and moral earnestness along the northern shores of the Mediterranean and in Italy, but the greatest gains were farther north. The Scandinavian peoples, known as Northmen or Normans, had swooped down on their more civilized southern neighbors in the preceding period, robbing, burning and destroying. They had thus harried the coasts of Germany and northern France, and had almost completely overrun England. They were then raw heathen. During this period they settled down, accepted the Christian religion and made themselves one of the most vital elements in the life of the nations where they made their home. In northern France they populated the important district henceforth known as Normandy. In 1066 William, the Duke of Normandy, made himself king of England, thus binding together sections of France and the English crown in a way that entailed endless bloodshed and suffering in later centuries.

The Normans also passed through the Strait of Gibraltar into the Mediterranean, overthrew the Greek power in southern Italy and the Mohammedan power in Sicily and established a Norman duchy which later became the king-

dom of Sicily.   For centuries they were an important political factor in the history of the Mediterranean.   Thus
order was being slowly established and civilization extended
over all of western Christendom.

§ 44

MISSIONS AND CULTURE

During this period the remainder of northern and western Europe was converted, becoming nominally Christian
from the Mediterranean to the Arctic Ocean.   The religion
was Catholicism of course and at every step it had taken
on some element of the heathenism it was conquering.   As
heretofore its advances had been made through opposition,
discouragement and suffering.   But the work was done.
A few centuries in the future these countries will take the
lead in throwing off the papal yoke, and will draw from
the Bible a spiritual and moral power which will crush the
ecclesiastical shell and liberate the spiritual kernel of Christianity.

There was in the period a religious revival which was
accompanied by growing intellectual activity.   *Monastic
and cathedral schools* were planted everywhere as the chief
means of transmitting to the Germanic peoples the culture
which had once belonged to the Latins.   In the eleventh
and twelfth centuries some of these schools began to grow
into *universities,* in whose class-rooms the ablest men of the
times lectured.   Thus Oxford, Cambridge, Paris, Cologne,
Bologna and others arose in these centuries.   They were
supposed to teach all knowledge and were often attended
by thousands of students.

In addition to the founding of schools this age produced
an *extensive literature* dealing almost exclusively with religious and theological themes.   It was in the Latin language and was intended for the learned only, for as yet
there was *no demand for a popular literature.*   It was
marked by acute and profound thinking, and still to this day

deeply influences the Roman Catholic church. Nearly all the distinctive Roman Catholic doctrines were worked out during this period, such as transubstantiation, the seven sacraments, purgatory, indulgences, etc. Judged by the quantity and quality of its output this must be termed an age of great intellectual activity. The foundation for the culture of modern Europe was securely laid. Much of the intellectual activity and output of this period is known as scholasticism.

§ 45

GROWTH OF PAPAL POWER

Beginning about 1050 the papacy grew rapidly in influence and power, reaching the very apex of its glory in the pontificate of Innocent III about 1215. Many things contributed to this growth, but the most important was a series of very able men in the papal chair. About 1050 Hildebrand, afterwards Gregory VII, began his fight for the reform of the church in head and members, that is from the papacy down to the parish priest. To accomplish this reform he believed it was necessary to free the church from all control by the state and indeed to make the state subservient to the church. Accordingly it was decreed by a council in 1059 that the pope must be elected in the future by the cardinal bishops and only be approved by the other cardinals and the clergy and people of Rome. This action relieved the papal elections of imperial pressure and also from the Italian factions that often disgraced the elections. In 1179 it was decreed by another council that two thirds of the cardinals were necessary to an election, thus making the election of two popes improbable in the future.

Other factors in this rise were activities of papal missionaries, the founding of great Catholic schools, the leadership of the crusades, the codification of canon law into a well articulated and consistent legal system which was ex-

tended over the whole Catholic world, the dispatch of
legates to all parts of the world as the pope's personal
representatives, the enlargement of the monastic orders and
their subjection to the direct authority of the pope and the
final triumph of sacerdotal celibacy which detached the
clergy from all social ties and attached them directly and
absolutely to their ecclesiastical superiors.

§ 46

STRUGGLE BETWEEN CHURCH AND STATE

The rise of the church precipitated a great struggle with
the state. The church had long since become a political
power that the world had to reckon with. Its immense
wealth in real property, which had been accumulated by
the gifts of the faithful through the centuries, its great moral
influence over men and the feudal authority of many of its
bishops, archbishops and abbots made it appear necessary
for the state to control it. For centuries this had been
accomplished by the appointment of the high ecclesiastical
officials by the princes. But the princes had frequently appointed unworthy men, and had sometimes sold the positions outright. The conflicting interests of these two mighty
powers occasioned the greatest struggle between church
and state that the world has ever seen. It began about the
middle of the eleventh century and raged for two hundred
years until the church and the empire (the country chiefly
involved), were both well-nigh exhausted. It began by the
popes forbidding the princes to appoint ecclesiastical officials; the princes responded by cutting off papal revenues
and deposing the popes. The popes again and again excommunicated emperors and kings, put their countries under
the interdict and forced them to obedience. Henry IV of
Germany stood before the castle of Canossa in midwinter,
in the garb of a suppliant pilgrim, beseeching the forgiveness of his holiness the pope; a century later Frederick Bar-

barossa at Venice led the pope's horse as a sign of his sub-
mission to the Holy Father; in 1215 John of England took
off his crown, handed it to a representative of the pope and
received it back as a fief of the Holy See. Lesser digni-
taries were treated accordingly. The papal theory was that
the church, being the spiritual power, must rule over the
state which is a secular power. The spiritual sword is
wielded *by* the church, while the temporal sword is wielded
by the state *for* the church and at the command of the
church.

On the other hand the state responded as energetically as
possible, and strong rulers were usually able to resist the
papal claims and assumptions. Still at the end of our period
the church seemed to have the better of the struggle. The
empire was in disorder while the church appeared to be
supreme.

§ 47

GROWTH OF MONASTICISM

This was preëminently the monastic age of Christianity.
All the old orders were reformed and enlarged, and many
new ones were founded. But the most significant phenomenon in this field was the appearance of a new type of
monasticism, namely that of the *brotherhood*. The older
monasticism remained within monastic walls, chiefly concerned with the salvation of its own soul and incidentally
rendering such service as it could within the narrow con-
fines of the monastery. The new monasticism took the
same vows of poverty, chastity and obedience, but its aim
was service. It went out into the world and devoted itself
to the service of the people, asking only bread and simple
clothing in return. These monks were known as *friars*
(brothers) and because they lived from what they received
from the people they were called mendicants or beggars.
The two great orders of this type founded at this time were
the Franciscans, founded by Francis of Assisi, in the year

1213, and the Dominicans founded by Dominic, a Spanish noble, in 1216.

Francis was a man of wonderful spiritual powers and unselfish devotion. He gathered around him and ultimately organized a body of likeminded men whose official title was *fratres minores* (Little Brothers),— an organization whose purpose was service in all possible ways. The official designation of the other order was *fratres predicatores* (Preaching Brothers), their special object being popular preaching primarily to meet the popular preaching of the Waldenses and other evangelical parties in southeastern France.

Both orders spread rapidly over the Catholic world and everywhere awakened new life in the church. They soon began to furnish the theological professors of the universities, the most effective popes, the missionaries and to fill most of the other positions of influence and importance in the church. Like the other orders they eventually became rich and corrupt, thus arousing opposition and resentment. They differed from each other in theology and in other respects and were often sharp and bitter rivals, but henceforth they did a large share of the hard work of the Catholic church. Each was controlled by a general who lived at Rome in close relations with the pope.

§ 48

CATHOLIC THEOLOGY

In this period the formulation of Catholic theology was virtually completed. It was the second great period of theological discussion and formulation, the fourth and fifth centuries being the first. In the first period those doctrines which are still accepted by nearly all Christians were stated; in this period the doctrines which are distinctively Catholic, separating that church from other Christian bodies, were drawn up. The church produced many able and famous men who are still held in great reverence by the Catholic church. Some of these are Anselm (1059–1109), an Italian of great learning and saintly life, who became archbishop of Canterbury in England and stated the doctrine of the atonement as most orthodox Christians, Protestant as well as Catholic, still accept it; Abelard (1079–1142), a Frenchman and one of the most famous teachers of all time; Bernard of Clairvaux (1091–1153), another Frenchman who was a great churchman, preacher and hymn-writer; Peter Lombard (1100–64) who compiled the most famous textbook of theology in the Middle Ages; Thomas Aquinas (1227–74), one of the profoundest thinkers of Christian history, a voluminous writer who is still regarded as *the* teacher of the Catholic church, its most influential theologian; John Duns Scotus (1266–1308), a Scotchman, subtle dialectician and bold thinker. The antagonisms of the last two named divided the whole Catholic world into two hostile schools of thought, known as Thomists and Scotists, for several centuries.

Several of the most characteristic doctrines of the Catholic church were discussed to a finish in this period. Some of these were *transubstantiation* (the change of the substance of the bread and the wine into the actual body and blood of Christ), formally adopted as the doctrine of the church at the fourth Lateran Council in 1215; the formal approval of substitutes for immersion as baptism at the same Council; the doctrine of purgatory, the seven sacraments, indulgences, etc., to be formulated at the Council of Trent. In short this was preëminently the Catholic period in doctrine and life.

§ 49

WORSHIP IN THIS PERIOD

The sacrifice of the Mass had now fully established itself as the center and heart of Catholic worship. As a ceremony it consists of the recital of texts of Scripture accompanied by symbolic actions intended to reproduce the events of the passion of our Lord from his arrest to his ascension. In the midst of the ceremony the bread and the wine are consecrated and thereby transformed into the glorified body and blood of our Lord, to be worshiped in the service and later taken in the communion. The whole ceremony of the Mass, however, is regarded as a repetition of the sacrifice of Jesus Christ on Calvary in every respect except that there is no blood. The Mass is "the unbloody sacrifice." Every Mass in all of Christendom is the repetition of that first sacrifice of our Lord. The cup was gradually withdrawn from the laity in this period to prevent the spilling of the consecrated wine, and infant communion, which had been practiced for centuries, was discontinued largely for the same reason. Some of the consecrated wafers were constantly kept at the churches to be administered to those who were in extreme need. In communion the wafer is placed on the tongue of the recipient by the hand of the priest and it is regarded as a mortal sin to remove it for any reason whatsoever. Thus the Mass and the communion became the most sacred mysteries of the church and its worship.

There is a revival of preaching in this period due chiefly to the Crusades and the activities of the new evangelical sects in southern Europe. They propagated their tenets by quiet preaching in the open air as well as in buildings. So successful was their propaganda that the Catholics felt constrained to follow their example and fight them with their own weapons. The Crusades had also stimulated preaching. They offered a great object to which men had to be persuaded by direct personal appeal. The result was the development of a number of really great preachers and much popular preaching of a lower order. Peter the Hermit and Urban II, the preachers of the first Crusade, Bernard of Clairvaux who aroused Europe to the second Crusade and others. The Dominican order was founded, we have seen, for the express purpose of preaching, and called itself "Preaching Brothers."

Much was made of the annual seasons of worship, thus overshadowing the Lord's day. Almost every day was devoted to some saint or to some event in the apostolic history or the life of Jesus. The adoration of the wafer at the elevation of the host was ordained in 1217 and the feast of *Corpus Christi* (the body of Christ), in 1264. The name of Mary was inserted in the liturgy and the *Ave Maria* began to come into use in the eleventh century, and about the same time the feast of the *Immaculate Conception* began to appear.

Perhaps the most notable achievement in the realm of worship in this period was the development in church architecture. Many of the most splendid churches and cathedrals of the world were erected in this period. In England, France and Germany all the artistic genius of Christendom was employed upon these glorious houses of worship. They were large, highly ornamented, enormously costly in time and money. The beauty and impressiveness of the great cathedrals and monastic buildings have never been surpassed in the history of architecture. They were built as places of Catholic worship and burial, being entirely unsuited to preaching and the church life of to-day. They were usually of stone, elaborately carved on the outside, sustained by massive pillars on the inside, surmounted with domes, tall spires or heavy towers and adorned with wonderful art-glass windows. These enormous piles were years, even centuries, in building, their purpose the glory of God. Some of the most notable of these great churches are Canterbury, York and Durham cathedrals in England, Notre Dame and Rheims in France, Strassburg in Germany and Milan in Italy.

§ 50

THE RISE OF EVANGELICAL SECTS

It is possible that evangelical Christians had existed at various places in western Europe through all the centuries of Catholic dominance as we have seen them in Asia Minor and eastern Europe. Certain it is that a number of sects appear in this period so powerful that the church was unable to suppress them. The opposition of these parties took many forms. Sometimes it remained in the Catholic church and attempted to reform that body. More often it was outside the Catholic church and was bitterly hostile to its doctrines, practices, worship and organization. The sects began to appear about the year 1000 and could never be stamped out entirely from that time onward. The earliest in western Europe were known as *Albigenses*. They appeared in southeastern France and opposed the Catholic church at almost every point, though they were themselves unscriptural in some of their doctrines.

A much more evangelical party appeared in the twelfth century in western Switzerland and eastern France known as *Petrobrusians* and *Henricans*. Still another party, known as *Waldenses,* originated about 1170 at Lyons in southern France. They were founded by Peter Waldo, a wealthy Catholic merchant converted by the Scriptures, who left his business, distributed his property and began itinerant evangelical preaching about 1178. He was joined by other likeminded men who called themselves the "Poor Men of Lyons." In 1179 they were forbidden by the Lateran Council to preach, and when they continued they were excommunicated in 1184. They then organized as a separate hostile sect, and spread rapidly over much of France, northern Italy, Germany, Austria and Spain. They were thoroughly evangelical, rejecting every distinctive doctrine and practice of the Catholic church. Notwithstanding fearful persecutions they were able to maintain their existence, and were a powerful evangelical leaven in all of central Europe. They are even to-day the strongest evangelical party in Italy.

§ 51

THE INQUISITION

Since the days of Augustine the church had been inclined to persecute heretics, feeling that the best interests of religion and society as well as the salvation of the heretic himself were thereby attained. Since the days of Constantine the state had been willing now and then to carry into effect the wishes of the church in this respect. Several times blood had flowed freely, the heathen governments having set the example followed by the Christians later.

For a long while the apprehension of heretics had been regarded as the duty of the bishops. But some of these, owing to kindliness or indifference, were negligent or inefficient in hunting down heretics. After several councils had vainly tried to stiffen the persecutions it was decided to create a separate agency whose sole duty it should be to extirpate heresy. This tribunal known as the Inquisition and organized by the pope, was in 1232 placed in the hands of the Dominicans. It was entirely independent of the bishops and directly subject to the pope, having a jurisdiction independent of that of the state and the local church officials. This was probably the most cruel and inhuman tribunal known to history. It could arrest without stating the reason, was not compelled to produce witnesses at the trial, and was permitted to use torture in extorting confessions from the accused or testimony from unwilling witnesses. Upon conviction of heresy the punishment for those who renounced their views was life-long imprisonment; those who refused to recant were condemned to death and turned over to the civil authorities who were required under .pain of excommunication to execute the church's sentence. Usually heretics were executed by burning or some other horribly painful and humiliating method. Rarely did one who fell under the suspicion of heresy ever escape. Thousands were put to death, especially in France and Spain where the government was more disposed to obey the church than in Germany and England. The Catholic church will never be able to cleanse itself from the shame of these bloody tragedies. Our period closes with the Inquisition doing its worst.

SIXTH PERIOD — 1300 TO 1517

A. EASTERN CHRISTIANITY

§ 52

INVASION OF THE MONGOLS OR TARTARS

ABOUT the beginning of the 13th century there arose in the interior of Asia north of China a new power which was destined to exert a profound influence upon eastern Christianity for centuries. Under the leadership of Genghis Kahn the Mongols, who were still utterly barbarous heathen, conquered all of northern China and all of Hindoostan to the Caspian Sea. After his death in 1227 his successors carried his conquests farther to the south, north and west. All of China was subdued and placed under a Mongol dynasty, which soon adopted Buddhism as its religion.

One section of them turned northward into Russia. All the southern and western portions were overrun about 1237, Kiev and Moscow were burned and the country subjected to the Mongol or Tartar yoke for the next two hundred and fifty years. These two and a half centuries under the heel of the " Golden Horde," as the Tartars called themselves, had a disastrous effect on the development of the life and religion of the Russian people from which they have not yet fully recovered.

From Russia this division of the Mongols moved westward through Poland into eastern Germany, burning and destroying everything in their path. At the great battle of Liegnitz their advance in this direction was stopped. They then turned southward into Hungary and along the Danube, their course marked by the smoldering ruins of towns and churches and by heaps of slain. Laden with spoil they finally withdrew to Russia.

But if the suffering of the Christians was great that of some Mohammedans was no less so. The Empire of Persia and the Caliphate of Bagdad were overthrown and destroyed.

The Mongol hordes then pressed on westward, destroying the Turkish power, and capturing and sacking the principal cities of Asia almost to the Mediterranean. This group finally accepted Mohammedanism and became staunch supporters of its persecuting measures.

The unified government of these western Mongols now broke up and for a time their power waned. But about 1400 another irruption of these people took place under the leadership of Tamerlane. All western Asia was again devastated almost to the Mediterranean. The slaughter of the helpless people was frightful, sometimes reaching into the tens of thousands in the sack of one city. The power of these Mongols finally came to an end in western Asia with the death of Tamerlane in 1405, but Russia continued to suffer.

§ 53

FURTHER ADVANCE OF THE TURKS

At the conclusion of the last period the empire of the Seljuk Turks had fallen into disorder and was on the point of dissolution. Its complete disintegration was hastened and completed by the invasion of the Mongols as related above.

But upon its ruins rose another Turkish empire, vaster and more powerful than the Seljuks had ever been. This new empire was founded by Othman or Ottoman in the heart of Asia Minor about the year 1300. From very small beginnings these Ottoman Turks, as they are called from their founder, rapidly enlarged their territory by conquests from both the Christians and the Mohammedans. Within forty years they had destroyed all Christian government

in Asia and in 1355 planted foot firmly on the continent of
Europe by the capture and fortifying of Gallipoli. In 1361
they captured Adrianople and made it their capital. In
1402 they received a severe backset when Tamerlane defeated them at the great battle of Ancyra and captured their
Sultan Bajazet. However they quickly recovered after
his death and the whole Balkan peninsula was then rapidly
reduced. On May 29, 1453 Constantinople itself was captured and made the capital of their empire, thus bringing to
a final end the old Roman empire. The extinction of this
ancient Christian empire is perhaps the greatest tragedy
that has ever befallen the Christian religion.

In the meantime the Ottoman Turks had been extending
their conquests eastward and southward over their Mohammedan neighbors, Turkish and Arabian, till at the end
of our period the Ottoman empire stretched from the Danube to the cataracts of the Nile and from the Euphrates to
the middle of the Mediterranean. For many years they
had been seeking to force the passage of the Danube which
was defended by the heroism of the Hungarians, and early
in the next period they will, under the leadership of Sulei-
man the Magnificent with whose reign the empire attained
its widest extent, lay siege to Vienna the capital of Austria
itself.

For several centuries the whole of the Greek Catholic
church with the exception of that of Russia lay helpless
under the heel of " the unspeakable Turk." Under them
the church was transformed into a political institution whose
chief duty was to serve its Turkish masters in the collection
of taxes and the preservation of order. The Christians
were compelled to support the government, to pay a tithe of
their sons who were reared as Mohammedans and organized into the famous Janizaries, the first standing army
of Europe. The Patriarch of Constantinople was selected
by the Turkish government and the bishops and lower clergy
were practically officers of the Turkish state. The church
buildings, many of the most beautiful of them, were taken

as mosques, conversion to Christianity was forbidden and in general the whole tone and spirit of Christianity was fearfully depressed. Christian worship was tolerated, but its effectiveness and power were nullified. Selim I obtained from Egypt the Caliphate or spiritual headship of all Mohammedans in 1517, since which date the Sultan has been both the political and spiritual head of most of the Mohammedan world. The tragedy of Turkish power in southeastern Europe was at its height at the end of our period. All Europe was trembling before what seemed to be an irresistible and ruthless foe.

§ 54

CHRISTIANITY IN INTERIOR ASIA

Many indications lead to the belief that Christians were to be found in considerable numbers in interior Asia in this period. They were mostly Nestorians and if Catholic writers can be believed they were active but lacking in the culture and character necessary to a successful Christian propaganda. The widespread rumor that an extensive Christian kingdom, lying to the north of China and ruled over by a priest-king, Prester John, seems to have had no foundation in fact. It was so far believed, however, that the pope sent an embassage to the interior of Asia in search of this supposedly Christian prince.

But a century later when the Mongols extended their conquests into the West the eyes of the pope were again turned to the Far East. From the middle of the thirteenth century missionaries were sent to eastern Asia in the hope of making some impression upon the barbaric heathenism of that region. These missionaries, and travelers like Marco Polo, found the Mongols tolerant of all religions, the three principal ones at court being Buddhism, Mohammedanism and Nestorian Christianity. Catholic missionaries finally reached the court of the great Kahn at Pekin in

1303. They were hospitably received and were permitted to erect two church buildings, one of them very near the royal palace and overtopping it. They translated the Psalms and the New Testament into the Tartar language and succeeded in baptizing 6000 converts in a very short time. All indications pointed to a successful mission for these Catholics, but the Mongols were overthrown by the Ming dynasty which suppressed Christianity in 1368. Many scholars believe that the Buddhism of central Asia was sensibly affected by this somewhat fleeting presence of Christianity. But in the providence of God the Far East remained practically closed to Christianity till Protestantism was able to take up mission work with a far more apostolic type of Christian faith than the Nestorians or the Catholics could have carried to these regions.

§ 55

CHRISTIANITY IN RUSSIA

Russia was under Mongol domination most of this period. But notwithstanding the stagnation and clog upon progress which such an invasion involved the Russian church made some progress. Most of the tribes in the frozen north such as the Laps and Finns were Christianized, the seat of the Metropolitan or head of the Russian church was removed from Kiev to Moscow in 1305 and after the fall of Constantinople was made entirely independent of the patriarch of that city. During all the earlier history of the Russian church its head had been appointed by this patriarch and naturally had been a Greek; henceforth the Metropolitan was elected by Russian bishops and was a native Russian, a great gain.

Monasticism had a remarkable growth and became the chief religious force in Russia. The buildings were enormous fortified outposts of civilization, fitted for both the defense and the propagation of culture and religion. They are still the most impressive buildings in the country, and manifest all the barbaric splendor of that great people. Russian monasticism does not show that great variety which we see in the West. All live under the same rule, that of St. Basil, and the ideal of service which is found among the western friars is not so manifest. Their aim is the cultivation of the contemplative life. Bishops must be unmarried men, hence all bishops come from the monasteries. On the other hand all priests must be married, hence no parish priest ever becomes a bishop.

Repeated efforts were made by the pope to bring about a union of the whole Greek church with the Roman church. The effort met with very little success in Russia or elsewhere except on paper. The culture and the religious direction and inspiration of Russia came from Constantinople. Ivan III (1462–1505), who was the first really great ruler of Russia, married the daughter of the Greek emperor and used all available means to induce scholars to lend their services to Russia. Constantinople had just fallen, and Ivan appropriated the double-headed eagle of the empire and called himself Czar, thus indicating his feeling that Russia was for the future to be the successor of the Byzantine empire. Our period closes with the country on the eve of its period of great expansion.

B. WESTERN CHRISTIANITY

§ 56

GENERAL CONDITIONS

In the West the history of this period was marked by no such great movements of the peoples as we have observed in earlier periods and in the East in this period. Racial and political conditions were fairly stable. The most notable events were the long and successful struggle of the Christians against the Mohammedans in Spain, and the

Hundred Years War between England and France. The Christian population of Spain gradually pressed the Mohammedan Moors back southward toward Africa from which they had originally come. The Christians organized themselves into small kingdoms as they freed themselves from their Mohammedan masters — Leon, Castile, Navarre, Aragon, Portugal. Together they forced the Moors into a small section of southern Spain around Grenada and then finally in 1492 destroyed the last remnant of Mohammedan political power. Thenceforth the Christians ruled over all the Spanish peninsula, though the Moors were permitted to retain their homes for more than a century longer. In the meantime the Christians had gradually united their own governments until there were but two kingdoms at the end of the period — Spain and Portugal, and these have remained to the present time.

It will be remembered that the Duke of Normandy, a district of France, conquered England in 1066 without giving up his land in France. Thus a large section of France was attached to the crown of England. By marriage and conquest these holdings were enlarged until the king of England actually held almost half the territory of modern France and ultimately laid claim to the crown itself. These conditions led to almost continuous wars for more than a hundred years. When the French were near despair they were once more heartened for the struggle by a peasant girl known as Joan of Arc or the Maid of Orleans. This girl believed herself called of heaven to deliver her country from the hated English invaders. Her enthusiasm and visions enlisted the support of the nation and the tide of English success was turned. In 1429 she fell into the hands of the English by whom she was convicted of heresy and burned at the stake. But her work was done. The English gradually lost ground and at the end of the period held only the city of Calais.

§ 57

DECAY OF FEUDALISM AND THE RISE OF CITIES

One of the most marked characteristics of the social changes of this period was the decay of the whole feudal system. The great nobles who had been so powerful in the preceding period as to overawe kings and peoples lose most of their power in this. The ruins of the mighty castles which make the landscape of England, France and Germany so picturesque in certain sections, are eloquent memorials of the predominant position which the nobility once held. These " Robber Barons " succumbed to the growing influence of the cities and the kings. As commerce and manufacturing rose the cities grew into powerful social units, able to defend themselves and their rights against nobles and kings and constituting the beginnings of modern democracy. They organized leagues, such as the Hanseatic League of northern Germany, for the defense of their rights and the extension of their trade, maintaining fleets and armies for the enforcement of their will.

At the other end of the social scale the king was also rapidly growing in power. The nations were unified and consolidated, and the people began to be represented in parliaments. Between the king and the rising cities the nobility rapidly sank into impotence, leaving room for a rising democracy in the state, in culture, religion and all the other departments of social life.

§ 58

THE DECLINE OF THE PAPACY

We have already seen that the papacy reached the zenith of its power and glory in the preceding period. From this dizzy height it plunged almost immediately into a slough of humiliation and division that robbed it of its influence and made it a stench in the nostrils of Europe. In 1305 the cardinals elected a Frenchman as pope. He did not go to Rome at all, but set up another papal court at Avignon on the lower Rhone. Here he and his successors, all of them Frenchmen, for seventy years were virtually the vassals of France whose interests they served. So notorious did the conditions become that Catholic historians have stigmatized this period as the " Babylonian Captivity of the Papacy."

In 1378 the cardinals were induced to elect an Italian at Rome so that the eternal city might again become the center of Catholic life. But the new pope, Urban VI, soon alienated the French cardinals by his rough behavior, and they proceeded to elect another pope, declaring that their former election was null and void because they had been coerced into the election of Urban. They chose a Frenchman who took the name of Clement VII and returned to Avignon, thus creating the most serious schism that the Catholic church ever had. Each of the popes, supported by a college of cardinals, declared himself to be the only legitimate pope, assumed to exercise all papal power and anathematized his opponent as the child of the devil and the devourer of the church. This unholy spectacle continued for nearly forty years. In 1409 at the Council of Pisa the cardinals voted to depose both the contending popes and elected another. But the popes declined to be deposed and the world had the delectable spectacle of seeing three men, each declaring himself the vicar of Christ and the infallible shepherd of the whole church, deluging the others with ecclesiastical vituperation and abuse. Finally by means of the ecumenical council of Constance and death all anti-popes were put out of the way and the unity of the church was restored. The last of the anti-popes died in 1449 and since then the Catholic church has never been afflicted by a schism.

But toward the end of the period several very unworthy men sat on the papal chair. Alexander VI (1492–1503), was a moral monster; Julius II was more of a warrior than a shepherd and Leo X was destitute of all knowledge of religion. The papacy, that institution that had once dominated kings and emperors and had seemed invincible under Innocent III, was now fallen and degraded. Princes and even Luther the monk of Wittenberg might defy it with impunity.

§ 59

THE DECAY OF MISSIONS

Missionary activity in the Roman church practically ceased in this period. This strange cessation was due to a variety of causes. In the first place the Christianizing of Europe, which had long been the sole field of missionary endeavor for the Catholic church, was nominally finished. All Europe was inside the church. In the second place the Greek Catholic church and the Mohammedans interposed an effective barrier between the Roman Catholics and western Asia and northern Africa, the only portions of the world accessible by land. In the third place the Atlantic ocean, screening all that new world of strange savage peoples, was still an unknown and untraversed waste of waters supposed to be peopled with the most frightful monsters. And finally the Catholic church itself was in such a condition of stagnation and decline that it had little spiritual life seeking an outlet in missionary endeavor. The church made repeated attempts to accomplish a union with the Greek church, but with insignificant results. Missions to the Mohammedans were out of the question on account of the bitterness of feeling on both sides.

§ 60

THE JEWS IN CHRISTIAN LANDS

As we have seen the Jews were the chief instigators of persecution against the Christians in the earlier centuries of

Christian history. But as the nations became Christian
the tables were turned and the Jews received double for
all the suffering they had inflicted on the Christians. Most
of the cities of the Roman empire had some Jewish population at the beginning of the Christian era. As a result of
the struggles with the empire in A. D. 70 and A. D. 135 the
national life of the Jews was completely destroyed and they
were scattered to the four winds of the earth. Henceforth
they wandered wherever life seemed most tolerable and the
prospects for wealth brightest, bound together only by racial,
religious and social bonds. With the spread of culture
northward from the Mediterranean lands they wandered
into Germany, France, England and other countries of
northern Europe. Here they settled as tradespeople,
money-lenders and retail merchants in the cities as they
grew up. Everywhere they were hated and despised, and
very often they were inhumanly treated. They were usually
confined to one specific section of the city, were often compelled to wear some distinctive dress and were heavily
taxed. Periodically furious persecutions would break over
them when they were mobbed and murdered with impunity,
and sometimes entirely banished by the government. Their
sufferings were great in all Christian lands, the Turks and
other Mohammedans usually being more tolerant of the
Jews than the Christians were.

The reasons for this cruel treatment were various. The
religious motive was probably the predominant one. The
Christians hated the Jews as the murderers of Jesus their
Lord, as the instigators of persecution in the early days
and as the despisers of the Christ and the Christian religion.
There can be no question that the Jews, despising the superstitions of Catholic faith and worship, often made themselves very obnoxious to Catholic feeling.

Added to the religious motive was the resentment aroused
by the haughty pride and the economic success of the Jews.
True to the instincts of their race they were always hard
and ruthless where gain was involved. Owing to the sen-

timent among Christians that one Christian should not lend money at interest to another, the whole business of money-lending fell into the hands of the Jews in most countries of Europe. The business was precarious if not illegal in the Middle Ages, and as a consequence the Jews charged very high rates of interest, usually 40% or more, to cover the risk. Not infrequently whole cities, distinguished nobles and even kings were at the mercy of the Jewish money-lenders. With this power came an unbearable haughtiness and egotism that was most exasperating.

Still further it was popularly believed that the Jews were accustomed now and then to murder Christian children for ritualistic purposes. There are on record numerous cases where the disappearance of Christian children was confidently charged to the murderous hatred of the Jews. Such an instance always caused an outbreak of frenzied persecution. These charges are probably entirely without foundation in fact, still they were confidently believed and added much to the accumulated hatred of the Jew.

Under these conditions Christian work among the Jews was practically hopeless and was rarely attempted. Neither Jew nor Christian was in a mood for mission work. Here and there Jews were forced to accept baptism on pain of death. Many died rather than submit and those who submitted scarcely ever became genuine Christians. Occasionally a Christian of purer spirit and wider vision arose and made some attempt to present to these people the Christ. The most notable of these, perhaps, was Vincent Ferrer (1350–1419), a distinguished Spanish Dominican scholar and ecclesiastic, who spent the last twenty years of his life in popular preaching in Spain and France. Of his wonderful power as a speaker there can be no doubt, and the lowest estimate of the number of converts from Judaism due to his work is twenty thousand. This is sufficient to show that other conditions might have produced numerous converts from these people who had lived among Christians but to suffer at their hands or fatten off their weaknesses.

§ 61

A NEW SPIRIT IN THE WORLD

About the middle of the fifteenth century a new spirit of personal independence, initiative and enterprise began to manifest itself in the European world. It was the beginning of the individualism which has been such a marked feature of the life of the latest centuries. Throughout the Middle Ages the two great institutions of society, the Church and the State, had completely dominated the individual, depriving him of his independence and significance. This new spirit asserted the significance of the individual as over against the institution and thus brought about the great intellectual, social and religious revolution known as the Renaissance and the Reformation. Some of the more striking manifestations of this new spirit will now be considered.

1. Beginning near the end of the fourteenth century there arose *a new education*. It started with the renewal of the study of the Greek language, literature and philosophy in Italy. Greek had once been well known in southern Italy and slightly in other Latin lands, but this knowledge had long since died out. A few Greeks from the East now began its revival. The awakening effects of the study were marvelous. A new world of thought and interest were opened up to the West, a new intellectual activity resulted. Students from other lands, hearing of the ferment in Italy, poured over the Alps to drink at these fresh and newly opened fountains. Along with the Greek came the revival of interest in classic Latin. The new studies were rapidly transplanted into France, Germany and England and soon became an important part of the curricula of all universities and other schools of higher learning. The intellectual quickening which accompanied this reform in education can hardly be estimated at this distance.

2. Along with the new education came *a critical spirit.*

Throughout the Middle Ages the individual had accepted whatever the state or the church gave him with little question. It was the " age of faith." The most unreasonable stories of saints, miracles, visions, etc., were accepted on authority without a thought of investigation or question. It was the atmosphere in which superstition flourishes, the atmosphere which was fostered by the Catholic church. The new spirit demanded a reason, asserted the right of the individual to question, to criticize, to judge for himself, to know. No more beneficent change ever came over the human spirit. Before this critical spirit the hoary superstitions and abuses which the " age of faith " had accumulated were destined to crumble, ushering in the modern world.

3. Renewed *interest in the Bible* was one of the striking manifestations of this new spirit. The Catholic church had done its work with meager use of the Bible. It remained in the Latin language, a sealed book to the unlearned. No efforts had been made to put it into the hands of the people or induce them to make use of it. On the contrary the church opposed its use by the laity. The new learning at once turned to this book. The first book that was ever printed was the Bible in the Latin language in 1455 ; in 1488 the Hebrew Old Testament was printed, and in 1516 the Greek New Testament.

More important for the people than this printing of the originals was the renewal of the work of translating the Scriptures into the languages of the peoples. In England John Wycliffe finished a translation of the entire Bible before his death in 1384, and it was widely circulated in manuscript. In France, Spain, Germany and other countries numerous translations of the Bible or parts of the Bible were made and diligently circulated in this period. But the Catholic church was usually hostile to this work and exerted its utmost efforts to suppress the Book for which the people were crying. The work of translating was done by the heretics or by Catholics who were out of harmony with their church.

Moreover the use of the Bible in the original languages began to find place in the class-rooms of the universities, as a substitute for the "Sentences" of the fathers and extracts from Aristotle, in the study of theology. Bible picture books, Bible stories and similar means popularized Bible knowledge.

4. *Inventions and discoveries* constitute the most striking feature of this revival of the human spirit. *The art of printing* was invented about the middle of the fifteenth century, the first printed book appearing in the year 1455. The use of the *mariner's compass* and of *gunpowder* in the West begin in this same century though they seem to have been in use in the Far East at an earlier date. Without these three inventions the modern world would have been impossible.

With the compass men began to venture out into the uncharted waters of the Atlantic. In 1492 Columbus, on his way to India as he supposed by a sea route, discovered America. In 1498 a sea-route to India was discovered by sailing around Africa, and in 1522 Magellan completed a voyage around the world. It is now impossible to realize the limitations of the knowledge which men had possessed of the world in which they lived or the tremendous shock which these discoveries gave to the world's thinking. It was as if all the foundations of thought had been shaken; it opened the way for changes in the realm of religion.

5. A worthy *vernacular literature* begins to rise in this period. During the earlier periods all the literature that was produced in western Europe had been in the Latin language. The masses were not educated and hence appeal to them through books was impossible. The beginnings of this vernacular literature signify that *the people* are beginning to think and that they are coming to be regarded by literary men as worthy of consideration. By

the time the Reformation broke over the world it was possible to reach a very wide public through the printed page. As culture spread among the masses they began to awake from abject subservience and demand some consideration for themselves. In Italy the great names were Dante (1265–1321), Petrarch (1304–74) and Boccaccio (1313–75), and in England that of Chaucer (1340–1400). These names have lived and will continue to live in the world's literature. But there were many other lesser lights in these countries and also in Germany and France. This new literature was not for the princes or the prelates but for *the people,* the common man. Moreover the very earliest of this literature is critical of the church. Dante does not hesitate to put some of the popes in hell, and other writers were scarcely less drastic in their criticisms. It was shocking, for the church had been exempt from criticism for centuries.

6. Another manifestation of the new power that was in the world was in the realm of *Christian* art. In the preceding period the church had erected magnificent buildings to the glory of God and the purposes of worship. In this the art of painting is put to the same service and is wonderfully developed. Again it was Italy that led the way. The greatest paintings were altar pieces used to stimulate the devotion of worshippers. They were based on biblical history, Catholic beliefs and legends of saints. The Virgin and the child Jesus were the most common subjects, and in the portrayal of the Catholic beliefs that gather about the manger at Bethlehem Christian art probably reached its highest attainments. Some of the names that made Italian art famous were Giotto d. 1336, Fra Angelico d. 1455, Leonardo da Vinci d. 1519, Raphael d. 1520 and Michael Angelo d. 1564. Christian art has never surpassed the work done by these men and it was all or nearly all in the service of the Catholic church. It was a wonderful manifestation of the new power that was so soon to transform the world in so many respects.

From the specifications above it will be seen that the middle of the fifteenth century really ushers in a new age. It was a Renaissance, a rebirth of the world, as it has been aptly called. The new intellectual movement has also been called *Humanism* because it was a new emphasis on humanity apart from the purely ecclesiastical aspects of life.

§ 62

REFORMATORY MOVEMENTS

The new spirit which was abroad in the world was bound to break out into efforts at the reform of the church " in head and members," to use a phrase that was common in those days. The most notable of these movements were in England and Bohemia. The subjection of the papacy to France during the " Babylonian Captivity " had alienated the sympathies of England and led to drastic efforts to curb papal power in that country. The literary leader of the country in these efforts was John Wycliffe (1320–84), a highly educated man, a professor in Oxford and a priest in the Catholic church. His opposition to the political pretensions of the papacy gradually led him to reject the whole religious system of the church — its doctrines, practices and organization. In addition to numerous anti-Catholic writings he translated the entire Bible into English and organized a body of men known as Lollards to circulate the Scriptures and preach evangelical doctrines. They made a powerful impression on the country and were never entirely suppressed till they were absorbed in the larger movement of the Reformation. Wycliffe is known as " the morning star of the Reformation," and his work undoubtedly prepared the way in England for the movement which ultimately put that country entirely outside the Catholic church. Both church and state did what they could to suppress the movement, and Wycliffe's bones were dug up and burned in 1429 at the command of the Council of Constance; but the seed was sown and the crop would mature in due time.

From England Wycliffe's writings were carried by students and others to Bohemia and there found enthusiastic acceptance in the University of Prague, especially in the persons of two professors, John Hus and Jerome. Hus was a great popular preacher, the rector of the university and a sort of national hero. He was, however, finally forced out of the university, condemned as a heretic at the Council of Constance in 1415 and burned at the stake. The next year the same treatment was meted out to Jerome, but this cruelty seemed for a time only to fan the flames of revolt from the Catholic church. The whole of Bohemia appeared to be on the eve of leaving the church. A crusade was finally preached against the reformers, their forces were cunningly divided so that they were defeated and their organization destroyed. A remnant of them survived and ultimately were able to organize another evangelical sect which has, however, exerted very little influence on the world. This great and promising movement of reform was thus strangled in blood. Doubtless some of its seeds still remain in the soil and may yet produce a rich spiritual harvest. Hus is a national hero, and his name must be reckoned with.

Reformers appeared at various places in Holland, and the famous Dominican monk, Savonarola, attempted the reform of Florence, the gay capital of Umbria. He was burned at the stake as a heretic in 1498, but he is now one of the heroes of this wonderful city.

The above is sufficient to indicate something of the mighty ferment that was now working in the world. What was the Catholic church doing to meet it? In a word it was doing nothing. Since the middle of the fifteenth century the popes had been patrons of the new learning and had vied with princes in the support of artists and literary men; but they had not responded to the demand for religious reform or for increased freedom among the people. The church was more corrupt than it had been for centuries, it was absolutely intolerant of dissent and ready to resort to the most cruel tortures to maintain its position of mastery. The monastic orders were decayed, the clergy were ignorant, indifferent to the needs of the people, greedy of gain, living in ease and luxury. The Bible was not circulated, the people were not taught, superstition was not opposed but rather fostered. In a word the world was in deep need and the church was not ready or willing to help.

SEVENTH PERIOD — THE REFORMATION — 1517 TO 1648

§63

WE come now to study the most tremendous upheaval that the Christian world has ever experienced. Before beginning the study of the details it will be well to make a brief survey of the Christian world as a whole. Looking about us at the beginning of the sixteenth century we observe that Christianity is divided into two large and several smaller groups.

1. *The Greek Catholic or Holy Orthodox Eastern Church,* situated in eastern Europe and western Asia composed principally of Greeks and Slavs, is organized into several distinct national churches of which the Russian is the most important. Nearly half of this church's territory is under the dominion of the Mohammedan Turks, and Russia has just been freed from the oppression of the Mohammedan Mongols. This church is religiously and intellectually stagnant, the renaissance of culture has not affected it in the least. It is fighting for its existence with barbarism, Mohammedanism and internal stagnation.

2. *The Roman Catholic Church,* covering western Europe and composed mainly of Latins and Teutons, is organized under one powerful head. It exercises political control over central Italy, and many of its bishops are princes of the realm in other lands. Many evangelical and hostile sects exist within its bounds, notwithstanding its vigorous and cruel persecutions, and they afford a leaven of purer religious life that will materially help the Reforma-

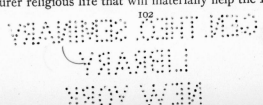

tion. Moreover there is within the church itself a ferment of intellectual activity, independent and even hostile to the church, which is transforming the thinking and intellectual atmosphere of the entire western world. The mental and spiritual stagnation of the East is not shared by the West.

3. The *Evangelical sects* of Europe mentioned above, found mainly among the Germanic peoples.

4. *The old heretical churches of the East* are still in existence but they too are under the heel of the Turk and capable of very small service in the future history of mankind. These are the Jacobite and Nestorian churches of Armenia and Persia, Syria, Egypt and Abyssinia. They remain uninfluenced by the Reformation as does the Greek church.

§ 64

THE ROMAN CATHOLIC CHURCH

The Reformation was wholly in the bosom of the Roman Catholic church, and in order better to understand that movement it will be well to get a clear idea of the church as it was at the beginning of the revolution that tore so many of its children away from its fellowship.

1. As a *system of government* it was a reproduction of the old Roman empire — the pope for the emperor, the college of cardinals for the old senate and curia, the archbishops, bishops, legates, etc., for the various officers of the old empire. Like the empire it was international, holding various races under the sway of one system of law and one system of executive government; but its authority was much more autocratic than the Roman government had ever been. Its political power had declined very materially in the last three centuries, but was still considerable.

2. Its *plan of salvation* was sacramental. It claimed that the church is the divinely appointed and sole agency for the salvation of men, all of whom are born in sin and under eternal condemnation. The chief and necessary instruments

used by the church are the seven sacraments, all of which are said to have been instituted by Christ. They are, in their logical order, Baptism, Confirmation, Eucharist, Penance — Marriage and Ordination — Extreme Unction. The first four and the last are for all Catholics. The other two exclude each other.

Baptism is the sacrament of regeneration without which — no one can be saved. It may be administered by any one — priest, layman or woman — and may be by immersion, pouring or sprinkling, but it must be in the name of the trinity. Faith in the recipient is not necessary, and hence it is to be administered to infants who would be lost if they should die unbaptized. It removes all guilt and punishment due to previous sin, both original and actual.

Confirmation must follow baptism, which it supplements and completes. It is administered with the imposition of the hands by a *bishop,* and it is believed to confirm the presence and effects of the Holy Spirit. It follows a period of careful catechetical instruction.

The *Eucharist* is the receiving of the host or consecrated bread. It can be administered by a priest only. This *host* is in the form of a wafer which is placed upon the tongue by the priest; it is believed to be the body, blood, soul and divinity of Jesus Christ, no longer bread at all, and hence must not be chewed or taken from the mouth on pain of committing a mortal sin. The wine or cup is not served to the laity. This sacrament is the medicine of immortality and greatly blesses and strengthens the soul.

Penance is the sacrament by which the guilt and the eternal punishment due to a mortal sin committed after baptism are removed, leaving only the temporal punishment still to be inflicted either in this life or in purgatory. It consists of sorrow for and confession of the sin to a priest, absolution or the forgiveness of the sin by a priest, and satisfaction for the sin by good works. *Absolution,* in which the priest says " *Te absolvo,*" (I absolve thee), is the essential part of this sacrament.

Marriage is a sacrament of the Church even though the unmarried state is regarded as the holier. It can be performed only by a priest of the Catholic church, and is in its very nature indissoluble. Hence Protestant and civil marriage are not normally recognized and divorce is never granted. Persons are permitted to live apart, and marriages are declared to have been illegal and null from the start, but a genuine marriage is never dissolved by divorce.

Ordination can be administered by the bishop only and confers mighty supernatural powers upon the recipient by which he, irrespective of his character, becomes a mediator between God and man.

Extreme unction is the final anointing by the priest just before death and is supposed to prepare the soul for the last great trial.

Good works of various kinds such as prayers often repeated, alms, pilgrimages, adoration of images and relics contribute to but do not effect salvation apart from the sacraments.

3. The *Mass,* described in an earlier section, is the center of Catholic worship, and the greatest mystery of the church, supremely beneficial to all, both living and dead, to whom its blessings may be designated.

4. *Catholic worship* is spectacular and dramatic, appealing to eye, ear and nose. It is in the Latin language and must be conducted by a priest. It appeals *to the eye* through the bodily movements of the priest and the congregation, the use of lights, paintings and other visible objects; *to the ear* through the chanting of the choir and the intoning of the priest; *to the nose* through the incense. *Preaching* is little cultivated except by some of the orders. The only visible object to which divine worship is given is the consecrated elements of the supper which are believed to be the actual glorified Christ and are therefore *truly worshipped.* Pictures, images and relics (that is parts of the bodies or objects connected with the bodies of Christ or the saints) are *adored* or *venerated,* and the saints are *invoked* for their

aid, but not truly *worshiped,* at least in theory.   The Catholic *cathedrals* are among the most magnificent and impressive buildings in the world.   Pious Catholics are much given
to *private worship* in the churches, when they can be seen
counting the prayers by the beads of the rosary which they
use for that purpose, believing that they will be heard for
their much speaking.

5. *Catholic theology* was virtually complete at the outbreak of the Reformation.   The church stood squarely on
the great ecumenical creeds as to the doctrines of God, the
divinity of Christ, the personality and the work of the Holy
Spirit; and most Catholics believed firmly in original sin
and the inability of men to save themselves apart from the
grace and help of God.   The distinctive Catholic beliefs
as to the sacraments and the plan of salvation had been
discussed to a conclusion but they had not yet been formulated into a creed.   That was done in the great Council of
Trent which met in 1545.

6. The *Future Life* was divided into five compartments —
hell for the unbaptized and the heretics, *heaven* for the
blessed, *purgatory* for those who die in communion with
the Catholic church.   They must remain here till the remnants of sin are purged away when they ascend to heaven.
The *limbo of infants* is a place in which all infants who die
unbaptized are kept perpetually, and the *limbo of the fathers*
a place in which the pious dead of the Old Testament were
kept till freed by Christ.   There is no escape from hell,
but purgatory will finally be left empty, since the souls as
they are completely purged ascend into heaven.

7. The *Confessional* was one of the church's secrets of
power and also one of its sources of weakness.   All serious
or mortal sins must be confessed and as many of the smaller
venial sins as can be remembered.   Every good Catholic
must go to confession at least once a year, preferably just
before Easter.   This baring of the soul and the life gave
the unworthy priest a power and an opportunity for evil
which was not infrequently utilized.

8. *Indulgences.* The power of the church over the soul was supposed not to cease with death, but extended into purgatory where the church could shorten the purgatorial sufferings by the use of the *indulgence.* An indulgence, as has often been asserted, was not a permission to sin. It had to do only with past sins of which the guilt and the eternal punishment due to them, had been removed by the sacrament of penance. The indulgence was the church's means of shortening the period of suffering in purgatory and transferring some of the (supposedly) superabounding good works, which Christ and the saints had laid up in the treasury of the church, to these bare and needy souls. These indulgences were sold at public auction and were one of the church's most important sources of revenue up to the Reformation, constituting one of the gravest scandals of the time. Their sale provoked the attack of Luther.

9. The *wealth* of the church was enormous. It consisted of church and monastic buildings, and extensive holdings in lands and slaves. It is estimated that in some countries the church held as much as one fifth of the property of the nation.

This then was the mighty institution which the Reformation attacked. It was ancient, wealthy, backed by civil government; it was the religion of princes and kings and the great of the earth, controlling all the schools, printing presses and learning of the world. The battle seemed utterly hopeless but God and truth were in it.

§ 65

THE REFORMATION

The Reformation began in Germany and gradually spread to the countries of western Europe ultimately affecting the whole of the territory that was held by the Roman Catholic church. It did not preserve unity, but took five different forms and also forced considerable reforms in the Catholic church itself.   These forms were Lutheranism, **Zwinglian-ism**, Calvinism, Anabaptism, and Anglicanism.

A. LUTHERANISM

§ 66

LUTHER

The first form of the Reformation to arise was that known as Lutheranism.   It is named of course from its founder Martin Luther, and originated in electoral Saxony in the heart of Germany at the university town of Wittenberg where Luther was then a professor.   Luther was born in 1483, the son of a miner, a plain man who succeeded in giving to his son Martin the best education that Germany could at that time furnish.   He intended Martin for the profession of the law and his education took that direction.   He had made a brilliant record as a student and his prospects were the brightest, but almost immediately on his graduation he renounced all his friendships and prospects and entered an Augustinian monastery, much to the chagrin and disappointment of his father and friends.   From the start he took his religious duties seriously.   So strenuous were his ascetic exercises that his superior was impelled to counsel moderation in the interest of his health and future usefulness.   His brilliant talents and earnestness won for him speedy recognition and he was made a professor in the new university of Wittenberg in 1509.   His work as professor did not prevent him from rendering further service to his order, and as a recognition of that service he was sent to Rome on business of the order in the year 1512.   This visit to the eternal city, the heart of the Roman Catholic world, brought serious disillusionment.   He found the living loose, the religious exercises perfunctory and lifeless, himself the butt of ridicule among the luxurious and careless priests of the city.   Returning to Germany he **gave** himself more earnestly to the teaching of the New Testament, expounding Romans and Galatians where the great doctrine of justification is most plainly set forth. Gradually he found himself becoming the critic of his church, and when Tetzel, a hawker of indulgences, appeared on the border of Saxony in the fall of 1517 he could no longer restrain his rising indignation. For years the popes had been in this way raising great sums of money most of which was wasted on the luxuries and immoralities of the papal court at Rome. It had become a crying scandal. Of the various means employed to extract money from the poor and superstitious the sale of indulgences was the most objectionable, because it seemed to be selling the grace of God, thereby fostering superstition and bringing religion into contempt.

§ 67

EARLY STRUGGLES

Accordingly on the last day of October, 1517, Professor Luther nailed to the door of the castle church at Wittenberg ninety-five theses attacking both the theory and the practice of indulgences as then current. These theses he proposed to defend against all comers. What he expected and wished was a discussion in academic and ecclesiastical circles which would result in restoring the theory and practice of indulgences to the position held years before. It was not in his mind to break with the Catholic church or even to condemn the use of indulgences; he only wished to remove what he regarded as abuses in their use. But we have seen that the world had been laying the train for a mighty explosion, and the theses were the spark that set this train off. Instead of an academic discussion they precipitated throughout the entire Catholic world a tremendous upheaval. Luther found himself at once the center of a mighty movement that was soon beyond his control and rapidly pushed him and most of Germany out of the Catholic church, made him the popular hero of the Fatherland and an object of execration to the church that educated and nurtured him.

At once a furious controversy broke out all over Germany. Luther was summoned to Rome where he would undoubtedly have been put to death in short order had he gone. Fortunately for the world his prince, who was a devout man, was unwilling to sacrifice to Roman pride his popular and brave professor, and so protected him in his refusal to go. Germany was at that time an aggregation of small semi-independent states which could control their own internal affairs in defiance of the emperor, and we probably owe to this political fact the preservation of Luther's life and the success of the Reformation at this time. Had Germany been a strongly centralized government as at the present time the emperor would undoubtedly have suppressed the movement at the behest of the pope, as he actually tried to do but found himself unable.

After a period of fruitless negotiations the pope excommunicated Luther in 1520 and ordered the German princes to apprehend him. Again his prince defended and protected him. In 1521 the new emperor Charles V, more a Spaniard than a German, was present at the diet of the empire at Worms. Luther was publicly heard before that august tribunal where he bravely held his ground, refusing to recant and uttering those memorable words, " Here I stand, I can no other. God help me." He was then put under the ban of the empire but still his prince protected him. It was at this time that he was arrested by his friends and carried to the Wartburg castle where he was kept in hiding for nearly two years. Luther had now defied the two mightiest powers of earth and yet he lived and was finally able to die in bed. A century before, as shown by the fate of Hus and Jerome of Prague, he would have died a martyr at the stake ; but there is now a new spirit in the world that is greater than the Catholic church and the German empire combined. Under the protection of that

spirit and the political conditions of Germany he was able
to proceed with his work.

§ 68

FURTHER PROGRESS OF REFORM

Luther soon renounced his monastic vows and married a
nun who had like him left her monastic life. In the year
1526 the movement had made sufficient progress to begin
the actual reform of the church in Saxony. This was done
with the approval and help of the civil government, not only
in Saxony but wherever the Reformation was successful.
The Reformers were firmly attached to the idea that religion is a matter of public concern to which the civil authorities must lend the weight of their influence and official
power. And as far as we can see the movement would
have been stifled in blood by the Catholic church but for
the protection of the state. Right or wrong the reformers
all threw themselves on the support of the state and everywhere the reforms were carried through with the help of
the state, everywhere there was a new and more intimate
union between church and state, a condition that laid the
foundation for much suffering in the future and created
problems that have not yet been solved.

With the help of the government Catholic worship was
abolished and a new evangelical service in the German language was imposed upon all ministers of religion; all priests
who would not accept the new régime were removed and
evangelical men were put in their places, the church buildings were taken over for Protestant worship, monasticism
was abolished and monastic buildings confiscated, a statement of evangelical doctrines was substituted for the Catholic doctrines, relics were taken out of the churches and buried
and the images and pictures removed from worship. The
new church in its government was then subjected to the
state by a system of *superintendents* answerable to the civil

authorities for their actions.   In governmental matters the
princes took the place of the bishops.

Very rapidly the reform was introduced into many other
states of northern Germany, so that by 1546 nearly half
of the country had left the Catholic church and set up new
territorial churches on the Lutheran model.   Only where
civil government had suppressed the movement had it
failed.

§ 69

LUTHERAN BELIEFS AND PRACTICES

The Reformation was at first more a reform of doctrines
and practices than of life among the people.   In fact for a
while the new freedom had a deleterious effect on the life
of the people.

In the matter of doctrine the reformers accepted the old
creeds in their teachings concerning God, the divinity and
the humanity of Christ, the personality and work of the
Holy Spirit, the corruption and lost condition of men, the
immortality of the soul.

The greatest change which Luther introduced was as to
the *plan of salvation,* the way in which the grace of God
reaches the heart and life of men.   He rejected the authority of tradition, insisted on the sole authority of the Scriptures, rejected the special priesthood and insisted on the
priesthood of all believers, rejected the whole sacramental
system of salvation declaring that justification is by faith.
Indeed justification by faith was the very center of his
system.   He retained the baptism which he had received
in the Catholic church including infant baptism and the
doctrine of baptismal regeneration.   This was a radical con-
tradiction of his doctrine of justification by faith, but he
does not seem to have felt the inconsistency.   He likewise
retained his Catholic ordination without reordination or
change.

Luther rejected the doctrine of *transubstantiation* and the sacrifice of the *mass,* but held that the glorified body and blood of Christ are really and sacramentally present in the bread and the wine, both of which are to be given to the laity. He retained *clerical dress, lights* in the worship, *confirmation* and a form of general congregational *confession,* abolishing auricular or private confession.

He rejected the doctrine of *purgatory* and all other doctrines dependent on it or related to it, maintaining that the future has only heaven or hell and that our destiny is fixed at death. *Good works* are a necessary fruit of faith, but are not in themselves a meritorious cause of salvation.

§ 70

LUTHERANISM IN OTHER LANDS

From Germany the Reformation spread to Denmark, Sweden and Norway where it was after a brief period of struggle completely triumphant. The Catholic church was abolished by law and a reformed national church of the Lutheran type was organized in each of these countries. In some instances the bishops of the Catholic church were converted to Protestant views. They were then permitted to retain their positions, thus creating in these lands Lutheran churches with bishops.

Along the eastern border of Germany in Poland, Bohemia and Moravia the Reformation made a very deep impression notwithstanding the hostility of the various governments. In Bohemia more than half the population was at one time Protestant. It was largely stamped out in these regions by the Thirty Years War.

In south Germany and the Austrian lands the various governments refused to allow the preaching of the gospel, proceeding with the most ruthless persecution against the reformers. As a consequence the Reformation made little impression in these lands. Bavaria, and the Austrian archduchy were kept comparatively free of Protestant views, but in Hungary the reformatory movement was more successful and was never suppressed entirely.

In Italy and Spain Catholic sentiment was strong and the governments were ruthless, but still these countries did not remain wholly unaffected. In northern Italy and around Naples there were many noble men and women who sought diligently if secretly to introduce reforms. Churches were founded in Naples and Venice and groups of reformers gathered elsewhere; but the movement was suppressed about the middle of the century.

In Spain the king, Philip II, honored the burnings called *autos da fé* (Acts of faith), with his royal presence, completely suppressing the movement in this country. Portugal was never affected, being the one country in Europe which remained entirely dormant.

B. THE ZWINGLIAN REFORMATION

§ 71

CONDITIONS IN SWITZERLAND

Switzerland was still nominally a part of the German empire at the beginning of the Reformation though as a matter of fact it had long acted in entire independence. It consisted as at present of a number of independent cantons, each with its own council managing its own internal affairs; these cantons were associated in a loose confederation whose business was directed by a large representative council. By this arrangement each canton was a political, social and religious entity living its own separate life but acting in concert with other cantons about matters of common concern.

The earliest and greatest of the Swiss reformers was Ulrich Zwingli, born in 1484 of a good family and educated in the best schools and universities of his time. One

year younger he began his reformatory work some three or
four years later than Luther. He reached his convictions
largely if not in entire independence of the work of Luther.
Certainly his system differed materially from that of Luther
in several important respects. Like Luther, Zwingli was
reared and educated in the Catholic church and became a
priest of that communion. He was a preacher of unusual
power and had been far more diligent in exercising his
preaching gifts than most Catholic priests. In 1519 he became priest of the leading church of Zürich, one of the principal cities of the country. Here he devoted himself to
diligent and careful study of the Scriptures in the course of
his preaching and under the influence of his own studies he
gradually left the Catholic position. His conversion was
more intellectual and less emotional than Luther's, and certainly far more thorough. His final position was more
radically Scriptural than Luther's. Luther's principle of
reform was the retention in the church of everything which
the Scriptures did not forbid; Zwingli's was the rejection of
all that the Scriptures did not warrant.

Under his leadership the canton of Zürich abolished the
Catholic church and set up a reformed church during the
years from 1523 to 1525.

Following this canton several others rapidly took the
same step. The most important of these were St. Gall,
Basel and Berne. The cantons in the center of the country,
known as the " forest cantons," remained staunchly Catholic. The tension between the two parties became so great
that war, narrowly averted in 1529, broke out in 1532. In
the one battle which was fought the reformers were badly
worsted and Zwingli was killed. The Catholics, finding
his body on the field, dismembered and burned it, scattering
the ashes to the winds. This was the first of the so-called
" wars of religion " that rose out of the great struggle to
emancipate the world from the thraldom of the Catholic
church. The progress of reform was thus stopped by force

in Switzerland, but the Catholics could not suppress the reform where it had already been established. The country remained divided between Catholicism and Protestantism.

§ 72

ZWINGLI'S VIEWS

Like Luther, Zwingli rejected the distinctive doctrines and practices of the Catholic church — its priesthood and sacraments, the authority of the pope and of tradition, the mass and transubstantiation, purgatory and all its related doctrines. He taught the sole authority of the Scriptures and followed the implications of this doctrine much more consistently than Luther; the priesthood of all believers; salvation by grace through faith and a future life that had only heaven and hell.

But on many points he differed from Luther. After some hesitation he retained infant baptism, but insisted that it had nothing to do with regeneration, being only the sign of the Christian covenant as circumcision was of the Jewish covenant. This was the first time in history, with the exception of Pelagius, that the baptism of infants had ever been practiced for any other reason than its supposed regenerative power. Zwingli marks a new stage in the history of infant baptism.

He differed also in his view of the Lord's supper. Luther maintained the real presence of Christ in the supper as firmly as the Catholics, differing only as to the manner of its presence. Zwingli declared that Christ was in no sense in the bread and the wine, but that they *represented,* set forth in a pictorial way, his body and his blood. They are memorials, reminders of Christ's death. They thus have great value for the spiritual life, but it is not by taking Christ into the mouth. On this point Luther and his followers were absolutely irreconcilable, looking upon Zwingli and his followers as rank rationalists who refused to accept the clear teachings of Scripture. The strife between the two was very bitter. Friends of the general Protestant cause brought the two great leaders together in 1529, when it looked as if the Catholics were about to attempt to suppress them all by force, in the hope that some kind of agreement might be reached at least to such an extent as to unite them in resistance to Catholic force. But they not only failed to agree, but Luther refused absolutely to have any communion with Zwingli or even to call him brother, saying they were of a different spirit. Thus came the first serious split in the ranks of the reformers.

Owing to the radical nature of his views as well as to his early death and the small and uninfluential country in which he lived Zwingli's views did not spread widely. South Germany was considerably affected, especially certain free cities of that region. His views also passed down the Rhine and made considerable impression on the Dutch. Doubtless, Zwingli's influence would have been much more evident if Calvin had not risen. Zwingli's followers were later absorbed by Calvinism and are known on the continent of Europe as " Reformed," while in English-speaking countries they are called Presbyterians.

C. THE CALVINISTIC REFORMATION

§ 73

JOHN CALVIN

John Calvin belonged to the second generation of reformers. He was preceded by Luther and Zwingli, upon whose work he built. He was a Frenchman, and his whole system shows the genius of the French. He was born in 1509, when Luther was twenty-four years old, in Noyon, France, of a rather influential and prominent family. Through the influence of his father he held positions in the Catholic church while he was still a boy. He was given the best education that France could afford at that time, everywhere making a brilliant record as a student. Like Luther he prepared for the profession of the law, but showed remarkable literary gifts during his university career. At one point in his educational training he had come into contact with a teacher who was imbued with the teachings of Luther, and it is supposed that his attention was first directed to the Reformation by this teacher. His conversion, as he himself tells us, was sudden. About 1533 he was so far known as a Protestant sympathizer that he was arrested and imprisoned. Escaping he wandered about France for a time and made a visit to some reformers in Italy. He then determined to leave France and take up his residence in Basel or Strassburg, where he would be safe and have opportunity to pursue the literary work to which he had resolved to dedicate his talents. On his way he was spending a night in Geneva, when the reformer Farel, who was then in a life and death struggle for the introduction of reform into that canton, made such a soul-stirring appeal that Calvin reluctantly decided to remain and assist in that work. This was in the year 1536.

Calvin's great ability and earnest efforts soon put him at the head of the civil as well as the religious life of the city. After reformatory opinion was sufficiently advanced the reformation was formally and legally introduced in the usual way. For a time there was strenuous opposition to the severe discipline which Calvin insisted on imposing on the whole population. He was driven into exile for a while, but the city soon learned that they could not get on and preserve their liberties without him; accordingly he was brought back in triumph and from that time to his death in 1564 he was the undisputed master of the city and the canton. So vast was his influence in the Protestant world that he was called the "Protestant Pope" and Geneva was known among Catholics as "Protestant Rome." From one of the gayest and most reckless cities of Europe Geneva was transformed into the soberest and most law-abiding and serious city of the world. It was virtually a theocracy, the church completely dominated the life of the entire community.

§74

CALVIN'S RELIGIOUS SYSTEM

Calvinism is usually regarded as a system of theology only, but it was this and far more. As a system of theology it was the most logical, consistent and thorough statement of Christian doctrine ever given to the world. It started from the sovereignty of God and from this controlling idea deduced all the other elements of the system, such as decrees, election, the security of believers, the helplessness of the unregenerate, etc. It leaned heavily on God who was all and in all. Man was utterly helpless except as God by his sovereign will helped him. Salvation depended on election, and the reasons for election were hidden in the inscrutable will of God. It was a stern system, but it gave to men a confidence in God and a sense of divine power that put red blood into their spiritual veins and nerved them for the mighty struggle that was upon them in the effort to overthrow the Catholic church.

As a system of *church government* Calvinism was a democracy — not an absolute democracy such as Baptists and Congregationalists have, but a *representative democracy,* consisting of a series of representative bodies ascending (with different terms in different lands) from the *Session* in the local church through the *Presbytery* and the *Synod* to the *General Assembly.* These various bodies exercise legislative, executive and judicial functions under the control of the Scriptures, but they derive their powers from the people not from the government. No officers were appointed by the government. The officers were ministers or teaching elders, ruling elders and deacons. The ministers were members of the presbyteries, not of the local churches.

The type of *Christian* life was rather stern and somber. Strict discipline was enforced, even by the civil authorities if necessary. As a type of life it was what we know as Puritanism. More than any other type of the reformation except the Anabaptist it sought to reform the life of the people as well as the theology and government of the church. It was preëminently ethical and practical, earnestly striving to improve the living of the people.

Calvinism established *national churches* wherever that was possible, and was unfortunately nearly as intolerant of dissenters as was any other type of Christianity. Anabaptists suffered as severely at the hands of the Calvinists as of the Lutherans.

As to *baptism and the supper* Calvin held a position midway between Luther and Zwingli. Like Zwingli he denied that baptism effected regeneration, but insisted that it was a *seal* as well as a *sign* of grace. Like both his predecessors he retained infant baptism, following Zwingli in the assertion that it was a sign of the covenant of grace and hence was to be conferred on none but the children of Christian parents.

As to *the supper* he denied that the body and blood of Christ are actually present in any sense whatsoever in the elements, but declared that the communicant does actually partake of the glorified Christ in a spiritual manner when he partakes in faith. Here again in his efforts to mediate between Luther and Zwingli his reasoning becomes confused and difficult to follow.

As to *future life* he rejected the idea of *purgatory* and all related doctrines, declaring that there was either eternal happiness or eternal misery in heaven or hell, and he did not shrink from the position that non-elect infants dying in infancy could not escape the pains of an eternal hell.

§75

CALVINISM IN OTHER LANDS

1. *In France.* Since Calvin was a Frenchman and used the French language it was to be expected that his type of reform would be the one received in France as far as that staunch Catholic country accepted any. France was already a strongly centralized government so that a reformer could not be protected by a semi-independent prince as Luther was protected by the elector of Saxony. This fact made it very difficult to carry on reformatory work, especially since the king Francis I was an exceedingly able prince and was bitterly opposed to the reform. All the work had to be done secretly and in the face of the severest persecution from 1535 onward. Notwithstanding the great difficulties good progress was made and in the year 1559 a national Protestant church was organized on the Calvinistic model, a Calvinistic creed was drawn up and Calvinistic worship was instituted.

Many of the higher nobility now gave in their adhesion to the new church, and political conditions were such as to force the reformers into the position of a political party. As a result of Catholic opposition civil war broke out in 1562. This was followed by other civil wars, and in 1572 the Catholics deliberately attempted to murder in cold blood all the Protestant leaders on the occasion of a royal marriage which had brought all the nobility together at Paris. Thousands of Protestants were butchered. This was the famous night of St. Bartholomew. It is said that its apparent success caused Philip II of Spain to smile and the pope to have a thanksgiving service in St. Peter's in Rome.

Before the end of the sixteenth century there had been eight separate civil wars over religion in France. This period of civil strife was brought temporarily to a close by the accession of Henry IV. He had been reared a Protestant but in order to obtain the throne gave in a nominal adherence to the Catholic church, saying that the crown was worth a mass.   In 1598 he granted to the Protestants the famous Edict of Nantes by which they received full civil liberty and a limited religious toleration.   In certain districts they were permitted to erect church buildings, found schools and seminaries, and in addition were allowed to retain four fortified cities with armed military forces for their protection.

Under the protection of this edict, at that time the most liberal arrangement that Protestants had been able to obtain for themselves in any Catholic land, they flourished for many years.   Finally persecution began again and in 1685 the edict was revoked.   Protestants then had no legal standing and thousands were hunted out of the land while thousands more endured unspeakable sufferings or returned to the bosom of the Catholic church under duress. It was a fatal blow to the religious and moral life of France and marks the beginning of her decline.   For one hundred and two years the whole power of the French state was engaged in uprooting these Huguenots, as they were called. Protestantism never recovered from this awful ordeal, neither did France.

2. *In the Netherlands.*   The Netherlands were early affected by the Lutheran and Zwinglian forms of the Reformation.   Persecution had broken out at once and the first martyrs of the Reformation were at Brussels in 1523. These lands were under the direct government of the emperor Charles V, who exerted his utmost energy in an effort to suppress the reformatory movement.   The fires of persecution were burning continuously for the next fifty years and tens of thousands perished at the stake.

Finally in 1555 the Netherlands were transferred from membership in the German empire to the crown of Spain and conferred on Philip II who was to succeed Charles in that country.   This transfer only sharpened persecution. In 1566 the infamous Alva was sent to the country with a large army of Spanish veterans to put down the reform finally and forever. The result was an open revolt under William of Orange who finally succeeded in freeing the northern provinces entirely from the yoke of Spain, its independence being acknowledged in 1648. The southern provinces, now constituting Belgium, were saved for Spain and the Catholic church.

In the meantime Calvinism had been introduced into the northern provinces about 1562. It had quickly absorbed the Protestantism that had preceded it with the result that a Calvinistic national church was organized and by law established. Holland, as we call the country, thus became a Calvinistic or " Reformed " people with an established Calvinistic church. The struggle for political and religious independence through which this country passed is one of the most heroic and thrilling chapters to be found in all the annals of mankind. Under the new régime the country flourished, exercising immense influence as champion of civil and religious liberty.

3. *In Scotland*. Scotland was independent at this time, but the king was weak while the nobles were powerful and the church was rich and corrupt. The country was bitterly hostile to England, and consequently was the friend and ally of France. These circumstances made it one of the last countries to accept the reform. The Scotch parliament forbade the circulation of Lutheran literature in that country at the very beginning of the German Reformation. In 1542 the king died leaving an infant daughter Mary to succeed him. Her mother who was a French princess became the regent and at once dispatched her daughter to be educated by her relatives in France.

Despite all the stringency of the government, reformatory ideas did get abroad. About 1544 a very remarkable man by the name of John Knox was converted to Protestant views. He was a university man and at that time a priest and teacher in the Catholic church. In 1546 he was implicated in the murder of the head of the Catholic church in Scotland, Cardinal Beaton, the profligate archbishop of St.

Andrews. With the help of the French he was captured and sent to the French galleys from which he was finally released through the intercession of the king of England. For a time he lived in England, then fled to the continent at the accession of Mary Tudor, living at Geneva and elsewhere as he could. At Geneva he became thoroughly imbued with the views of Calvin and was henceforth one of his most vigorous exponents.

By 1556 enough Scotch nobles had accepted the Reformation to form a " Covenant " and a union for their own protection. Supported by them Knox was able to return to Scotland in 1559. Under the powerful impression made by his preaching and leadership the Scottish Parliament formally adopted the reform in the year 1560. Catholic worship was abolished, monasteries were dissolved and the property confiscated for the erection of schools and hospitals, the churches were supplied with evangelical ministers and a Protestant form of service was drawn up. A national church was thus organized on the Calvinistic model, expressing its will through a General Assembly which was to be entirely independent of the crown. Scotland thus became a Calvinistic country, the church being called Presbyterian.

Mary Stuart, who had grown to womanhood in France and had married the king of France, was left a widow in 1560. She then returned to Scotland to take up the reins of government there. She was an uncompromising Catholic, and almost immediately she and Knox were at war. She at once set up Catholic worship in her palace, Holy Rood. Knox thundered against the " new idolatry " from his pulpit in St. Giles near by, and for months the great struggle went merrily on. Mary's doubtful character, the attachment of the Scotch to the Reformation and the great power of Knox as a fearless champion of Calvinism, gave him the victory. In 1566 she was deposed and her infant son James was proclaimed king. She fled to England, threw herself on the mercy of Elizabeth whose crown she had long claimed, was imprisoned and finally executed in 1587 after an imprisonment of twenty years.

Under James the Presbyterian church was finally legally established as the national church of Scotland, though he and subsequent rulers strove hard to destroy its democracy and subject it to the state more completely by transforming it into an Episcopal church whose ruling officials should be appointed by the crown.

4. *Calvinistic influences elsewhere.* Calvinism made a deep impression on other lands where it was not finally successful. It spread back into *Germany* over several of the states along the Rhine where Lutheranism had already been established. The Zwinglian parts of *Switzerland* formally accepted the Calvinistic reform about the middle of the sixteenth century while the Protestant elements of *Hungary* went over almost entirely to the Calvinistic position. Beginning about the middle of the century *England* was deeply affected by Calvinism both in doctrines and ideals. The Calvinistic movement was known here as Puritanism. It began to affect the church under Elizabeth, growing in power under James. It demanded various reforms of the Anglican church along with the adoption of the Presbyterian form of church government. It finally in 1642 precipitated the Civil War in which Charles I lost his head and the monarchy was overthrown. With the death of Oliver Cromwell it lost its hold on the government, but it had stamped its impress on the English people permanently. Out of its ranks arose several of the English denominations, such as the Congregationalists, the English Baptists, the Quakers and still others at a later period.

D. THE ANABAPTIST REFORMATION

§ 76

The question of the relation of the Anabaptists to earlier evangelical sects is still in dispute. Undoubtedly they held many of the same doctrines and practices as those held by the Waldenses and other evangelical sects of the Middle Ages. On the other hand they never united with these sects or seemed conscious of any connection with them; moreover, the Anabaptist leaders are known to have come out of the Catholic church rather than from the sects.

Around both Luther and Zwingli there arose a radical party of reformers who demanded that the reform should be carried through to its logical conclusion in an attempt to reëstablish apostolic Christianity without waiting for the assistance of the state. This involved the adoption of a program so radical and revolutionary that all the great reformers shrank from it, though Zwingli hesitated for a time.

When these radicals finally came to the conclusion that there was no hope for a genuine scriptural reform with either Luther or Zwingli they renounced all connection with both the Catholic church and the Reformers and undertook the reëstablishment of primitive Christianity on their own responsibility. They began at infant baptism. Declaring that it was an invention of man, was unscriptural and anti-Christian, the foundation of the papacy and the source of the worst corruptions from which Christianity had suffered through the ages, they renounced it and fellowship with all who practiced it, and began faith-baptism. That baptism they did not get from the Catholic church, but believed they had it from heaven through the Scriptures. Because of this *rebaptism,* as their opponents called it, they were dubbed *Anabaptists* which means *rebaptizers,* a name which they always repudiated, calling themselves *disciples* or *brothers.*

This position on baptism involved radical changes in other respects. It necessarily involved a church of regenerate members who have voluntarily associated themselves together in the faith and fellowship of the gospel; it involved also a separation between church and state and a citizenship based on civil rather than religious considerations; it meant the secularization of the state by excluding it from the field

of religion and consequent religious freedom; it led to religious democracy in the government of the church and ultimately to democracy in the state. All these positions
seemed extremely dangerous in those days. Persecution
broke out at once and was carried on in the most ruthless
manner not only by the Catholics, but also by all parties
of Protestants. Thousands of Anabaptists perished at the
stake in Switzerland and various parts of Germany; nearly
every one of the leading reformers favored persecution;
hundreds of books and pamphlets were written against them
and every creed condemned their doctrines. They were
burned, drowned and allowed to die in prison. Against
such opposition it was not long possible to make progress.
But notwithstanding their terrible sufferings they were able
to maintain their existence and still continue in small groups
in Switzerland. Under the name of Mennonites they are
still known both in Europe and America. They were a
harmless people whose chief offense was their piety and
their religious views.

Some of their doctrines have been indicated above. Their
fundamental peculiarity was their individualism in religion.
They believed that every soul possessed the right to decide
all religious questions for itself, a right which could not be
alienated or assumed by any institution whatsoever. This
is also the view of Scripture and so they insisted upon the
sole and sufficient authority of the Bible. Standing on this
foundation they rejected infant baptism and practiced faith-
baptism, demanded religious freedom and the separation
between church and state, a church of the regenerate kept
pure by the exercise of discipline, a church free and able to
conduct its own affairs.

In the social and political realm they opposed war and
refused to bear arms or pay war taxes, refused to take the
oath for any reason whatsoever, did not believe genuine
Christians could hold civil office, opposed capital punishment and trade in alcoholic liquors being the first prohibi-

tionists of modern times, objected to Christians lending money at interest, and many of them believed and actually strove to establish community of goods.

E. THE ENGLISH REFORMATION

§ 77

POLITICAL CONDITIONS

England was already a strongly centralized government with a young, ambitious and vigorous king, Henry VIII. With the exception of the revolt of Wycliffe the country had been most loyal to the Catholic church. In the early days of the Reformation in Germany rigorous measures had been taken against reform in England, the king himself writing a scurrilous pamphlet against Luther. Manifestly the introduction of reform would be possible only by the conversion of the ruler, which at first appeared to be a remote contingency.

But about 1527 Henry decided that he wished a divorce from his wife Catherine. She had been the widow of his elder brother Arthur who had died a few weeks after the marriage. The alliance between England and Spain had appeared so important to both countries that the governments had united in requesting from the pope a dispensation for the marriage of Henry to the widow, it being contrary to Catholic law for a man to marry his brother's widow. The pope had granted the request and had declared the marriage with Henry entirely valid. Now Henry demanded the annulment of this marriage. Naturally the pope was greatly embarrassed by the demand since his predecessor had decided that the marriage was valid. Still more serious perhaps was the threat of Charles V, nephew of Catherine, that he would certainly punish his Holiness if the divorce was granted. In the midst of these difficulties and dangers the pope attempted to delay, hoping that something would "turn up" to relieve the embarrassment. At last Henry lost all patience, and on the advice of Thomas Cromwell decided to take matters into his own hands and secure a divorce in his own realms. To make this possible it was necessary to abolish papal jurisdiction and establish a tribunal in England which would have authority to grant the divorce. Accordingly in 1531 he began a course of legislation which speedily transferred to the crown of England all the authority which had once been exercised by the pope. Courts were then created which granted Henry the desired divorce, and in 1534 he was declared to be the head of the English church.

§ 78

INTERNAL REFORMS UNDER HENRY

Henry's activities were purely political, but parallel movements which would ultimately lead to the reform of the church itself were beginning. John Tyndale, a priest in the west of England, undertook to translate the Scriptures into the English tongue. Driven out of the country by persecution he fled to the continent where he finished the New Testament and got it printed. It was then smuggled into England and distributed by merchants as they could in their business. Tyndale was at last apprehended and martyred, his last words being "O Lord, open the king of England's eyes." In answer to this prayer and almost as an echo of his words the very next year the entire Bible appeared in print with the king's approval. This first printed English Bible is known as Coverdale's Bible, from the translator who prepared it. In 1537 Matthew's Bible appeared without official sanction and in 1539 the Great Bible, so named from its large size, was officially printed and chained in the churches, though it was not yet used in the services. People were permitted to read it and made large use of the privilege.

In 1535 Henry, who was a great spendthrift and always heavily in debt, decided to confiscate the property of the monasteries and abolish the monastic life in England. This tremendous change was carried through in four years, greatly enriching the crown. Most of the money was lavished by Henry on his favorites but his action put an end in England to one of the most objectionable features of mediæval Christianity. Henry died in 1547 leaving the church still Catholic in every respect except that it had been cut off from the papacy, had received the Scriptures in the English tongue and had suffered the abolition of monasticism. Of course the circulation of the Scriptures and the preaching based upon it had begun to leaven the mass of the English people, but Catholic faith and worship were regnant at Henry's death.

§ 79

REFORM UNDER EDWARD VI

Henry was succeeded by his only son Edward. He was but ten years of age, but he was highly gifted and was a Protestant in sentiment. The regency was given to his uncle who was also Protestant in sentiment. The work of abolishing the Catholic church and introducing Protestantism officially and legally now went swiftly forward. A new service book called the " Book of Common Prayer " was drawn up by Thomas Cranmer, archbishop of Canterbury, assisted by other scholars, and was legally imposed upon all ministers of the church. That book and no other must be used in all the churches of England. It was based upon older liturgies with the distinctively Catholic elements eliminated and is unquestionably one of the most satisfactory service books ever produced by Protestants. If a written service is to be used at all this one can hardly be improved upon. It is still with slight modifications in use in all Episcopal churches throughout the world.

A Protestant creed was also drawn up and imposed upon ministers. Thus Catholic worship was forbidden, Catholic priests in so far as they refused to accept the new régime were expelled. Protestant ministers were installed and Protestant services set up in all the churches. Catholicism like other sects was made illegal and outlawed.

§ 80

UNDER MARY AND ELIZABETH

Edward was succeeded by his sister Mary, the daughter of Catherine. She regarded Protestantism as the cause of all the sufferings and disgrace of her mother and herself, and came to the throne with the one master passion of restoring England to the bosom of " Mother church " and punishing the Protestant leaders who had been instrumental in overthrowing it. As soon as she was firmly seated she induced Parliament to rescind all the laws which had abolished Catholicism and established Protestantism, thus reëstablishing Catholicism as the religion of England. But she could not induce Parliament to reconstitute monasticism or restore to the church the property that had been confiscated.

She then married Philip II of Spain, the most fanatical and at that time one of the most powerful rulers of the world. By his help the country was formally absolved and received back into the church. Several Protestant leaders were then tried and executed as heretics, the most notable being Bishops Latimer and Ridley and Archbishop Cranmer. As the two former were led to the stake Latimer cried, " Let us play the man to-day, Master Ridley, for by the grace of God we shall light such a fire in England as shall never be put out."

Shaken by a long imprisonment and by seeing his friends die Cranmer was persuaded to recant, but in the final scene bravely recanted his recantation and at the stake firmly held his right hand in the flames till it was consumed, thus reasserting his Protestantism in the most effective way possible. Under Mary's régime several hundred were executed at the stake as heretics. This cruelty fixed upon her the stigma of " Bloody Mary," making Catholicism forever impossible for Anglo-Saxon countries.

Elizabeth had been reared a Protestant, but had conformed to the Catholic church during the régime of Mary. On her accession it was not known what religious attitude she would take. Slowly and cautiously she turned toward Protestantism. Mary's legislation was repealed, the reformatory legislation of Henry and Edward, slightly modified, was revived, the English church again restored to Protestantism. This was accomplished by 1562 and constituted the beginning of the glorious " Elizabethan Era " in which England forged to the front as one of the great European world powers. Elizabeth reëstablished the English church on the Protestant foundation which it has retained substantially unchanged to the present.

§ 81

CHARACTERISTICS OF THE ENGLISH CHURCH

The new English church was in many respects nearer to the Catholics than any other form of Protestantism. The old Catholic organization was unchanged except that the sovereign instead of the pope was made the head of the church and all papal activity was cut off. Catholic property was all taken over for the use of the new church, while the Catholic succession of ordinations and baptism was continued unchanged. The mass, penance and extreme unction were abandoned; the doctrine of purgatory with all related doctrines and practices were abolished, while a Calvinistic doctrine of the supper was incorporated in the ritual and articles of faith. Private confession was abandoned but confirmation by the bishop and a form of general public confession was retained. Archbishops and bishops were henceforth to be appointed by the king, while new English courts took over all the business once transacted by the pope.

Anglican worship is very ornate and resembles that of the Catholic church very closely, but on examination it will be found that the distinctive Catholic elements were largely eliminated. It is but just to state, however, that the Catholicizing or High Church party have in recent years interpreted the Prayer Book in a Catholic sense, thereby causing much bitterness and strife in the church.

The new church was completely subjected to the state, the two institutions henceforth combining to suppress all forms of faith and worship other than that authorized by law. These regulations obtained for over a century and a quarter, Catholics, Puritans, Congregationalists, Baptists and Quakers suffering alike as illegal and intolerable sectaries till toleration was granted in 1689.

§ 82

PURITANISM

Puritanism which was simply Calvinism working in the English church appeared as early as the middle of the sixteenth century. It was greatly stimulated by the return of English refugees from the continent on the death of Mary and the accession of Elizabeth. Many of them had lived in close personal contact with Calvin and his work at Geneva and had imbibed his views. Moreover they brought back with them a new translation of the Bible made at Geneva and hence known as the Geneva version. It was an excellent piece of work, translated in the Calvinistic sense, provided with Calvinistic notes and printed in convenient form for home use. It became the Bible of the English homes and undoubtedly exerted a powerful influence for the spread of Calvinistic convictions.

Elizabeth succeeded in keeping Puritanism suppressed, but

it blazed out under James I.   It demanded purity of life, a
revision of the Prayer-Book in the direction of simplicity
and brevity, freedom of action about many of the ceremonies, and a Presbyterian form of church government.   The
controversy finally precipitated the Civil War in 1642 in
which Charles I was overthrown and deprived of his head.
For a short while it looked as if Puritanism would master
the government, but Cromwell was opposed to the intolerance and the church government of the Presbyterians and so
nullified their efforts.   On the accession of Charles II the
Episcopal church was reëstablished and all forms of dissent were suppressed.   Under the repressive measures of
the government Presbyterianism disappeared as a party in
the state church.

§ 83

RISE OF THE INDEPENDENT ENGLISH DENOMINATIONS

While Puritanism disappeared from English life as a
unified force it had made impressions and sown seeds that
were destined to have far reaching results in the production
of independent bodies.   Three of these come within this
period.

1. *Congregationalism* was founded by Robert Browne.
He had been a student in Cambridge University during the
height of the agitation aroused by the Puritans.   He had
thus been forced to consider questions connected with the
nature and government of the church.   After leaving the
University he had visited Holland where he had met
Anabaptists and learned something of their views.   He
then settled in eastern England where there were many
Dutch Anabaptists with some of whom he must have been
acquainted.   It was probably through these influences that
he finally reached the conviction that the church was a local
body, composed entirely of regenerated people, completely
separated from the state and from all other ecclesiastical
bodies, endowed with authority to perform all ecclesiastical
functions — preaching the word, administering the ordi-

nances, disciplining its members, ordaining its officers, etc.—
and wholly democratic in its government. He came to the
further conclusion that the English church could not be reformed and that it was sinful to be longer connected with it.

Accordingly he separated from it and set up a new
church at Norwich apparently in the year 1580. It was
soon broken up by the authorities and Browne fled to Holland where in a number of pamphlets he set forth with
great force and clearness the position which the Congregationalists have held to the present time. Finally he returned to England and reëntered the state church, but his
work was done. His followers were long called Brownists
in derision.

About 1587 a second independent church was formed in
London on substantially the same model. It too was broken
up, some of its members being martyred in 1593 and others
fleeing to Holland. Still a third church was organized at
Gainsborough and Scrooby under the leadership of John
Smyth and John Robinson. This also was driven to the
continent and settled in Holland about 1607. Smyth and
a part of his congregation turned Anabaptist, while a part
of Robinson's church came to America in 1620 in the *May-
flower* and founded New England and American Congregationalism.

Many of the Congregationalist fugitives in Holland remained and died there; but in 1616 Henry Jacob returned
to London and began work there. The body was persecuted and grew very slowly until the outbreak of the Civil
War in 1642 when they became one of the leading factors
of the national life. This was not because of their numbers but of the high character of the body, of their principles
of freedom for which the English were struggling at that
time and of the great ability of some of their representatives,
the most notable of whom were Oliver Cromwell and John
Milton, each in his sphere among the greatest men England
has produced.

With the return and accession of Charles II they suffered

like other dissenters until the adoption of the Act of Toleration in 1689.

At Plymouth, Mass., some of Robinson's church founded Congregationalism in America. They were joined by many thousand Puritans in the next few years fleeing from the persecution of Archbishop Laud, and falling away from their principle of religious freedom and separation between church and state, they made Congregationalism the established church in New England and became almost as intolerant as the English church from which they fled had been. Baptists were persecuted, and Quakers were actually put to death on Boston Common.

2. *The English Baptists.* As we have seen, persecution had driven some of the continental Anabaptists to England early in the sixteenth century. They were being persecuted by Henry VIII as early as 1530. They continued to maintain their existence, however, and some of the English may have been converted to their views inasmuch as some of the English Baptist churches claim to have originated in the sixteenth century. If so they have left no contemporary evidence of their existence. The English Baptists as a denomination date their existence from the year 1611, and relate their history about as follows:

John Smyth and his party, as we have seen, settled at Amsterdam in Holland. Here Smyth of course came into contact with the Anabaptists. He was speedily convinced of the scripturalness of their position on at least two points, viz., their Arminian theology and their rejection of infant baptism. Accordingly he and about forty of his members instituted faith-baptism and set up an English Anabaptist church at Amsterdam. Smyth soon came to regard this action, which had been taken in entire independence of the Anabaptists, as improper. He and a few others made application for admittance into the Anabaptist or Mennonite church and eventually most of them were received and thus lost to the Baptist cause. The larger part of the group stoutly asserted their conviction that they had acted properly under all the circumstances. Accordingly they issued a confession of faith in 1611 and about the same time returned to England under the leadership of Henry Helwys and John Morton to begin work in the home land.

They were still called Anabaptists and were bitterly persecuted. The major points in their contention at this time were insistence on faith-baptism with the rejection of infant-baptism, religious freedom for which they wrote and suffered nobly, the salvation of all infants dying in infancy which was then strenuously denied by the Calvinists, and the assertion that Christ died for every man or a general atonement which was also denied by the Calvinists. They grew slowly till the Civil War when they also had more freedom and opportunity. In 1660 they claimed to have 20,000 members. After the accession of Charles II they suffered with other dissenters till freedom came with the Act of Toleration in 1689.

The group just discussed were Arminian in theology and connectional in church government. The English Calvinistic or Particular Baptists began a little later in England. It will be remembered that Henry Jacob had returned from Holland to England in 1616 to begin a Congregationalist work in London. Naturally this group also had been more or less affected by the Anabaptists in Holland, and consequently it occasions no surprise when we learn that the question of infant baptism was agitated among them till it led to a split in 1633. The new church abandoned infant baptism and soon adopted faith-baptism. Another congregation of like faith seems to have been established about 1638, and by 1644 there were seven in London and environs. In that year they drew up and published their first confession of faith a good deal of which was taken from an earlier Congregational confession. It is vigorously Calvinistic.

The Continental Anabaptists had practiced both immersion and other modes of baptism, but these English Anabaptists, as they were still called, insisted on immersion only and at least a part of them sent Richard Blount to Holland to secure baptism for himself and them.

The Arminian Baptists were called General, the Calvinistic were called Particular. They were agreed in practicing a faith-baptism, insisting on a converted church membership, separation between church and state with complete religious freedom, church independence and democratic church government, etc. But they differed absolutely on theology and had no communion with each other.

The Calvinistic Baptists were much more favorably received by the English, that type of theology being dominant at that time in England. They grew rapidly during the period of the Civil War and Cromwell's régime, having several leaders of ability and culture the most notable of whom were William Kiffen, Hansard Knollys and John Bunyan. On the accession of Charles they suffered with the other dissenters. Bunyan was in prison for twelve years beginning in 1660, during which time he wrote his immortal allegory, " Pilgrim's Progress."

In 1677 a new and more elaborate confession was drawn up and in 1688 formally adopted by the first general meeting of the Calvinistic Baptists. It is an adaptation of the Westminster Confession, whole sections of it being taken over almost without change. With the Act of Toleration in 1689 Baptists obtained toleration with other dissenters. There were then more than one hundred churches in England and Wales.

American Baptists originated nearly as early as their English brethren. The General Baptists seem to have been planted by immigration, but the first Calvinistic Baptists originated on the soil of Rhode Island. Roger Williams, a Congregational minister of Massachusetts, was banished from that colony because of his criticisms of the government of the colony. He took refuge at Providence where in 1638 he organized an Anabaptist church by instituting faith-baptism anew. Williams did not remain in communion with the church long, but it lived and still exists as the First Baptist Church of Providence. The colony of Rhode Island had absolute religious freedom and separation between church and state, the first government in the history of the world to be founded on that basis. Everywhere else the Baptists were persecuted except in the later Quaker colonies. They grew very slowly, however, due to their meager equipment and the prejudice which they met everywhere. The two parties remained separate in America as in England and developed several other parties such as Seventh Day Baptists, Six Principle Baptists, etc. At the end of the period there were only a few thousand in both England and American and they were still usually called Anabaptists. The prefix *Ana* was gradually dropped in the next period.

3. *The Society of Friends* or Quakers was founded by George Fox, an English Puritan youth. He had a remarkable religious experience in which he could find no relief for his burdened conscience in any of the churches till he threw himself on the mercy of Christ apart from all ecclesiastical ordinances. The glorious truths of the gospel were then " opened " to him by means of an inner illumination of the Holy Spirit. Ever afterwards he relied upon this " inner light " for salvation and guidance. He rejected and seemed to hate the churches, which he called " steeple houses," because he believed that they actually stood between the soul and God. With the churches he rejected all ecclesiasticism — baptism, the supper, ordination, prepared services, dedicated buildings, etc. This meant absolute religious freedom, absolute religious democracy which put women on complete equality with men in all religious duties and privileges. He would have no church but organized his followers into a society of friends.

They were bitterly persecuted from the start and were soon dubbed Quakers. It is estimated that as many as 14,000 were imprisoned in England between 1650 and 1689 when they also obtained toleration by the Act of Toleration. In the meantime several hundred had died in prison.

They began their work in America in 1656 and met the same treatment as in England. Four were actually hanged on the Boston Common, one of them being a woman. In the early days they showed wonderful zeal in preaching at home and also in mission work abroad. But after they obtained peace they lost their aggressiveness and became a retiring, pietistic body who were highly respectable but little influential. In 1682 William Penn founded the great colony of Pennsylvania on the basis of religious freedom. It was the most notable single act of Quaker history.

They opposed oaths, war, slavery, intemperance, luxury, extravagance in dress, urged prison reform and contributed in other ways to the betterment of living conditions.

F. REFORM IN THE CATHOLIC CHURCH

§ 84

DURING THE EARLY DAYS OF THE REFORMATION

At first the Catholic church seemed to be stunned by the magnitude of the disaster which was threatening to overwhelm it, and did nothing to stem the tide that was setting so strongly against it. Luther and the other leaders were excommunicated, but nothing effective was done to stop the movement itself. Had it not been for the activity of some of the Catholic princes of southern Germany the entire Teutonic people might have been swept out of the Catholic church forever. The Dukes of Bavaria and the rulers of the various Austrian lands forcibly and successfully resisted the introduction of reformatory ideas and doctrines into their lands. The emperor tried unsuccessfully to prevent its spread in other parts of the country. As we have seen, the rulers of Italy, France and Spain succeeded in suppressing the movement. It is not too much to say that it succeeded wherever it had a free opportunity and failed only where it was suppressed by force.

§ 85

THE SOCIETY OF JESUS OR JESUITS

One of the most fateful events of this wonderful era was the organization of the Jesuit order. Its founder was Ignatius Loyola, a Spanish nobleman whose career as a fighting man had been brought to an end by a gunshot wound in the siege of Pampeluna in 1523. Unable longer to follow the life of a soldier he determined to devote his talents to the service of the church. Having obtained some education in the schools of Spain he became a student in the University of Paris. While there he gathered about him a group of likeminded young men, French and Spanish, who bound themselves together to go on a mission to Palestine as soon as the way opened. They made their way to Venice, but the road to the East remained closed. As a consequence they went to Rome and there were formally constituted into a society to be known as " the Society of Jesus." It was essentially a monastic order of a new type. Members were to be admitted only after a rigid examination and long preparation; they took the usual monastic vows and in addition the vow to go anywhere on a moment's notice; they were to be thoroughly educated and fitted for mission work anywhere.

The organization was military. There was a general at Rome in absolute command, with subordinate officers throughout the world. The militant spirit of fighting Spanish Catholicism was infused into it from the start. Its weapons were to be missions, the confessional, education and where necessary the free use of force. More than one sovereign was assassinated by them. They sought to reach and influence the upper military and ruling classes, and through them to control the destinies of nations. Almost from the beginning of their history they became, as they have remained, the controlling influence in determining the policies of the papacy. It was largely their efforts that put a stop to the progress of the Reformation in southern Germany and finally precipitated the Thirty Years War. They have not been able to suppress Protestantism, as they planned, but they have succeeded in exalting the papacy to the dizzy and blasphemous claims which it now makes for itself.

§ 86

THE COUNCIL OF TRENT

The reformers had frequently demanded a free ecumenical council before which they could lay their grievances. The emperor also demanded such a council. It had been frequently promised but the pope could not forget the unhappy experiences of his predecessors in dealing with councils, and so constantly found means for postponing its call. At last the emperor Charles V, who believed that a council could heal the Protestant schism, threatened to call a German council to deal with the situation unless the pope acted. To avoid this danger the pope finally very reluctantly called a general council to meet in the little city of Trent in 1545.

It was not largely attended and from the first session was completely under the domination of the pope. The Jesuit order had just been organized, and at once they distinguished themselves as the protagonists of the highest papal pretensions. In alternate sessions the council took up the work of reforming the church and formulating a new creed. The latter was its most important work. It sat at intervals from 1545 to 1563, during this time formulating all the distinctive Catholic doctrines except the dogmas of the immaculate conception of Mary and the infallibility of the pope. The most important of these doctrines have been stated above. Upon the creed here drawn up the Catholic church still stands. It contains the peculiar doctrines which characterize Catholicism.

§ 87

CATHOLIC GAINS

Through the efforts of the Jesuits, the activities of the inquisition and the various religious wars that were instigated by the Catholics they were able to put a stop to the progress of the Reformation before the end of the sixteenth century. They stamped it out in blood in Spain, Italy, the Austrian lands and most of eastern Europe. They made a long and bloody effort in France but without complete success. Ireland and Belgium they saved for the Catholic church. In other Protestant lands they were able to bring about serious Catholic reactions, but were never able to overthrow Protestantism. In Sweden the queen became Catholic but resigned the crown; in Saxony the Elector became Catholic but Protestantism remained the religion of the people; in England James II was Catholic but he was overthrown and the Protestant William and Mary seated on the throne.

But during this sixteenth century they won vast additional territories by colonization. The West Indies, the southern part of the United States, Mexico, Central America, the whole of South America and the Philippine Islands were populated by the Spanish and Portugese Catholics. Moreover for nearly two centuries it looked as if Canada and the interior of the North American continent would be preëmpted by French Catholics, though it finally passed into Protestant hands.

Moreover the Catholics were filled with zeal for the conversion of the heathen while the Protestants did nothing in this direction for more than two centuries. Every expedition that set out for a new country was fitted out with a religious equipment to do mission work among the natives. Vast numbers of Indians accepted Catholicism in a nominal sort of way in the Americas. Missionaries filled with fiery zeal like Xavier turned to the far East and planted flourishing missions in India, China and Japan. This work seemed to be most promising, but the shallowness of the conversions and the political activities of the missionaries eventually brought their work to ruin in most of their fields of labor. Ultimately the Catholics had to reorganize their work almost everywhere.

§ 88

INTERNAL REFORMS

The stress of Protestant criticism forced the Catholic church to make some reforms. The *sale* of indulgences was abolished, though the principle and use of indulgences was retained; education of the clergy was emphasized and a stricter control over their morals was established; preaching and the catechetical instruction of children was materially enlarged and improved; in some countries the Scriptures were translated into the vernacular and provided with Catholic notes to offset the circulation of the so-called " Protestant Bible," though the Latin Vulgate remained the " authentic version " and only the Latin text was translated. In every land where Protestantism is strong the Catholic church has stood on a higher level than in those lands which are Catholic. Since the Reformation there has been no pope of scandalous life such as many pre-Reformation popes lived. Monasticism was also reformed and many abuses removed. In short the Catholic church prepared itself for a new struggle for world domination under circumstances more difficult than it had ever before faced.

§ 89

WARS OF RELIGION

On account of the close union between church and state the Reformation became a political question in every land into which it was introduced, thus creating the danger of civil and international war over the whole of Europe. Actual hostilities were not far behind the feet of the earliest reformers. The earliest " religious war," so-called, broke out in Switzerland in 1529. This was followed by a second one in 1531 in which Zwingli was killed and the progress of reform in this country was brought to an end.

The first war in Germany broke out in 1547. It was known as the Schmalkald War and was very short. The Protestants were completely defeated by the Catholics under the emperor and Catholicism was restored in south Germany. In 1551 war broke out again and this time the Protestants were victorious, securing the Peace of Augsburg by which Lutherans established for themselves a legal standing within the empire.

We have seen how France was torn by eight civil wars from 1562 to 1598. During the same period the provinces of the Netherlands were involved in a struggle in which Spain was a participant and which eventuated in a partition of the country and ultimately in the independence of the northern provinces and their erection into a new state.

Toward the end of the sixteenth century and in the first half of the seventeenth there were revolts and attempted revolutions in many Protestant lands as a result of the efforts made to restore Catholicism. But the most fearful of all the wars of religion was the Thirty Years War in Germany. It broke out in 1618 as a result of Catholic efforts to overthrow Protestantism in Bohemia and with brief interruptions lasted till 1648 when it was brought to an end by the famous Treaty of Westphalia. All Germany was devastated, France, England, Sweden and other lands were deeply affected, Catholicism was restored in eastern and southern Germany. Catholics suffered, however, almost as much as the Protestants and in the end were compelled to acknowledge that they could not suppress the Protestant movement.

By the Peace of Westphalia two new and independent

Protestant states were created, Switzerland and the Netherlands or Holland; Calvinism was recognized as a legal religion beside Lutheranism; in the possession of church property Jan. 1, 1624, was recognized as the "normal year,"
that is those who held a piece of property on Jan. 1, 1624,
were confirmed in its possession thus putting Protestants
in permanent possession of enormous quantities of property;
finally the prince was still recognized as the arbiter of religion, that is the religion of the prince must be accepted as
the religion of the people.

The pope rejected the treaty, stormed at and anathematized its framers but all to no purpose. The effort to
suppress Protestantism by force had failed and the Catholic
powers were ready to acknowledge that fact. Never since
that day has the pope played any important part in international politics. Catholic and Protestant powers have
lived as good neighbors, have made war and concluded
treaties without asking his advice or consent.

§ 90

EXPANSION OF CHRISTIANITY THROUGH COLONIZATION

Up till the beginning of this period Christianity was almost confined to Europe. It had once been the religion of
North Africa but Mohammedanism had stamped it out
there. It still existed in western Asia, but under the heel
of the Mohammedan Turks it had lost all power and significance. Cut off from other peoples by the ocean on
the west and by the Mohammedans on the east Christianity
had spread but little for several centuries, missions had
almost ceased.

The discoveries of the Spanish and Portuguese opened up
a new world into which Christianity was not slow to enter.
These discoveries led to the exploration, exploitation and
settlement of vast areas of land hitherto unknown, carrying

Christianity with settlers and extending it among the natives by missions.

The Spanish and Portuguese at once began attempts at conquests and colonization. They carried their religion with them and as a consequence all of America south of the United States is now solidly Spanish and Portuguese Catholic. They also took possession of the Philippine Islands and made them Catholic. A little later the French Catholics took possession of the region around the St. Lawrence and the Great Lakes and planted Catholicism there.

The Protestant powers were much slower in their efforts at colonization. More than a century after the discovery of America, Protestants made their first permanent settlement at Jamestown in Virginia. Gradually the middle portion of the eastern coast of North America was occupied by the various nationalities and types of Protestantism at that time in Europe. Later Australia and New Zealand were discovered and settled by Protestants, almost exclusively English. In like manner South Africa was populated by the Dutch Protestants and later by the English. At first the various Protestant parties in North America were hostile to each other, but gradually they consolidated or otherwise eliminated friction, and eventually most of them passed under the dominion of the English.

Thus not only Europeans but European religious parties were planted in all the new lands which were held by savage or barbarous peoples. By this means the territory of the Caucasian stock and the Christian religion was enormously enlarged. The new territory was ultimately divided almost equally between the Roman Catholics and the Protestants, the Spanish and the Portuguese being the leaders of the Catholics and the English being the leaders of the Protestants.

Before the end of this period Russia had begun that wonderful period of expansion which has carried her people entirely across northern Asia. With them went the

Greek Catholic church so that all northern Asia is now Greek Catholic. Not only did the Russians remain loyal to this faith, but they also converted many of the natives to the same faith. This territory constitutes the sole important gains made by the Greek church since its separation from the Roman Catholic church in 1054. But this expansion constitutes enormous gains in territory and numbers.

EIGHTH PERIOD — 1648 TO 1789

§ 91

INTRODUCTION

FROM the Reformation to the present it is almost impossible to present the vast and complex material in a form that will at once be clear and comprehensible and at the same time show the progress of events. The unity of Christianity is gone. In its place has arisen division and strife not only between Catholics and Protestants but among the various Protestant parties themselves. The numerous Protestant bodies have been continually multiplied by new schisms. This has been especially true of English Christianity where there was originally less consistency and more freedom. Christianity has been paying a high price for liberty, but time has proven that the blessings of liberty are worth all the cost.

§ 92

RISE OF SKEPTICISM

The great body of the Reformers had broken away from the Catholic church without, however, weakening the principle of authority in religion. In the room of an infallible church they asserted an infallible Bible. At first the right of private judgment in the interpretation of that Book had been claimed; but in a short time the principle of tradition had reasserted its power, leading to the formulation of creeds that must be accepted under civil and religious penalties. Intolerance became almost as inflexible and savage in Protestant as in Catholic lands. Only the Socinii of northern Italy and their followers had shown any tendency to break away from the old orthodox creeds, and they were but a small and uninfluential party.

But by the middle of the seventeenth century the world had become unutterably weary of theological strife and religious wars. Men began to think that religion, and especially the Christian religion, was the cause of all their woes. If people would only reject these superstitions, they said, and live by reason we should have a new world in which peace and brotherhood would reign. The principles of church authority, credal authority and scriptural authority must be thrown aside that men might live by the light of human reason. It was the age of Rationalism, reasonableness, "illumination." As it came on its advocates thought they were ushering in a golden age, free from superstition and ignorance, blessed with peace and enlightenment. How little we can know in advance of the fruits of our actions!

Skepticism took many different forms. Among them was *Deism,* a view of God which practically banished him from the universe. He was supposed to have created and set it in motion, but he now exercised over it no providential control. This completely nullified the fundamental assumptions of religion itself. Much was said about *natural religion,* which was supposed to be religion reduced to its lowest terms — belief in the existence and holiness of God, in the obligation to righteousness, in the immortality of the soul, in future rewards and punishments. This was good as far as it went, but it made belief in revelation and in the distinctive doctrines of Christianity impossible. *Arianism* and *Socinianism* minimized the person and work of Jesus Christ in such a way as to regard him as little more than a good teacher and example.

This skepticism, begun in England as *Deism,* spread to France where it became so powerful as to control for years almost the whole of the literary and intellectual life of the nation. Thence it passed into Germany where it became almost as strong as in France. The whole of life was rationalized — church, state and social life.

During the latter half of the eighteenth century the same views of religion, brought to America by British and French officers, deeply affected our own intellectual and religious life. Our schools and many of our pulpits were full of French infidelity. In France Voltaire and in America Tom Paine were the popular representatives of this type of thinking.

As was to be expected under these conditions the most serious religious and moral decay began all over the Christian world. Religious fervor cooled, evangelical elements were eliminated from song and worship generally, the evangelical note disappeared from preaching, religion became purely formal and intellectual. Even those who retained their orthodox theological beliefs lost the vitality of their message, becoming mere theological debaters.

Along with this decay of faith went a rapid decline in morals. Vice, drunkenness, gambling, robbery and all other forms of evil living were so terrible that many good men despaired of the race. It was a common opinion that Christianity was on its last legs; soon all religion would be dead and then men would be left free to live according to reason, that is as their whims and passions might dictate. These conditions with variations prevailed in both Europe and America.

§ 93

DECLINE OF THE PROTESTANT DENOMINATIONS

Under the influence of the prevalent conditions it was to be expected that the individual churches and denominations would show serious decline. The state churches, notwithstanding the security of their position, languished. The two extremes of a dry and lifeless theological *orthodoxy* and a cold and paralyzing *rationalism* sapped these churches of all vital piety and active benevolence.

The free churches of England and America were in little

better condition. Congregationalists, Baptists, Quakers and all others suffered. *In England* the majority of the General Baptists became Socinian while the Calvinistic wing developed a hyper-Calvinistic theology which was fatal to all Christian effort. Among American Baptists the same two tendencies were operative, especially the latter which is to have such fateful results in the anti-mission, anti-effort views of the next period. Unitarian views, which appeared among the Congregationalists and Quakers, are to become a serious menace to the existence of these bodies in the next period. Lutherans, Reformed and others on the continent, shared the same general experience.

Toward the end of the period all parties began to feel the refreshing effects of the great evangelical revival which was sweeping over the English speaking world. The membership of the churches began to increase in numbers, their piety became more fervent and actively benevolent, their standards of living higher.

§ 94

THE CATHOLIC CHURCH SUFFERS DECLINE

It was not alone the Protestant churches and denominations that suffered from the growth of Rationalism. The Catholic church was also greatly weakened.

1. *In France* there was serious friction between the government and the church of France on one side and the papacy on the other, during much of this period. Louis XIV (1643–1715) was especially determined to control the French church, and in this effort he was supported by the church itself. The struggle was carried to such lengths that the French bishops in 1682, under the leadership of the famous scholar and bishop Bossuet, drew up a statement which was virtually a " declaration of independence " and which has been called the " Gallican Liberties." It was declared that the power of the pope is confined to spiritual

matters, that the seat of final authority is in the Council not the pope, that even in spiritual matters the pope's authority is limited by the canons and the ecclesiastical customs of France and that the pope's judgment is not irreversible. A few years later, however, these views were rescinded.

There was also a revival of the evangelical views of Augustine in the French church. It was known as Jansenism and for a time gave the ecclesiastical authorities much trouble. Many of the leading literary men of France were, either because of Rationalism or a more evangelical faith, opposed to the Catholic church. During the first half of the eighteenth century France had a number of great Catholic preachers, in fact some of the greatest preachers that the Catholic church has ever produced. The most notable were Bossuet d. 1704, Bourdaloue d. 1704, Fenelon d. 1715 and Massillon d. 1742. But by the end of the period faith had almost perished from the French people, a condition of unbelief from which they have never yet recovered.

2. *In Austria* free thought advanced so far that the Emperor Joseph II (1780–1790) introduced sweeping reforms into that intolerant and priest-ridden country. He granted toleration to Protestants, prohibited appeals to the pope, suppressed pilgrimages, religious processions and many of the monasteries, forbade the publication of papal communications till they were approved by the government, etc. Finally a gathering of German clergy called the " Congress of Ems " took steps looking toward the severance of the German Catholic church from the papacy. So threatening did the situation appear that the pope journeyed all the way to Vienna in an effort to avoid the disaster.

Unfortunately all these struggles were more the result of rationalistic skepticism than of evangelical faith and so soon came to naught. Rationalism had the power of destroying, but could supply little that was constructive and able to meet the religious needs of men.

3. *Suppression of the Jesuits.* As we have seen the Jesuits, on account of their organization, their *esprit du*

corps and their splendid educational equipment, exercised an immense influence over the fortunes of the papacy and the destinies of the European countries. This influence became so great in the church and the order meddled so continually and in such obnoxious ways in the affairs of civil governments that Catholic ecclesiastical and civil authorities united in a demand for the suppression of the order. They were banished from Portugal in 1759, from France in 1762, from Spain and her possessions and from Naples, Parma and Piacenza in 1767 and were finally suppressed and dissolved by the pope in 1773. Free thought thus scored one of its greatest triumphs.

§ 95

ELEMENTS OF GAIN IN THIS PERIOD

It would, however, be a grave mistake to suppose that the results of this period were altogether evil. On the contrary there were mighty gains which have permanently enriched the life of the world. Freedom is a dangerous possession to those who have not learned how to use it, but it is a precious treasure nevertheless. This is the period in which the world was gaining its freedom and learning how to use it. Naturally there were excesses and mistakes. But there were gains also.

1. In this period much of the world gained its *intellectual freedom,* gained for the individual the right to think for himself without danger from the state or the church. Man broke away from the tyranny of creeds and confessions and ecclesiastical organizations and began to seek for the truth for himself. He created a philosophy entirely independent of the church, he criticized the church, its creeds, its ministry, its worship, its theology and even its Bible. Superstitions, errors and wrongs that were hoary with age were melted in the fierce heat of this crucible and disappeared forever. Unfortunately men sometimes went too

far and attacked things that were true and essential, but such things were safe and the gain was indisputable.

2. *Political freedom.* In this period the long and bitter struggle for political freedom was begun. The remnants of feudalism were abolished and all men attained to equality before the law. The American colonies succeeded in breaking the galling yoke of the mother country, and set up a government by the people and for the people, a republic. Kings and princes began to be limited by constitutions; not the will of the prince but the will of the people was to be the law of the land for the future. This was an unspeakable gain whose fruits have as yet not all been gathered.

3. *Religious freedom.* From time immemorial religion and the state had been united. "Throne and altar" had often been allied against the people who between the two had suffered the most horrible treatment. For the first time in human history Roger Williams set up in the colony of Rhode Island in 1638 a government under which absolute religious freedom was guaranteed so long as its exercise did not disturb public order. The established churches of the other colonies were attacked during the latter half of the eighteenth century, an effort which eventuated in the adoption of a federal constitution which guaranteed religious freedom and secured the disestablishment of the various churches in Virginia, Massachusetts and other states.

From this beginning the movement looking toward religious freedom has spread until religious toleration is enjoyed in nearly all lands and the work of disestablishment is going steadily forward, giving absolute equality before the law to all forms of religious belief and practice. Indications are that another hundred years will see complete disestablishment the world over.

4. *Popular education.* The education of the Middle Ages had been aristocratic. No attempt had been made to educate all the people; as a rule only churchmen and the nobility had been educated. Luther and other reformers had begun a movement for general education supported by

the state. During the rationalistic period of the eighteenth century this movement began to be realized. The rationalists were generally democratic in their feelings, believing in the dignity and rights of the people. Naturally they favored the education of the people.

Along with the diffusion of education came the freedom of the press and the right of public assembly and open discussion. These are among the most valued blessings of our day, the most tremendous safeguards of liberty and justice possessed by the modern world.

§ 96

EVANGELICAL REVIVALS

The lamp of evangelical truth and life seemed for a time to be flickering towards extinction, but it was only dimmed, not quenched. In due time it would again be placed on the lampstand to shine with new splendor and power. The night of skepticism and moral decay was the precursor of the most splendid day in the history of Christianity. This day began with the revivals of the seventeenth and eighteenth centuries.

1. *The German revival.* The earliest of these revivals was in Germany and is known as *Pietism.* Its leader was Philip J. Spener, a highly cultured pastor, who began the work of reform in the city of Frankfort on the Main about 1666. He turned away from the prevalent theological type of preaching to simple, practical, vital sermons, intended to reach and bless the lives of the people. He encouraged Bible study, stimulated the activities of the laymen, emphasized the necessity for a religious experience, for a converted and educated ministry, for practical reforms.

Spener's ability and culture recommended his views to the cultured circles of Germany, but the official church was usually bitterly opposed to his views and his practical measures. It was felt to be a depreciation of the church and its sacraments, of the pastoral office, and to be dangerous to good order and religion. Some of the young professors who embraced Spener's views were driven out of the faculty of the University of Leipsic. They proceeded at once to found the University of Halle upon the basis of Spener's teachings. In connection with this new school, A. H. Francke founded the famous Halle Orphan House, one of the most noted homes for orphan children in the world and the beginning of such work among Protestants.

Unfortunately Spener's movement lacked popular support. It was almost confined to university and cultured circles and so never took firm hold upon the life of the German people. Soon after the end of the century that gave it birth it was stifled by the rising tide of Rationalism which was sweeping over the world. It left few traces behind it, and Germany has had no real revival since.

2. *The American revival.* Moral and religious conditions in the American colonies were aggravated by the isolation of the people and the hard conditions of frontier life. Undoubtedly the decline was most serious, the old piety was well-nigh gone. The downward tendency was stopped by the "Great Awakening," which began in Northampton, Mass., under the preaching of Jonathan Edwards, pastor of the Congregational church at that place. Edwards was one of the ablest thinkers that America has yet produced, saintly in life, earnest and searching in his preaching. In the midst of his regular ministrations there broke out a great revival, which swept over most of the colonies with markedly beneficial effects on the whole life of the colonies, both public and private. It was taken up by other and less notable men, thousands were converted, many of the old churches were revived, some of them were split by the new wine of spiritual life, new evangelistic churches were founded.

The movement was strengthened by the work of George Whitefield, the great English evangelist, who made many evangelizing tours of the country and spread the good news of the gospel from one end of the land to the other. In all, he visited this country seven times and finally died here in 1773.

3. *The British revival.* About the beginning of the eighteenth century England was in a most distressing state of moral and religious decay. Life was unspeakably gross and evangelical faith seemed to be dead. Out of these conditions arose an evangelical revival which changed the whole tone of life and doubtless saved the country from the horrors of a catastrophe similar to the French Revolution, which burst upon the world at the close of the century. The leading instruments in the hands of God in the promotion of this revival were John and Charles Wesley and George Whitefield. They were all Oxford men, the Wesleys coming out of the Episcopal rectory of Epworth, and Whitefield being the son of an inn-keeper. While in the University they had formed, among the students, an organization for the cultivation of the religious life which had earned the title of " The Holy Club " from their fellow-students, who had also called them " Methodists," on account of their methodical devotion to their university duties.

All three were ordained to the ministry of the English church, of which they were members. But about the year 1737 they were all, each in his own way, converted and led to a much more evangelical position than that held by the English church. Their preaching soon became so emotional, vigorous and vital as to render them obnoxious to the authorities of their church. Being excluded from the churches they began to preach in the open air and in rented halls, always at hours other than those at which the services of the church were held. They were striving to remain good Anglicans.

They preached a glad, emotional gospel, full of song and movement, free to all men, with assurance based upon experience. John Wesley and Whitefield were great preachers, while Charles was a notable hymn-writer and singer. Soon there were hosts of converts. These Wesley, who was a marvelously gifted organizer, gathered into *societies* for the cultivation of the spiritual life and the propagation of the gospel. The societies were divided into *classes,* under the direction of *class leaders,* who were responsible for their moral and religious instruction and spiritual welfare. Careful supervision and instruction were thus established to conserve and supplement itinerant evangelism. These local leaders were laymen and women, while the few ministers who were converted to his views, along with some laymen, were given oversight over a number of these societies in a circuit and thus became *circuit-riders.* In 1744 the first conference of the preachers was held in London, thereafter becoming the *Annual Conference.* Wesley, at this time, had no thought of founding a new church; his only purpose was the creation of an organization which would conserve and propagate his revival movement. The Wesleyan *type of piety* came from the Moravians through Wesley's personal contact with that organization in London, the *ritual* and some other features were derived from the Anglican church, the *organization* arose out of the exigencies of the movement reacted upon by Wesley's organizing genius.

The *organization of the Methodists* into a body independent of the Episcopal church took place in America in 1784, while their separation from the mother church in England did not occur till after Wesley's death in 1791. The movement thus ultimately gave rise to a new denomination, but the whole religious life of Great Britain, as represented in all denominations, was greatly quickened and elevated by the Methodist movement. By the end of the century, skepticism had largely passed away, moral life was much improved and the mighty modern foreign mission movement was at the birth. Never since these revivals has the religious and moral life of the English-speaking world sunk back to its former low level.

§ 97

BEGINNINGS OF PROTESTANT MISSIONS

The Catholics had never ceased to engage in mission work even in the midst of the storm of the Reformation. For a time they had been very successful in India, China and Japan, enrolling thousands of converts. But the work was superficial, and the missionaries meddled with the governments and quarreled among themselves. As a consequence further work in these lands was forbidden, the missionaries were banished and Christianity almost perished. They were, however, still making progress in Central and South America.

On the other hand the Protestants were just making a beginning of foreign mission work in this period. In all cases their earliest efforts were in connection with colonial enterprises, for the colonists and the natives in the colonies. Before the middle of the seventeenth century a few Dutch in the East Indies and two or three English in America had made some effort to evangelize the natives, the earliest in America being Roger Williams. These were the efforts of individuals and amounted to little.

But early in the eighteenth century *concerted effort* began in Germany for the propagation of the gospel in foreign lands. Frederick IV, king of Denmark which had colonies in both the East and the West Indies, became deeply interested in the preaching of the gospel in connection with these enterprises. Unable to find Danish preachers who would go two Germans from Halle were sent out to Tranquebar in the East Indies in 1705. This mission, supported by the government of Denmark but manned by German missionaries and hence known as the "Danish-Halle Mission," flourished for nearly a century till the growing Rationalism destroyed its home support. Many missionaries were sent out and for a time beginning in 1710 a missionary magazine was published, the first of its kind.

There was organized in 1727 on the estates of Count Zinzendorf in the heart of Germany the *Unitas Fratrum* or *"United Brethren."* The organization was composed of fragments of persecuted peoples from various parts of Europe, remarkable for their piety and their steadfast devotion to principle. Under the guidance of Zinzendorf they decided in 1728 to undertake foreign mission work and in 1732 they sent their first missionary to the West Indies. Soon their missionaries were to be found in many lands. In general they have chosen the most difficult and neglected fields of the world. No other organization of Christians in the whole history of Christianity have exhibited equal devotion and sacrifice to the cause of foreign missions.

NINTH PERIOD — 1789 TO 1917

A. GENERAL CHARACTERISTICS OF THE PERIOD

§ 98

THE POLITICAL HISTORY

JUDGED from any standpoint the last is the most glorious period of Christian history. In many respects the world made more progress in the brief span of this period than in all previous ages combined. Moreover life became ever more and more complex as ease and rapidity of communication and transportation brought the nations with all their manifold divergences into more intimate and continuous contact. Only the most important features of this wonderful age can be noticed and these only in a brief and inadequate way.

The peoples of the world have made marked political progress during this period. The points of change and improvement have been so many and important as to defy description in the brief space that is here available. Only the most significant features will be mentioned.

1. *Constitutional government* has been established in every civilized land, though in a somewhat rudimentary form in Russia and some other countries. Only England and the United States were governed by constitutions at the beginning of the period, and the American government, still in its infancy, was regarded as an experiment. To-day all civilized peoples have succeeded in protecting themselves

from the capricious and arbitrary will of their rulers by a statement of fundamental law which all are bound to observe.

2. *The Republic* as a form of government has made wonderful strides. At the beginning of the period the United States and Switzerland were the only two governments in the world that were in any sense republican. Now all the new countries of the Western Hemisphere are republican while the old world kingdoms of France and China and Russia have adopted that form of government, and all the others have been compelled to give to their subjects almost as much freedom as if they were republics.

3. *Internal democracy.* Within the nations there has gone on a constant development of democracy. The people have wrenched from their rulers and the upper classes an ever increasing share in the actual processes of government. Cabinets and advisers have been made responsible to the people, lower officials have been made elective; the right of suffrage has been extended in many countries to include all men over twenty-one, and the women are rapidly winning the right to vote. The right of all the people to be represented is a principle which is now firmly embedded in the political thinking of the world.

4. *Colonization.* Russia continued to expand until the whole of northern Asia is now in her possession and she has ports on the Pacific. England continues to hold and exploit India, though few Englishmen other than officials reside there. Most of Africa has passed into the hands of European nations and the more salubrious portions are being colonized. England, France, Germany, Belgium, Italy and Portugal held most of the continent at the end of the nineteenth century. During the Great War England and France have taken Germany's colonies and it is announced that they will not be restored at the conclusion of peace.

5. *Rise and fall of powers.* The most notable declines have been in the cases of Turkey and Spain. At the begin-

ning of the period Turkey ruled over all southeastern Europe, western Asia and northern Africa. She has now lost all of Africa, all but a very small fraction of Europe and much of her Asiatic possessions. What will be left to her after the conclusion of this war remains to be seen.

Spain held all of South America except Brazil and the southern portion of North America and all the Philippine and West Indian Islands at the beginning of the period, and was accounted one of the Great Powers. During the period she has lost all her colonial possessions and is now almost confined to the Spanish mainland.

The most notable national growth has been seen in the expansion of the United States into a world power, the growth of Russia, the expansion of Prussia, the rise of Japan and China into the position of world powers, the latter because of its size and potentialities rather than its military strength.

The old German empire was dissolved in the midst of the Napoleonic wars and a new German empire was founded in 1871 which has shown marvelous powers in the development of the sciences and the application of scientific knowledge to the practical affairs of life, in military power and social organization. She has built up the mightiest military machine the world has ever seen.

The Italian peninsula, for so many centuries divided into petty and hostile states, was finally amalgamated into a united kingdom in 1870, since which time it has been prospering and expanding in such a way as to promise a happy future.

6. *Expansion of the Functions of the State.* During this period the state has very generally taken over many functions which were once performed by the church or left undone. During the Middle Ages the church had provided the only public educational facilities that existed; it had solemnized marriages and granted divorces; it had cared for the sick, the poor, the defective, the widows and orphans. In general it had been the agency for the care of

the vital interests of human society. It had been recreant to its high trust and had been deprived in large measure of its privileges and its wealth by the Reformation.

During this last period the state has been rapidly taking over these forms of service. It has founded a system of state schools which are universal, free and excellent; it alone can marry and divorce people; it takes care of a large proportion of the defective, distressed and dependent classes; it seeks to develop the health, happiness and prosperity of all the people.

§ 99

SOCIAL PROGRESS

The social progress of this great period has been no less striking than the political. We live in a new world vastly different from that of the seventeenth century, and it is a vastly better world to live in. Some of the points of improvement follow.

1. *Living conditions* have been wonderfully improved. The people are better housed, better fed, better clothed, enjoy more leisure and they have a larger per capita of wealth. During the last century they have crowded into the cities depleting the purely rural life of America and the village life of the older countries, but notwithstanding this crowding the living conditions have improved along almost every line.

2. *Old Social Distinctions and Feudal Rights* have been weakened and in many cases have disappeared. Never before in a period of equal length has the world made such strides in the process of democratizing society. There is no nobility in any of the newer lands and the nobility of the older countries has been abolished or stripped of its ancient privileges and immunities. The titles remain as the sole distinction.

Slavery and serfdom have practically disappeared from

the earth. Moreover laboring men have banded themselves together into unions which are as powerful as the nobility used to be, and, it must be admitted, sometimes just as dangerous to the public welfare. During the course of this entire period there has been going on a mighty process of leveling up and leveling down.

3. *Diffusion of Education.* Education in the Middle Ages was aristocratic. Only the clergy and the nobility regularly obtained an education. The common people were utterly illiterate, periodicals did not exist, books were few and very costly. The only means of reaching the mind was the spoken word. In this last period the state has taken up the work of educating the masses, furnishing a complete and excellent education entirely at public expense and in the more advanced countries compelling all children to make use of the advantages thus afforded. The consequence has been an immense improvement in the general intelligence of the people, a tremendous multiplication of books and periodicals and the opening of the avenues of the human mind to exploitation from a thousand angles. The problems that depend on illiteracy are disappearing, but the problems that arise from the misuse of letters are increasing in seriousness continually.

4. *Militarism.* Since the Napoleonic wars and especially since 1870 there has been an astounding increase in the preparations for war. Learning war has become one of the greatest burdens of mankind. In many lands the manhood of the nation has been trained from one to three years as soldiers; every discovery of science has at once been put at the service of war; in time of war the entire nation is mobilized. It is to be hoped that the horrors of this present struggle will strip war of all its glamor and reveal it so hideous and destructive as to make future wars so improbable that learning war can be diminished if not abandoned altogether.

5. *Use of Machinery.* It is well-nigh impossible for us to realize that all the applications of steam and electricity

to the work of manufacture, travel, transportation, communication and illumination have been made in the last period of Christian history. Progress in the mastery and use of the powers of nature in the service of man has been greater in this period than in all previous history combined. By the use of machinery one workman now accomplishes more than dozens could have done a century and a half ago. These changes in the way of doing the world's work have effected mighty social changes. It has led to powerful combinations of capital and equally powerful combinations of labor; it has multiplied travel and migration many fold; it has created cities and emptied the country and villages; it has brought to the tables of all the products of all climes making the luxuries of a few years ago the necessities of to-day; it has brought the world's doings of yesterday to the breakfast table this morning; it has given to the working man from fourteen to sixteen hours out of the twenty-four to be employed as he sees fit; it has eliminated the small manufacturer and is eliminating the small farmer thereby forcing coöperation, reducing independence and compelling interdependence. In other words there have been both gains and losses, but there is no probability that we shall ever go back to former conditions.

6. The *progress of women* in this period amounts almost to an emancipation. At the beginning of the period there were no provisions for her education except in private schools. Not a single college or university in existence was open to her. As a rule she was uneducated except in the most elementary branches and in household economics and manual labor. No career was open to her in the professions, in teaching or business life. Her rights of person and property rested for the most part in others. Naturally her part in the religious life was comparatively small.

During this period she has obtained the right to a full and thorough education and is now taking large advantage of that privilege. Most of the professions are now open to her, and in all forms of commercial and manufacturing she is taking large place. She has become the teacher of child life in school and church almost exclusively. In this world war she is bearing her share of the burdens and sufferings as heroically and fully as the men. She is rapidly securing the right of suffrage and may be expected to take an ever increasing part in the public life of the world.

§ 100

REFORMS OF THE PERIOD

1. *Slavery.* The greatest single reform has doubtless been the abolition of slavery which has disappeared from all Christian lands. Serfdom has gone with it, so that whatever hardships men are now compelled to suffer they are no longer mere chattels to be bought and sold as pigs or cows.

2. *Alcoholism.* At the beginning of this period drunkenness was opposed as it had been through the centuries, but it was frightfully prevalent. Nobody opposed the use of alcoholic beverages as such or believed that they were hurtful when taken in moderation. Drinking was interwoven with the social and even the church life of the world. Ministers and church officials indulged and the total abstainer was very rare. The idea of saving the individual and society by prohibiting the manufacture and sale of these liquors because they are in themselves and always hurtful and dangerous had scarcely entered the minds of the most advanced thinkers, and had not affected the masses in the least degree.

Now the world is struggling with this monstrous evil with good prospects for complete victory in the near future. Not only in the United States but throughout the entire world liquor is being abandoned and prohibited.

3. *Gambling.* By its very nature it is impossible to suppress entirely gambling in private. But public gambling has been greatly reduced in the course of this period. The

lottery, which has been the popular and legal means of gambling, has been entirely suppressed in America and most other Christian lands, while at the beginning of the period it was not infrequently resorted to by churches in raising money. The evils of racetrack and other forms of gambling have also been sharply curtailed.

4. *Duelling.* At the beginning of the present period the duel was the honorable method by which gentlemen settled personal difficulties often very trivial. Public sentiment approved the practice so thoroughly that an honorable man dare not decline to fight if challenged, or to send a challenge if offended in certain ways. The death of Alexander Hamilton in a duel with Aaron Burr early in the nineteenth century gave duelling the death blow in America. It still lingers in milder form in Germany and to some extent in France.

5. *Vice, or the "social evil."* Less progress has been made in combating the ravages of this evil than any other of the great open sores of humanity. Under modern conditions of living it actually seems to be on the increase. It has become commercialized and organized into a business, so that man's cupidity reënforces the demands of his lust. In all the great cities young girls are constantly lured to their ruin, disappearing in the most loathsome slavery that the world has ever known. Of all the public and private evils that afflict humanity this has been the most stubborn and difficult to conquer.

§ 101

SOME GENERAL FEATURES OF THE RELIGIOUS LIFE
OF THE PERIOD

1. *Religious Freedom.* Organized persecution has ceased almost everywhere, the Inquisition has been dissolved. Full civil rights with freedom of worship and propaganda are quite generally conceded to dissenters. But many Christian

countries still have established churches which enjoy more or less of state patronage and other advantages while dissenters are permitted to carry on their own independent work, in some cases exempted from paying taxes for the support of the establishment and in other cases not. In many cases all forms of religion are granted state aid.

Complete disestablishment has made remarkable progress bringing with it the full adoption of the voluntary system of church support and the absolute equality before the law of all forms of religious faith. The colony of Rhode Island was the first government ever established on this basis while the United States was the first of any size and importance. It has been followed by nearly all the governments of the New World, and by France, Geneva, Ireland and Wales in the Old World. No government has ever tried this plan and then returned to the establishment. Many religious and non-religious elements of the modern world are demanding this freedom in other lands and there is reason to believe that it will gradually extend to the whole world.

2. *Protestant Missions.* Dutch and German missionaries had done some work in connection with colonial establishments in the East in the preceding period. At the very opening of this period began the most remarkable era of missionary effort and growth which the world has seen since the apostolic days. It started in connection with colonial enterprises but quickly extended to all sections of the world. The pioneer in the English speaking world was William Carey the Baptist who in 1792 succeeded in organizing the Baptist Missionary Society for the propagation of the gospel in foreign parts. He was but a cobbler without university education, but in India he became one of the greatest scholars and most remarkable missionaries of all time.

The beginning was quickly followed by the organization of similar societies in both England and America by all the leading denominations and churches. English and

American Christianity has taken the lead in giving and working, but there are many deeply interested friends of missions in all Protestant lands.

During the period missionary organizations have been created, a missionary literature has been produced, the history and the religious and social customs and beliefs of the unevangelized have been learned, the fields have been equipped with church buildings, schools and printing-presses, the Bible has been translated and the foundations for a Christian literature have been laid. Several hundred thousand converts have been gathered into churches and the very life of at least two nations has been profoundly changed. China and Japan have come out of their seclusion and radically modified their fundamental ideals in the last century, largely as a result of Christian missions. Africa has been explored and the beneficent effects of the gospel are already felt in wide stretches of " the dark continent." Foreign missions are to-day the greatest inspiration of the churches at home, the reflex influence of the devotion and success of the missionaries having been of incalculable value to every good work in the home land.

3. *Study and Circulation of the Bible.* As we have already seen the Reformation had rescued the Bible from the neglect into which the Catholic church had relegated it, had translated it into the vernacular of the European peoples and had set it in circulation again. But as a matter of fact it was not largely circulated. Preaching was theological, religious instruction was given from the catechism; the impulse to its circulation was simply the demand of the people. Very little definite knowledge of Bible lands and people existed, and there was no organized effort to teach the Bible.

During this period every nook and corner of Palestine and other Bible lands has been explored, the history of the peoples mentioned in the Bible has been in some cases discovered and in all cases rewritten, the social and religious customs of the inhabitants have been studied on the ground. All this work has made the Bible a living and vital book as it had never been before. It was possible to understand its doctrines before, but their setting had never been known by western peoples.

Along with this intensive study of the Bible has gone increased efforts to bring it to bear on the life of the people. Great Bible societies like the " British and Foreign Bible Society," the " American Bible Society " and others now print the Bible in all the principal languages and dialects of the world, circulating more copies in one year than all Christendom had produced in the first seventeen centuries of Christian history. The original text of the New Testament has been established and the best possible translations of both Testaments have been made. Commentaries, Bible dictionaries, Bible histories, Bible stories have made the book available to everybody who cares to know its contents.

In the last half century the Sunday school has become the chief agency for the direct study of the Bible by the people, the catechism having almost disappeared as the text-book of religious education before the increasing use of the Bible. In summer assemblies, Chautauquas and similar popular gatherings the Bible is taught by the most scholarly and skillful teachers of the land and studied by hosts of men and women actuated by the single motive of knowing the will of God and becoming more efficient in the work of the kingdom. Probably no phase of the religious life of to-day is more promising of vitality and efficiency than this.

4. *Extra-ecclesiastical Religious Organizations.* Up to the beginning of the last period Protestant activities were confined almost entirely to the various church organizations. But as the tasks enlarged and the interest intensified the life broke over ecclesiastical bounds and created many non-ecclesiastical organizations. The new wine was bursting the old bottles. The earliest of these extra-ecclesiastical

organizations were the missionary and Bible societies already mentioned.

Following these came temperance and anti-slavery societies, tract societies, Sunday school societies, etc. But perhaps the most notable of all are the various organizations which are intended to minister to and utilize the religious possibilities of the young. Foremost among these in time and efficiency was the Young Men's Christian Association organized by George Williams in England in 1844. Later but hardly less important is the Young Women's Christian Association and the numerous young people's societies which are now found in all the churches and denominations. These Protestant organizations have been imitated by the Catholics and even by the Jews.

The motive of all these organizations is religious and practical and they form one of the most striking and significant features of the religious life of to-day. This marks the religious life of America more than that of any other country.

5. *Activities of Laymen.* The mediæval church had no place for the activities of laymen. The priesthood was believed to be endowed with all religious responsibility and power. The layman was expected to do nothing but fill the position of an obedient and dutiful son of the church, humbly and unquestioningly receiving its grace and liberally furnishing it with money.

The Reformers were also rather suspicious of the layman, permitting to him functions which were but little more important than those granted by the Catholic church. Only the Quakers abolished ecclesiasticism altogether and sought to establish a purely lay Christianity, though the Anabaptists went far in that direction. In consequence the layman lost his interest and sense of responsibility for the spiritual welfare of men and the progress of the kingdom. Individual effort gave way to corporate effort, all of life except that under direct ecclesiastical control was utterly secularized.

The nineteenth century witnessed a great change in this regard. The gradual weakening of ecclesiastical ideas has afforded a constantly enlarging place to the layman. His earliest work was in such extra-ecclesiastical organizations as the Young Men's Christian Association, and these still afford him large opportunity. In addition the missionary field and the Sunday school movement have provided him with important fields of labor. As medical missionary, as teacher, as business manager, in laymen's missionary societies, and in many other ways he is making his contribution to the spread of the kingdom at home and abroad. In the Sunday school he is superintending, teaching, training teachers, arousing and enlisting. Occasionally he becomes an evangelist of rare power as was the case of D. L. Moody. Few features of present day Christianity are more significant than this increased freedom and activity of the layman.

6. *Activities of Women.* During the Middle Ages all women who desired to render active service in the work of the kingdom were compelled to enter a convent where they were permitted to teach children, serve in hospitals and perform other such tasks suited to their strength and endowments. The ordinary woman could do little more than count her beads and attend the services of the church. Woman was taboo in the Catholic church. Ecclesiasticism and the priestly conception of the ministry banished her from the service of her Lord in the church. Her education was neglected till she was not prepared either by experience or training to accomplish much.

Protestantism abolished the convent, thereby destroying the institution through which woman had done most of her work, without creating any other for her. Most Protestants were as unwilling to have woman take any part in the distinctive work of the church as the Catholics had been. Consequently she was long debarred from any important part in the work of Protestants. Only the Quakers, who swept away every vestige of ecclesiasticism, gave her freedom for Christian activity. And it must be said that the manner in which she used that freedom did not recommend it. The Anabapists, Baptists and later the Methodists also granted considerable freedom, at least to the extent of permitting women on occasion to exhort in evangelistic services.

The nineteenth century has brought a great change in this regard. The religious movement which enlisted her most enthusiastic interest was the cause of foreign missions. At its very beginning she organized societies for prayer, study and giving. Anne Hasseltine Judson went with her husband to the foreign field and displayed as much heroism and efficiency as he, soon making of herself one of the most heroic figures of Christian history. Other less notable women had similar experiences. On the foreign fields they escaped those prejudices which such activity at home would inevitably have excited, and their achievements gradually broke down objections at home. The women have now become the chief distributors of missionary information; they raise considerable sums of money for the cause; they furnish more than nine-tenths of all the teachers of the young in the Sunday schools, they are conducting neighborhood houses, caring for the sick and needy in hospitals. In short they are in many Protestant communions the principal support of the pulpit in all the spiritual and benevolent work of the kingdom, in some cases, notably in the work of the Salvation Army, sharing the work of preaching to the full.

During this time educational privileges and facilities have been so extended that women are becoming on the average better educated than the men. This naturally better fits them for the service which they wish to render. Every woman who desires to serve her Lord and fits herself to do so effectively will now find an open field among nearly all the denominations. At home and on the mission fields they are rendering noble service.

7. *The Religion of the Young.* Infant baptism brought

children into relation with the church while they were still infants, but it did not give them a religious experience or enlist them in the work of the kingdom. Evangelical denominations, for some inexplicable reason, did not expect conversion before children had reached the late adolescent or even the adult age. Doubtless this view was due to a reaction against belief in baptismal regeneration which was the negation of the evangelical principle.

Whatever the cause certain it is that the decline of belief in baptismal regeneration was accompanied by a conviction that children could be brought to evangelical faith much younger than the custom had been. As a result of earlier effort the average age of conversion has been pushed back several years in this period.

But early conversion must be followed by early training and service. As a consequence all evangelical churches are now giving far more attention to the conversion and training of the young than they have ever done before. Major attention is directed to them in the Sunday school, and numerous societies have been organized to meet their special needs; church music has been greatly altered in their interest; preaching to them distinctly has been encouraged and the whole tone of evangelical Christianity has been modified in the direction of youth. This change, if wisely safeguarded, ought materially to increase the efficiency of Christian workers.

8. *Growth of Evangelism.* Evangelism might be defined as a direct presentation of the gospel, in whatever way, to the intelligence for the free and voluntary acceptance of conscious and responsible human beings. It is the antithesis of sacramental salvation which is supposed to be effected by the use of certain ceremonies which are believed to operate to the salvation of the soul in the moral unconsciousness of infancy. Thus defined evangelism is employed as at no time since apostolic days. All denominations and churches, even the Catholics and Episcopalians, have engaged in evangelistic effort.

The reason for this evangelistic activity is not far to seek. The Catholic church in the Middle Ages and the Protestant state churches were supposed to embrace the entire population. From the beginning of life they were within the pale of the church, under its tutelage, partakers of its grace. On the contrary the voluntary principle leaves vast numbers of the population outside of church relations, constituting a mighty mission field around the door of every church in the land. Vigorous evangelism, under these conditions, becomes absolutely necessary not only to the growth but even to the existence of the churches. This is especially true of Baptists and those other bodies that reject infant baptism. Without evangelism they would die in a generation.

This evangelism has taken many forms at different times and places. In America, where the voluntary principle has been operative longer than elsewhere and evangelism has been more actively pushed, we have had the " camp-meeting," the annual " protracted meeting," the work of great evangelists like Moody and Sunday, pastoral evangelism in the regular services of the church, Sunday school evangelism through the efforts of teachers and officers, personal evangelism where individual Christians seek to win men and women to Christ through personal contact and influence. As the years have gone by the conception of the scope and character of evangelism has been elevated and enlarged. It is certain to be more and more widespread and important as the voluntary principle is extended over the world.

9. *Decline of Infant Baptism.* During the Middle Ages infant baptism was well nigh universal. It was supposed to be the chief, indeed the one indispensable, means of salvation. Both the Catholic churches practiced it universally and many of the sects did likewise. It was the nexus between the church and the state, the instrument by which society as a whole was incorporated into the church. To reject or neglect it was to bring down upon one's head the wrath of both state and church in the form of bitter perse-

cution and religious coercion. Only individuals and small persecuted parties opposed its practice.

At the Reformation all the great Protestant churches retained it as they left the Catholic church, though some of them altered its meaning in an effort to bring it into harmony with their evangelical principles. The Anabaptists were the only party that sought to abolish it, and they were speedily crushed by the combined power of the various churches and states of that era.

So effective was this effort at suppression that faith-baptism made no headway until religious toleration was established in England and America. Toleration was followed by complete religious freedom in America and by an ever increasing degree of freedom in England and other countries. This progress of freedom has been accompanied by a marked decline in the practice of infant baptism. This decline has been due to several causes. One of the most important has been simple indifference and neglect. An irreligious man will not take the trouble to have his infant baptized, thus stultifying himself, if he is free to neglect it without imperiling the civil or social status of his child.

More important than this religious indifference has been a rapidly growing body of pious people who are conscientiously opposed to infant baptism, believing that it is not only unscriptural but actually antiscriptural and dangerous to evangelical faith. They regard it as the foundation of both the great Catholic churches and a constant and serious menace to the spirituality and evangelical character of all other churches that practice it, though they gladly recognize the fact that some of the Pedobaptist bodies have eliminated the most serious elements of the practice.

At the beginning of the present period the body of people who opposed infant baptism was small and confined almost entirely to English speaking countries. At the present time there are eight to ten millions who are organized into churches or denominations based upon faith-baptism, and it is estimated that there is an antipedobaptist population of at least twenty-five millions in the United States alone.

10. *Practical Beneficence.* For a long time the Protestant churches seemed to be more interested in theology, forms of worship and church order than in the service of mankind. Moreover they were fighting for their existence. The Reformation had swept away much of the church's wealth and all the institutions through which its beneficence had been administered. Protestants lacked, therefore, the inclination, the means and the agencies for such work.

The general spirit of the nineteenth century has been preeminently practical, and this tendency has manifested itself in religious life. The emphasis on systematic theology and church peculiarities has waned while thought has been fixed more and more on service. Church people have led in most of the great reforms of the nineteenth century, while creeds have been altered or neglected even by the most rigidly theological churches. Many good people have been alarmed by this decline of emphasis on theology, but the tendency continues unabated and the results on the whole seem to be good.

11. *Opposition to Christianity.* During the Middle Ages and the Reformation era there was no open opposition to Christianity. The church and the church's officials were often criticized, but all classes were theoretically religious and Christian. During the last period Christian lands have witnessed an enormous growth of antichristian sentiment. It has taken many forms such as blank materialistic *Atheism* or denial of all spiritual reality; *Agnosticism* or the refusal to make any assertions either positive or negative concerning spiritual things; *Pantheism* or the assertion that everything is essentially God, a view which is almost as deadly to the value of religious faith as Atheism; *Unitarianism* which, while holding to the fundamental beliefs of Theism, strips Jesus of all significance other than that of a remarkable teacher.

In all these forms of thought Christian ideals and ethics

were usually accepted by men who did not accept Christianity in any other sense. But about the middle of the nineteenth century the ethical ideals of Jesus were viciously attacked by the mad German philosopher Nietzsche who apotheosized force and made might right. His doctrine of the superman, justifying all selfish aggression, was exceedingly gratifying to the carnal man and he has had a large following especially in Germany.

In addition to active opposition there is much indifference and neglect in all Christian lands, due to preoccupation and absorption in material interests. Leisure, comforts, amusements and luxuries have engaged the thought and attention of men more and more in the latter part of the nineteenth century.

12. *Christian Divisions and Christian Union.* The principle of freedom and voluntarism introduced by the Reformation has been the source of innumerable schisms and sects. This has been especially the case in English and American Christianity where the voluntary principle has enjoyed fullest scope and application. Not only have the old divisions coming down from the Reformation been perpetuated into the last period, but others have arisen. The causes of these schisms have often been trivial and sometimes wholly unworthy, but the intensity of feeling and the strictness of separation have not been diminished thereby. There are in the United States many Presbyterian churches, an equal number of Methodist and many types of Baptists and other similar bodies.

More recently an opposite tendency has set in which seems to be working towards coöperation and even union of the Protestant forces. An unusually long " era of good feeling," an increasing emphasis on the practical tasks of the Christian world, a deepening sense of the immensity of the work to be done together with a declining emphasis on the minutiæ of theology and church order have combined to bring the denominations nearer together and in some instances to effect actual unions. The most notable evidences of this tendency in recent years have been the union of the United and the Free churches of Scotland into the United Free Church of Scotland, the union of several types of Methodists in England, the union of the Cumberland with the Presbyterian Church in the United States of America and the union of the Free Baptists with the Baptists in the North. In a free congregational body like the Baptists there is a process of union going on all the time. By this means the Hardshell Baptists have been largely absorbed in the regular body.

Even where union is not contemplated there is much coöperation in Christian and reformatory work. A notable effort in this direction was the organization of the Federal Council of Churches of North America in 1908 in which all the greater bodies of Protestants except Southern Baptists are represented. Through this organization the voice of American Protestantism finds expression concerning many matters of common interest. Another notable example of coöperative activity is seen in the Edinburgh and the Panama conferences to study the common problems of the mission fields. Few tendencies in American Christianity are stronger to-day than this sentiment for fraternal relations and Christian coöperation where no fundamental convictions are imperiled.

B. THE GREEK CATHOLIC OR HOLY ORTHODOX EASTERN CHURCH

§ 102

INTRODUCTION

The so-called Greek Catholic or Orthodox Eastern church contains most of the Christian population of eastern and southeastern Europe, northeastern Africa and western, southwestern and northern Asia. Its membership belongs chiefly to the Greek and Slavic races, and number in all from one hundred to one hundred and thirty-five millions. As a whole they are behind the peoples of western Europe and America in culture, economic efficiency, political development and moral standards. For centuries they have been in a continual struggle with Arabic and Turkish Mohammedanism, which doubtless accounts in large measure for their backwardness. In this struggle they first arrested the advance and then during the nineteenth century have turned back this flood of barbaric fanaticism, a service for which the rest of mankind should remain eternally grateful.

The Orthodox Eastern church is not united under one head as the Roman Catholic church is governed by the pope. It is organized into sixteen independent churches, each under its own governing body, but all constituting one church with essentially the same doctrines, practices and sacramental system, and all looking to Constantinople as their spiritual head. The Greek church is sacramental and sacerdotal as the Roman, but there are several more or less important differences. Like the Roman church it has seven sacraments, but the rituals differ. Baptism is a three-fold immersion; confirmation may be administered immediately after baptism and by a priest; the wine as well as the bread (which is leavened) is granted all baptized persons even infants; crucifixes and graven images other than the cross are forbidden while pictures (ikons) are extensively used in worship; instrumental music is not permitted, but singing (by men only) is wonderfully developed and impressive; the holy mysteries (mass) are celebrated in a sanctuary separated from the body of the church by a partition; the people pray standing (except at Pentecost) and facing the east; monasticism is highly developed under the rule of St. Basil but not organized into orders as in the Roman church.

Of the sixteen churches those that are still Greek in language are those of Constantinople, Alexandria, Greece, Cyprus and Sinai; seven are Slavic, those of Russia, Bul-

garia, Servia, Carlowitz, Bosnia-Herzegovina, Bukowina
and Montenegro; two are Roumanian, those of Roumania
and Hermannstadt; two are Arabic, those of Antioch and
Jerusalem. Six of these are national churches established
more or less firmly by law. They are the churches of
Russia, Greece, Servia, Bulgaria, Montenegro and Roumania; four are in Austria, viz., Carlowitz, Bukowina,
Bosnia-Herzegovina and Hermannstadt; the others, with
the exception of Cyprus and now Alexandria, are subject to
Turkey.

§ 103

PATRIARCHATE OF CONSTANTINOPLE

This church is bounded by the limits of the Turkish empire. Its head is the patriarch of Constantinople who, with
the assistance of a Holy Synod of twelve Metropolitans
and a Mixed Council consisting of four Metropolitans and
eight laymen rules over the church in both spiritual and
temporal things. The patriarchs of Antioch and Jerusalem
report to the Turkish government through the patriarch of
Constantinople. The church numbers perhaps four million
souls and is in a very depressed condition.

The patriarchates of Antioch, Jerusalem and Alexandria
have together fewer than half a million members. The
patriarch of Antioch resides at Damascus, that of Alexandria at Cairo.

The church of Sinai is only a small monastery, but it is
entirely independent.

The church of Cyprus, independent since 431 A. D., in
1911 had about 180,000 communicants.

§ 104

RUSSIAN CHURCH

Russia has made striking progress in many ways during
this last period. It has continued to expand in territory and

increase in population till it covers all of northern Asia
and had a population at the beginning of the war of approximately 170,000,000, very diverse in race, religion and culture.
Serfdom was abolished in 1861, but no system of general
primary education has been established and not more than
20 per cent. of the population are literate. Higher and
technical education is fairly well developed.

The Russian church is not very missionary but it has
made some progress during the period through the expansion of the government. It has a population of between
eighty and ninety millions. The Czar, up to his abdication,
was the head of the church while the governing body was
the Holy Synod composed of ecclesiastics and laymen appointed by the Czar. This Synod is subjected to the government by the presence of the Procurator who is a minister in the government and has power to quash any business which may come before the Synod. The powers of
this Synod are enormous and by it the church is made more
completely subservient to the state than that of any other
country in the world. The church is supported by the government only in part, the lower clergy being but poorly paid,
poorly educated and little regarded. The bishops are unmarried while the priests are married once only. The
church has produced few scholars and has done little intellectual or practical work of any kind, but recently it has
been showing some signs of an awakening.

Besides the established church there are many sects, some
of whom do not differ essentially from the Orthodox
church, while others, as the Stundists, are thoroughly evangelical. The total number of these dissidents is not known
but is certainly several millions.

In addition to these there are some eleven million Roman
Catholics chiefly Poles, five million Protestants chiefly
Lutherans in the western provinces, fourteen million Mohammedans, six million Jews and some Pagans, Buddhists,
etc.

In 1905 religious freedom was assured, but in practice

it has been much curtailed.   Baptists and others have suffered real persecution.   These paragraphs are written in
the midst of the revolution that has overthrown the autocracy and which may bring lasting freedom to the Russian
people who are among the kindliest and most religious
people in the world.

§ 105

THE "CHURCH IN GREECE"

At the beginning of the present period Greece was still
under the heel of Turkey.   Through terrible sufferings in
a revolution which extended from 1821 to 1829 she conquered her freedom and organized a constitutional monarchy with a Bavarian and then a Danish prince as king.
Since her emancipation she has made notable progress in
education and other reforms.

Her national church was organized independent of Constantinople in 1833.   It is governed by a Synod modeled
after that of Russia, consisting of five members appointed
by the king, exercising almost complete control over all
ecclesiastical affairs.   The population of between four and
five millions is almost solidly Orthodox, there being only
about twenty-five thousand Christians of all other confessions.   In addition there are about five thousand Jews and
twenty thousand Mohammedans.   Like the Greek people
the Greek church is poor, its buildings small and unim-
pressive, its clergy indifferently educated and exercising
little influence.

§ 106

THE OTHER BALKAN STATES

1. *Bulgaria* did not obtain complete freedom from Turkey
until 1908, but under the semi-independence of earlier years
she had made considerable progress in education and social
reforms of many kinds.   Her church was organized in

independence of Constantinople in 1870 while she was still a Turkish province, but this proceeding precipitated a schism from the patriarch of Constantinople which has not as yet been entirely healed.   The head of the Bulgarian church is an Exarch who resides at Constantinople, while the governing body is a Holy Synod of four members.   Religious freedom is assured by the constitution and the ministers of all denominations are paid by the state.   While the great body of the population are Orthodox there are Jews, Mohammedans, Roman Catholics and a few thousand Protestants.   American Methodists have been doing school work in this country for some years with some success.

2. *Servia.*   Like the other Balkan states Servia endured a long and painful struggle in her efforts for freedom from the Turkish yoke, finally and fully secured by the Treaty of Berlin in 1878.   Her church was organized the next year.   It is governed by a Synod and is supported and largely controlled by the state.   The free exercise of all forms of worship is guaranteed, but conversion from the state church is forbidden.   The Serbs have not made such progress as the other Balkan states.   Her school system is still very imperfectly developed and less than 20 per cent. of the population is literate.   Out of a population of about five millions nearly all are Orthodox, though there are Mohammedans, Jews and a few Roman Catholics.

3. *Roumania.*   This country, long under the heel of Turkey, has been an independent kingdom since 1881 with a population of between seven and eight millions.   Its church, which had already secured its independence in 1864, is governed by a Synod modeled after that of Russia whose members are chosen by the government.   Religious freedom is assured by the constitution, education is encouraged and much progress has been made.   The great bulk of population is in the state church but there are one hundred and fifty thousand Roman Catholics, twenty-five thousand Protestants, nearly three hundred thousand Jews and fifty thousand Mohammedans.

The other Orthodox churches mentioned above are comparatively small and unimportant, all of them except the church of Montenegro being under the domination of Austria-Hungary.

§ 107

RELATIVE GROWTH OF THE ORTHODOX CHURCH

Attention should be called in closing to the tremendous relative growth of this church during the last period. It is now one of the mighty forces of the world. At the beginning of the period Russia was the only country professing the Greek religion that was not under the tyranny of Turkey and Russia was hardly one of the great powers of the world. To-day she stands in the very first group of nations, and several other Orthodox kingdoms have risen to independence and world-wide significance. Only a small part of the Orthodox Christians of the world are now subject to the Turkish yoke. Undoubtedly this division of Christianity is destined to be a factor to be reckoned with in the future history of the world. If the Russian revolution consummated March 16th, 1917, stands it means a mighty emancipation and a tremendous leap forward in one of the large and influential sections of the human race.

C. THE HERETICAL CHURCHES OF ASIA

§ 108

INTRODUCTION

This group of churches have for centuries been continuously under the Mohammedan governments of the Turks and Persians and at times have suffered frightful oppressions. They have had an uninterrupted struggle for existence and hence have shown little missionary or other activity beyond heroic tenacity in holding on to their faith and nationality. Their existence has been in some instances one long martyrdom. They are neither Greek, Roman Catholic nor Protestant, but hostile to all these churches.

§ 109

THE ARMENIANS

The Armenians do not constitute a nation, but are a people scattered in Turkey, Russia, Persia and other lands. At times, especially in 1895-6 and again since the outbreak of the Great War, they have suffered frightful butcheries at the hands of the Turks. There are between three and four millions all told.

The head of the Armenian church is the Catholicos who resides at Echmiadzin in Russian Armenia. Under him are a number of bishops who with him constitute the government of the church. They hold that Christ had only one nature, that the Holy Spirit proceeds from the Father only; baptism is administered by a threefold sprinkling and a threefold immersion and is followed immediately by confirmation; the supper is celebrated with wine and leavened bread which must be dipped in the wine; extreme unction is administered to ecclesiastics only and then only after death; the worship of saints is practiced but purgatory and related doctrines are rejected; the Bible and the liturgy are in the old Armenian language but preaching is in the modern speech of the country. The Armenians are tenacious of their religion, language, race and social customs, in fact are the most virile race in Turkey and for this reason they are hated intensely.

During the nineteenth century the American Congregationalists have done a great work in the way of education and spiritual stimulation among the Armenians. The object has not been to found Congregational churches but to infuse new life into the existing organization.

§ 110

THE NESTORIANS AND JACOBITES

The Nestorians, now numbering some three hundred thousand, are found chiefly in Kurdistan, Persia and India, and most of them are in a very depressed and backward state. All nationalities and religions have oppressed and persecuted them. They have a head known as the Catholicos, living in the mountains of Kurdistan, and several metropolitans and bishops. The Nestorians are much nearer the Protestant position than any other form of oriental Christianity, believing that Christ had two natures, rejecting transubstantiation, purgatory, the veneration of saints and images, practicing the marriage of the clergy below the bishop. The Scriptures and their liturgy are in the ancient Syrian language which unfortunately they are no longer able to understand. They take communion in both kinds and have no monasticism.

The American Presbyterians have for many years had a flourishing mission among them at Urumiah, Persia. Lately several have turned to the Baptist position in this region.

The Jacobites, numbering some two hundred thousand, are the remnants of the early Syrian Christianity now living in Syria and Mesopotamia. They are Monophysites, believing that Christ had only one nature; but in other respects they approximate the doctrines and practices of the Greek church. Once very influential in this region they are now weak and despised by all.

§ 111

CHRISTIANS OF NORTHEASTERN AFRICA

1. *The Copts.* The descendants of the ancient Egyptians are now known as Copts. They live for the most part in the cities of upper Egypt and number nearly a million.

They have suffered fearful persecutions at the hands of both the Orthodox Christians and the Mohammedans and are now comparatively weak and fanatical. They are Monophysites, believing that Christ had only one nature. The church is governed by a Metropolitan residing at Cairo. They practice circumcision, baptize by immersion, celebrate the communion by dipping the bread in the wine. Their services are very elaborate and lengthy, their fasts numerous and rigid.

Lately the Presbyterians have been carrying on a successful work among them.

2. *The Abyssinians.* Abyssinia is an independent kingdom lying in east Africa with a mixed population of several millions. They are descendants of the ancient Ethiopians who were of Semitic origin; Ethiopia is still the native name for the country. Their church, which dates from the middle of the fourth century, has been corrupted by absorptions from heathenism more completely than any other church in existence. It is largely dependent on the Coptic church of Egypt, whose patriarch always names the *Abuna* or ruler of the Abyssinian church from among the Coptic monks of Egypt. The priests are allowed to marry, but there are many monks and nuns. They practice circumcision, keep the Sabbath, eat no swine's flesh, baptize adults by immersion and infants by aspersion and celebrate the supper with grape juice only. They reject the doctrines of transubstantiation, purgatory, the worship of images and related views. They have the Scriptures in the ancient Ethiopic language, which is now a dead language. So far they have resisted successfully all attempts of both Catholics and Protestants to win them away from their old national church.

§ 112

THE UNIATS

Among all the churches of the East, especially the various Orthodox churches, the Roman Catholic church has succeeded in making some converts to Romanism, working assiduously at the task for many years. These people who leave their own and join the Roman church are known as *Uniats*. They acknowledge the supremacy of the pope and adopt some other slight changes in faith and ritual and often become bitterly partisan for Rome. They are usually allowed to retain their native language in worship and are sometimes permitted to continue a married priesthood and communion in both kinds. These together amount to six or seven millions. They are sometimes called Catholics of the Greek rite.

D. THE ROMAN CATHOLIC CHURCH

§ 113

GENERAL INTRODUCTION

1. *Temporal Power Lost.* At the beginning of the last period the Roman Catholic church was facing one of the most serious crises of its history. The Rationalism of the eighteenth century had cut deep into its vitals, especially in France and Austria. The French Revolution which broke out in 1789 for a time swept the church entirely out of existence in that country. Its property was confiscated, its organization was overthrown and subjected to state control, its recalcitrant officials were murdered or chased out of the country, and finally it was legally abolished. On the restoration of order Napoleon recognized Catholicism as the religion of the majority of the French people and arranged to control as well as support it by the state without, however, restoring all of its confiscated property or permitting the return of monasticism.

Friction soon began again and led Napoleon, in 1809, to invade Italy, confiscate and incorporate the papal state into France. When the Pope protested he was arrested and imprisoned till he signed an agreement dissolving the papal state and transferring the papal court to Avignon. After the fall of Napoleon the Congress of Vienna in 1815 restored the Catholic church as far as possible to its former status. A period of reaction set in and for a time the pope gained rapidly in power, but before the middle of the century the democratic movement was again aggressive. Beginning in 1848, the great year of revolutions, the various states of Italy were gradually amalgamated into a united kingdom; at last, in 1870, Rome was captured by the patriots and the papal state outside the walls of the Vatican was also incorporated into the new kingdom and the temporal rule of the pope was brought to an end. His protests have availed nothing and there is no indication that the world will ever again consent to his becoming a temporal ruler.

2. *Increase of Spiritual Power within the Church.*   While the pope's temporal power was waning, his power over the Catholic church was growing.   In 1854, without calling a council, he declared the Immaculate Conception of the Virgin Mary to be a dogma of the church and a Doctrine of the Faith which could not be doubted without peril to the soul.   Never before had a pope dared to define a doctrine, but his bold action in this instance was accepted without a murmur.

In 1864 he published a Syllabus of Errors in which nearly every object for which modern democracy has been struggling was condemned and anathematized and this too was accepted, though not without some misgiving.   Finally, in 1870, at the famous Vatican Council the pope was declared to be infallible when he officially speaks on any subject pertaining to faith or morals.   Against this assumption there was considerable protest, several thousand Catholics of Austria seceding and setting up an independent church known as the " Old Catholic Church." But it availed nothing. The great mass of the church accepted the blasphemy without a tremor and even with joy.   The result has been a mighty strengthening of the pope's position in his own church.   Practically he is regarded as infallible on all subjects, he is the universal bishop having direct access to every diocese in the world.   The entire church is directly dependent on his Holiness, who is the vicar of Christ on earth and the source of all power, the organ of the church's unity and infallibility.   No other ruler in human history has approached his pretensions.

3. *The Size and Location of the Church.*   Relatively to both Protestantism and the Greek Catholic church the Roman church has declined during the last period.   And yet it is the largest and mightiest single body of Christians in the world.   It counts about two hundred and fifty millions of population, about half the nominal Christians of the world.   Its adherents are found in every land, but the masses of its membership are in southwestern Europe and South and Central America, where it is still supreme.   It is predominantly a Latin church, the only other considerable bodies of Catholics being the south Germans, Poles, and southern Irish.   It uses the Latin language in its services throughout the world except among the Uniats.   The countries where it is predominant are Italy, France, Spain, Portugal, Belgium, all the countries in America from Mexico southward, the Philippines, and to a less degree in Ireland, Austria, and south Germany.

4. *Gains and Losses.*   The church has made some rather striking gains during this period.   For example, it has been permitted to return into all the Protestant lands from which it was expelled at the Reformation.   In the United States it has made huge gains, chiefly by immigration.   By the freedom of Belgium in 1830 and the emancipation from Spain and Portugal of Mexico and all the Central and South American States, and by the unification of Italy in 1870, there has been a great gain in the number of independent Catholic states.   By means of missionary efforts, which have been actively prosecuted, several million converts are claimed in Asia and Africa.

But there have been great losses.   The Catholic states of Spain and Portugal have lost practically all their colonies

and have fallen far behind the greatest Protestant states —
Great Britain, the United States, and Germany. Austria
has lost the leadership of the Teutons and is now barely
able to hold together. Moreover, in many of the Catholic
states the church has lost enormously in privileges, power,
and wealth. In France and most of the American Catholic
countries it has ceased to be the established church, and everywhere it has been compelled to grant toleration to other
Christians. Monasticism has steadily declined in numbers
and influence and has been completely abolished in France
and some other lands. Moreover, where the church is still
nominally supreme large elements of population, sometimes
a considerable majority, have lost all religious interest and
are for all practical purposes lost to the church. This is
notably true in France, Italy, Mexico, and Argentina. Protestants are actively engaged in mission work in nearly all
the Catholic countries and they are meeting with marked
success. Some of the most prosperous Protestant missions
in existence are in Catholic countries. With the exception
of France all Catholic countries are very backward in education, and in social and moral reforms.

5. *Modernism.* The Catholic church, knowing how dangerous enlightenment and Bible study are to its hold on the
minds and hearts of men, has done its utmost to isolate its
people. It anathematizes Bible societies and all efforts to
circulate the Bible in the vernacular, it discourages its members from attending Protestant services, warns them to
accept nothing but what the church gives them, creates
organizations to keep them from association with Protestants, maintains parochial schools to prevent Catholic children from attending the public schools with Protestant children, maintains a Congregation in Rome for the censoring
of all books and periodicals. And yet, notwithstanding this
elaborate effort to keep their membership from touch with
the world, modern thought and Protestant ideals are here
and there penetrating the Catholic church. So serious was
this in 1907 that the pope undertook a vigorous campaign

against what he termed Modernism. This Modernistic movement was in part due to the philosophical, scientific and critical thinking of the time, but also largely to the study of the Bible and church history, and to the spread of the Protestant spirit of freedom and spirituality. For the present the pope seems to have triumphed, but those who profess to know declare that the movement is not quenched but only driven to cover and that it will flame out again in due time. It seems certain that the very existence of the Catholic church depends on its ability to isolate itself from the world in which it lives.

6. *Learning, Literature, and Art.* During the last period the Catholic church has not been intellectually as productive as in former eras. Its scholastic and mediæval outlook necessarily put it out of harmony with the striving and learning of the modern world. It has steadily excommunicated and silenced its greatest men, and as a consequence has made few contributions of any importance in any field of intellectual endeavor. Liberal statesmen and rulers are never in good standing with the hierarchy. Freedom which is necessary to any real achievement is abhorrent to the very genius of the Catholic church. It demands obedient children, not developed and independent personalities. It is not likely that the Catholic church will ever again produce a really great man.

§ 114

ITALY AND THE ITALIAN CHURCH

Italy, the home of the papacy, has experienced remarkable changes during this period. At the beginning the peninsula was still cut up into many independent and semi-independent states, the papal state holding the center. Much of this was overturned by the French Revolution and the Napoleonic régime, but was largely restored by the Congress of Vienna. Central Italy was again put under the control of the papal state and Lombardy and Venice were given to Austria. But liberal aspirations were not dead. Led by the great patriots Mazzini, Garibaldi and Cavour, all Italy was gradually freed from its oppressors and united under one government, Rome being captured from the Pope Sept. 20, 1870, and subsequently made the capital of the united kingdom. The Pope has steadily refused to acquiesce in this " robbery," as he and his partisans term the incorporation of the papal state into the nation. To the pope was left the Vatican palace with St. Peter's church and the Lateran palace and church in Rome and the Castle Gondolfo near Rome. The nation also guaranteed to him a large annuity, and the privilege of free communication with the world outside of Italy. His person is inviolable, he has his own guards, his own postal system, diplomatic corps, etc. In short he is not a subject of Italy, but an independent sovereign in his own small domain.

In the years since its unification Italy has made progress from the economic, political, and educational standpoints. She has also extended her sway over large sections of north Africa, at the present time holding three colonies there — Eritrea on the Red Sea, a part of Somaliland, and Tripoli taken from Turkey in 1912.

Italy has a very homogeneous population of some thirty-six millions, nearly all of whom are nominally Roman Catholics. By the last census there were sixty-five thousand Protestants, most of whom are Waldenses and foreigners, with a few thousand Baptists and Methodists; thirty-five thousand Jews. But the upper classes are generally indifferent or hostile to religion, as are the Socialists; the government is officially atheistic, all references to God being carefully avoided in state papers and addresses. Beginning in 1855 most of the monastic establishments were gradually confiscated and turned over to the state for various religious, educational, and charitable purposes. Some of the most historic and artistic buildings, such as Monte Casino, have been preserved as national monuments. Elementary education is little developed and the majority of the people, especially in southern Italy, are illiterate. Since 1877 religion has been excluded from the schools, religious instruction being given only when demanded by the parents; theological faculties in the universities have been abolished.

Italy has the most splendid and impressive church buildings in the world. St. Peter's and St. Paul's at Rome, St. Mark's at Venice and the cathedral at Milan are among the most imposing architectural monuments of human history. Many others scattered from end to end of the land are marvels of beauty and artistic merit. The Vatican Library and Galleries are filled with much of the world's greatest work in painting, sculpture and other arts. Italy is a beautiful land, but it is cursed with the poverty, illiteracy, beggary, and other evils which centuries of papal domination have entailed. Few lands suffer from greater spiritual destitution and religious indifference than this one where the Catholic church has had its supreme opportunity to show by its fruits what it can do for humanity. It has constructed a great ecclesiastical organization and mighty and beautiful church buildings, but it has failed to produce a nation notable for the quality of its men.

§ 115

CHRISTIANITY IN FRANCE

This has been a remarkable period in the history of France. At the conclusion of the Napoleonic wars France was restored to a monarchial form of government and the Bourbons were again set upon the throne. The monarchy was overthrown in 1848 and France became a republic for the second time. In 1851 the President succeeded in having himself made Emperor Napoleon III. In 1870 he was overthrown by the Germans and deposed, France again taking the form of a republic. The stability of this third republic has steadily grown and during the Great War its power and efficiency have been the admiration of the world. In 1911, the date of the last census, the population was about forty millions; recently the birth rate has been very low and declining, while the divorce rate has been high and increasing. Vice and drunkenness have been increasing. France also has extensive colonial possessions in northern Africa, southern Asia and elsewhere, with a population of some forty-four millions. What the extent and population will be at the close of the war no one can tell, but she has been materially increasing her holdings in Africa.

Under the arrangement made by Napoleon in 1801 Catholicism was recognized as the religion of the majority of the French people and was controlled and supported by the government. Substantially the same treatment was accorded to the Lutheran and Reformed churches and to the Jews. This arrangement continued till 1905, when a complete separation between church and state was effected, making all forms of religion free and equal. All financial support of the church was withdrawn, church property was rigidly limited as to amount and put under strict governmental supervision. On the other hand the church was entirely freed from state control as to its worship, doctrine, and internal affairs generally. The Catholic church did not accept the new arrangement as to property, and the deadlock continues.

The great struggle between church and state in France has been over the schools and the monastic orders. Notwithstanding the fact that the return of the orders was never authorized after their suppression during the Revolution, they had gradually returned in such great numbers that in 1901 there were over one thousand establishments and more than one hundred and fifty thousand monks and nuns in the country, most of them there illegally. They were largely engaged in teaching, but many of them had extensive commercial establishments. Their influence was generally exerted against the republic and liberal institutions of all kinds. This attitude generated such hostility that the teaching of religion was banished from the public schools in 1882, and in 1886 all clerical persons were made ineligible for a teaching position in the state schools.

The orders at once established private schools in great numbers and were soon educating a large percentage of the children of France and these from the ruling classes. Their hostility to the republic was endangering the stability of the government. Accordingly in 1901 a law was enacted requiring every order desiring domicile in France to secure articles of incorporation from the French parliament. Many orders recognized the impossibility of securing such permission and made no application; many applications were refused. By this means monasticism was practically abolished in France, even as the Jesuits had been expelled in 1880. The educational system, which is one of the best in the world, is now completely secularized or laicized and illiteracy has ceased. The government is officially atheistic and the masses of the people are largely indifferent or hostile to religion. Such are the fruits of the Catholic régime in another land where that church long had undisturbed control over the life of a great people.

Many of the most beautiful church buildings in the world are in France, as for example the cathedrals of Rheims, recently almost destroyed by the Germans, Bordeaux and Notre-Dame in Paris; but the church under the leadership of the Jesuits has fostered superstition to a remarkable degree. The Catholic church produced a few scholars of note during the nineteenth century, but they were usually in bad repute with their church and not a few have been silenced and their books have been suppressed.

There are about six hundred thousand Protestants in France, most of them Reformed (Calvinists) and Lutherans, with a few Baptists, Methodists, and others. They exert an influence upon public life out of all proportion to their numbers, holding very many of the highest positions in the government. But they are not increasing in numbers, are divided into conservative and liberal wings, the latter being practically Unitarian. In recent years they have produced some notable scholars and literary men. There are also from seventy to one hundred thousand Jews in the country.

The French government no longer undertakes to be the protector of Catholic missions in the East. For years France furnished the chief missionary zeal of the Catholic church as well as a very large share of the men and women who did the work. Lately there has been a dearth of priests in France itself.

In the French colonies nearly all the great religions of the world are represented — Mohammedanism, Buddhism, Confucianism, etc. Naturally Catholic missions are being vigorously prosecuted also, but entirely without state aid.

The religious condition of France has been deplorable. It has seemed to be slipping into blank atheism. Vast numbers of the people have long been completely irreligious.

§ 116

CHRISTIANITY IN SPAIN

No other country of the world has been so loyally Catholic during the last period and none has declined in territory and significance so rapidly as Spain. At the beginning her colonies included nearly half of North America, all of Central and South America except Brazil, most of the West Indies, the Philippines and many other islands. During the period she has lost the whole of this vast colonial empire and has fallen far back in the scale of the nations. She now has a population of about twenty millions. During the period there have been frequent struggles between the liberal and clerical elements, with the latter usually successful. According to the latest census about 66% of the population is illiterate, though recently the government has established compulsory primary education under government control and with government support.

The entire population with the exception of about thirty

thousand is Catholic, most of them fanatically Catholic, though there is some free thinking. The Inquisition, the most cruel and inhuman judicial tribunal in history, was not finally suppressed till 1834, when its property was confiscated and applied to the payment of the national debt. Religious freedom is now guaranteed to all religious beliefs, but all others than Catholicism meet powerful prejudices. Monasticism is still in full swing in Spain, the monks and nuns numbering something over fifty thousand. The church is supported by the state treasury.

Since 1868 Protestant missions have been carried on in Spain with increasing success. There are now some seven thousand Protestants — Presbyterians, Congregationalists, Anglicans, Baptists, and Methodists. In no land have the Jews suffered more barbarous treatment than in Spain, and yet there are still about four thousand Jews in the country.

According to the best testimony available great numbers of the more intelligent people of Spain are disgusted with or only nominally attached to the Catholic church and are turning rapidly to liberal and free thinking views. It would seem that the opportunity for Protestantism is now very great, and certainly the moral and spiritual need is great.

§ 117

CHRISTIANITY IN PORTUGAL

Portugal has a population of about six millions, besides considerable colonies in Africa, India, and China. The people are extremely backward, more than 75% being wholly illiterate. The royal government had a rather stormy career throughout the nineteenth century and in 1910 was overthrown and succeeded by a republic. The new government has undertaken to organize a system of compulsory primary education, but the moral condition is said to be very low.

Portugal was the only country of Europe to remain wholly unaffected by the Reformation, and in modern times it has been influenced by liberal and Protestant ideas less than any other country. Some progress has been made, however. In 1834 the monasteries were abolished and their rich property confiscated; some returned and were recently confiscated again by the republic. Still there are nearly one hundred thousand ecclesiastical persons in Portugal, or one to every fifty-seven inhabitants. The church was disestablished in 1911, which will probably serve automatically to reduce the relative number of the Catholic clergy.

Protestants have been doing work in a small way since 1845, but there are now but about one thousand Protestant communicants, divided among Anglicans, Presbyterians, Baptists, and Methodists.

§ 118

CHRISTIANITY IN BELGIUM

Up to the outbreak of the French Revolution Belgium had been attached to the crown of Austria. By the Congress of Vienna it was, in 1815, united to the Kingdom of the Netherlands under the Protestant House of Orange. But differences of religion, racial characteristics, language, and economic interests caused continual friction and finally led to separation in 1830 and the establishment of an independent constitutional monarchy in 1832, when the neutrality and safety of the new government was assured by agreement of the great powers. Until its invasion by Germany in 1914 it had lived in peace, engaged in internal development. At the outbreak of the war Belgium had a population of about eight millions and in addition an extensive colony in central Africa known as the Belgian Congo, with a population estimated at fifteen millions of Bantus.

The Belgians were a quiet, industrious, and thrifty people, engaged in agriculture and manufacturing. The country enjoys entire religious freedom, but the government grants considerable subventions to all the recognized churches, Catholic, Protestant, and Jewish.   The great bulk of the people are Catholic, some thirty thousand are Protestants (Lutherans, Reformed, Presbyterian, Anglican, Methodist, and Baptist) and several thousand Jews.   The Catholic church has many beautiful and impressive church and school buildings, several of which have been ruthlessly destroyed by the Germans.   Monasticism is allowed, and there are more than thirty thousand monks and nuns largely engaged in teaching and hospital work.   The chief feature of the internal politics of the nation has been the struggle between liberals and clericals for the control of the schools. Few countries are more solidly Catholic than Belgium.

§ 119

RELIGION IN AUSTRIA-HUNGARY

Austria-Hungary, the only important non-Latin Catholic country, is the last remaining remnant of the old Holy Roman Empire founded by Charlemagne on Christmas Day, 800.   At the beginning of the last period it still contained Belgium and all northern Italy in addition to the territory which it now has.   As a result of the French Revolution and the Napoleonic wars these outlying territories were lost and much of its power destroyed.   In 1806 Napoleon (who had himself assumed the title of Emperor in 1804) compelled the emperor to resign the title of emperor of the Holy Roman Empire, thus dissolving the oldest government of Europe.   Henceforth the sovereign styled himself Emperor of Austria.   The dissolution of the empire left the German states without any bond of union or central government whatsoever.   In the room of the empire there was formed a confederation of German states with Austria as the leading member, an arrangement which continued for nearly half a century.   By the Congress of Vienna in 1815 Austria recovered her Italian territories and some additional lands along the eastern shore of the Adriatic.   For a time she seemed about to recover her old prosperity, but her government was reactionary and unfavorable to democratic movements. Beginning in 1848 a revolutionary period set in which lasted till 1867, when virtual independence was bestowed on Hungary.

The sovereign is now Emperor of Austria and Apostolic King of Hungary, but the two countries are largely independent, each having its own constitution, its own parliament and executive departments. The matters which the two states regulate in common are foreign, military and naval affairs, coinage, weights and measures, tariffs, currency. In all other respects the two states are independent.

With the help of France the Italians succeeded in gradually driving the Austrians out of Italy beginning in 1859. In 1866 Austria was defeated by Prussia and excluded from the German confederation and from the empire at its formation in 1871. In 1878 it was entrusted with the administration of the two provinces of Bosnia and Herzegovina, just then being freed from the tyranny of the Turks. In 1908, during the confusion in Turkey due to the Young Turk movement, Austria seized the opportunity to incorporate these two provinces into the empire, a proceeding which in large measure occasioned the outbreak of the Great War in 1914.

Austria-Hungary is in area the second and in population the third state in Europe. The total population at the beginning of the war was about fifty millions, of whom about three-fifths were in Austria and two-fifths in Hungary. The population is singularly mixed. The largest homogeneous contingent are the Germans, of whom there are about twelve millions; the next largest are the Hungarians, of whom there are more than ten millions; the twenty-two million Slavs are divided into various names and languages; three and a quarter million Roumanians, two and a quarter million Jews, and a million or more of other nationalities complete the medley.

Religiously the people are as diverse as they are racially

and linguistically.   Roman Catholics predominate, constituting about thirty-five millions of the population; the emperor
must be a Roman Catholic and the influence of the court has
been steadily and powerfully with that church.   The church
is richly endowed but not state supported or state controlled
in its internal affairs.   During the century it has been one
of the most vigorous and effective divisions of the Catholic
church, though even here the church has lost control over
the schools and marriage, and religious freedom has been
wrung from it since 1868.   Monasticism is still held in honor
and there are many monks and nuns.   There are theological
faculties in most of the universities and many seminaries
for the training of priests.   The church has shown much
intellectual and charitable activity, creating a great many
organizations for these purposes, producing an extensive
literature, even translating the Bible for the use of Catholics, of course publishing it with careful instructions as to
its use.   Austria has been decidedly reactionary in both
church and government, but for more than half a century
now liberal ideas and liberal laws have made progress as a
result of popular demand.   The new emperor is said to be
much more liberal than Francis Joseph was.   A rather vigorous " free from Rome " movement has since 1897 carried
a good many Catholics over to the Lutheran church.

Of the Roman Catholics more than four millions are
Uniats or converts from the Greek Catholic church who
are still permitted to use the Greek rite.   In addition there
are about four million Greek Catholics, more than two million Jews, an equal number of evangelicals, chiefly Reformed (Presbyterians in Hungary) and Lutherans.   Recently the Baptists have been working with remarkable success in Hungary, having secured freedom and safety
throughout the empire.   Half a million Mohammedans and
a few scattering parties complete the religious complexion
of this wonderfully heterogeneous and mixed country.   If
the government holds together through the strain of this
war great changes are likely, and all indications point to

increasing liberalism in religion and politics, no matter what the outcome of the military struggle may be.

§ 120

SPANISH AND PORTUGUESE AMERICA

Space forbids more than a cursory glance at Latin America stretching in one unbroken mass from the southern boundary of the United States to Cape Horn. At the beginning of the last period this whole vast domain was under the governments of Spain and Portugal. Beginning about 1816 one province after another won its independence and set up government for itself as an independent state. At first Brazil was a kingdom but transformed itself into a republic in 1889. The history of most of these countries has been politically turbulent and stormy. Violence, bloodshed, and instability have been their most striking characteristics.

Very early Negro slavery was introduced into all these countries so that the major portion of the population is now composed of a mixture of the native Indians, who were the only inhabitants when the Europeans came, the European Spanish and Portuguese and the Negroes who were imported as slaves. In the remoter interior districts there are still many pure-blooded Indians, while there is an element which has preserved its Spanish and Portuguese blood pure. In all these countries there has been much European immigration of various nationalities in recent years. Slavery has been abolished in all these countries during the nineteenth century, and in some of them progress has been made in the direction of education and culture.

In all of them the Catholic church is the dominant religion and in some it enjoys the privileges of a state church. However, all forms of faith are permitted and guaranteed their freedom. In many of the countries there is rampant infidelity and intense hostility to the church. Few of these countries have adequate school systems and there is much illiteracy and superstition. Nowhere else in the world is the Catholic church in a lower state of morals and intelligence than in the majority of these countries. The mixture of races, the isolation, the hot climate, the frontier conditions have combined to make this group of nations among the most needy in the world. Civil marriage has lately been made compulsory in most if not all these countries, an arrangement which will doubtless improve moral conditions. The Catholic church is provided with church buildings which are, however, in some of the countries, the property of the state, which suffers no religious corporation to hold property. Most of the countries have numerous monastic establishments, but lately monasticism is on the decline here as elsewhere in the Catholic world. The priesthood and the ignorant classes generally are fanatically devoted to the Catholic church, but the more intelligent and cultured are turning away from the church into infidelity or indifference.

Peru is the only country which does not have toleration and even here some Protestants are tolerated in actual practice. In every Latin-American country Protestant mission work is being pushed with more or less vigor and success. Brazil has about one hundred thousand Protestants, Mexico eighty thousand, Argentina a large contingent, and other countries smaller numbers. There are Baptists, Methodists, Presbyterians, Episcopalians, Lutherans, and others.

§ 121

THE WEST INDIES AND THE PHILIPPINE ISLANDS

Spain succeeded in saving these island groups from the wreck of her great colonial empire till 1898, when as a result of the Spanish-American War she was compelled to relinquish her control. Up till that date they had been kept solidly Catholic with the exception of a large Mohammedan and pagan element in the Philippines. They were ignorant, superstitious, and fanatically Catholic. Since passing under the control of the United States a good public school system has been organized, religious freedom has been established, Protestant work has begun and very marked improvement is everywhere apparent. Cuba, which did not come under the sovereignty of the United States, has also received Protestant missionaries with open arms. Evangelism and school work are being fruitfully prosecuted by Baptists and others.

§ 122

CATHOLICISM IN PROTESTANT LANDS

In this era of religious freedom Catholicism has had the opportunity of penetrating Protestant lands just as Protestanism has obtained freedom to operate in Catholic countries. This opportunity has been vigorously utilized so that there is a considerable body of Catholics now in every Protestant land, even those where Catholicism was suppressed at the Reformation.

1. *Germany.* Catholicism was never entirely suppressed in Germany. The "ecclesiastical reservations" act of 1555 secured to the Catholics the permanent control of such bishoprics as Cologne, while some of the lands of southern Germany, like Bavaria, were never reformed. In addition to these remains of Catholicism which have come down from the Reformation there have been some trifling gains by conversion and colonization in purely Protestant territory. But the proportion and the distribution of Catholic population is substantially the same as at the conclusion of the Thirty Years' War. The famous Kulturkampf of 1872, a struggle of Bismarck to control the political activities of the Catholic church, was only measurably and temporarily successful. They have long composed a compact political party known as the Center, which have usually been able to secure

what they wished. The Jesuits are not tolerated in the country.

The Catholics constitute about 36% of the population of the empire. In only three of the twenty-six German states do they have a majority — Bavaria, Baden, and Alsace-Lorraine; of the other states, only Prussia has more than one-third of its population Catholic. The Catholics are found chiefly in south Germany, along the Rhine and among the Poles of eastern Prussia. They receive state support and in general have been a rather intelligent and progressive type of Catholic.

2. *Scandinavian Countries.* Denmark has only about ten thousand Catholics in a population of two and three quarter million; Norway has only about two thousand in a population of two and a half million, and in Sweden only twenty-five hundred in a population of more than five millions. In other words, these countries are freer from Catholicism than any other in the world.

3. *Great Britain and Ireland.* By the legislation of the Reformation era Catholicism was suppressed entirely in all divisions of this country. Actually it was made illegal on paper, but continued to exist in fact, especially in Ireland, which was made more Catholic by its intense hatred of England. Agitation for the removal of restrictions upon the Roman Catholics began before the end of the preceding period. They continued at intervals until 1829, when by the so-called Catholic Emancipation Act full civil rights were finally granted them. In 1853 the hierarchy was restored in England amid much excitement, so that Catholics now enjoy equal freedom with others, except that the king and some of his most intimate advisers must be Protestants.

During this last period Catholics have increased in numbers rather rapidly in the United Kingdom; this increase has been largely from immigration, but there have also been many notable conversions among them, as John Henry Newman, one of England's greatest preachers and literary men. The Catholic population of England and Wales is estimated at 1,900,000, that of Scotland at 546,000, and that of Ireland at three and a quarter million. Perfect freedom is now enjoyed by the Catholics as by others in all these lands. The English Catholics have been among the most intelligent in the world with considerable scholarship and productive ability.

Catholics of course enjoy perfect freedom in all British colonies, where they have been even more prosperous than in the mother country. Of a population of about eight million in Canada, nearly one-half are Roman Catholics of many nationalities, immigrants from many lands. In Australia and New Zealand from one-sixth to one-fifth of the population exclusive of the aborigines is Roman Catholic, while in the South African Union less than one-tenth are Catholics.

4. *The United States.* The most phenomenal growth of Catholics in Protestant lands has been in the United States, largely because of immigration. At the beginning of the last period they were very weak and were almost entirely English speaking Catholics. Out of a population of about one hundred millions at the present time, about fourteen millions are Roman Catholics, or approximately one-seventh of the people. The church has three cardinals, the hierarchy is thoroughly organized, and the church provided with parochial schools and other institutions of learning, hospitals, monastic establishments, organizations of laymen and women, numerous periodicals and vast quantities of real estate. In many of the cities the church controls a majority of the petty municipal offices, such as positions on the police force and in the fire department, but has held comparatively few important positions in the government of the States or the nation. The church has remained in large measure a foreign institution under the constant suspicion of the native American element of the country, on which it has made very little impression. Its membership is composed of many nationalities and languages, making for it grave difficulties. The conversions of Protestants to this church have been

comparatively few and unimportant, while hosts of people have been converted from it to the various Protestant churches. Its membership has been below the average in culture and social position. At times a liberalism which has been termed "Americanism" has threatened to make a breach between American Catholics and the papacy and between the laity and the hierarchy. But these have been smoothed out, and Catholics now seem to look hopefully to America as the home of a future Catholicism of immense significance.

§ 123

CATHOLICISM IN NON-CHRISTIAN LANDS

During the last period Catholics have prosecuted missions more or less successfully in most non-Christian lands. They are under the general direction of the Congregation of the Propaganda at Rome, the actual work being done by the members of the various monastic orders. There are numerous colleges and schools in Europe and America for the training of missionaries. Formerly various governments were accustomed to subsidize Catholic missions, but practically all this has been withdrawn during the last period and they must now be supported by voluntary gifts. To collect these offerings several societies have been organized during the last three quarters of a century. There are no statistics on the amount of Catholic gifts, but they are probably far below those of the Protestants.

Much of the Catholic work is exceedingly superficial, though contact with Protestant missions has improved the quality of the work done. All told they claim about six million adherents in non-Christian lands, though this is probably a considerable exaggeration.

E. PROTESTANTISM IN THE LAST PERIOD

§ 124

The last has been the glorious period of Protestantism. The leadership not only of the Christian part of the world but of the entire world has passed into their hands. The whole world recognizes that the United States, Great Britain and Germany are the three leading nations of the earth. Moreover, the smaller Protestant powers are their equals in all respects except size and military power — in the freedom, contentment, and happiness of their people, in moral standing and intellectual activity and productiveness. Protestants are far more tolerant and liberal than Catholics, but no whit less convinced or keenly active. They lead in culture, in missionary gifts and activity, in moral and social reforms, in all movements for the uplift of humanity, in the alleviation of suffering and distress. It is true that they are divided into many denominations and churches and not infrequently there is friction and waste of effort; but when all is said it still remains true that they are as much united as the Catholics and that there is among them a larger and ever growing unity of feeling and spirit of cooperation. Less and less they work at cross purposes, more and more they regard themselves as divisions in a common army. Protestantism is in closest sympathy with the aspirations and strivings of the modern world at every point. It promotes enlightenment and freedom, does not fear investigation and thought, trusts the individual and seeks to develop him into the completest personality.

(A) THE LUTHERAN CHURCHES

§ 125

The largest group of Protestant Christians is the Lutherans, who number all told about seventy millions. They are substantially agreed in doctrine, polity, worship and general type of Christian life, but they are by no means one church in the matter of organization. On the contrary, in those lands where Lutheranism is the state church each government has its own church and in countries where there is no established church, like the United States, there are often several organizations. The whole group is, however, homogeneous and compact, more so than most other groups. Lutheranism is almost entirely Teutonic, spreading only with the migration of the Teutons. It has been very vigorous during the last period.

GERMANY AND ITS CHRISTIANITY

The German empire is predominantly Lutheran. In 1817, the three hundredth anniversary of the posting of Luther's theses, a union of the Lutheran and " Reformed " (Presyterian) churches began and was gradually carried to completion in Prussia and many of the smaller German states. The resultant church is known as the " Evangelical Church," and is the state church where it exists. Each of the individual states composing the empire has its own state church supported from the state treasury and controlled by the state authorities, but religious freedom under government oversight is assured to all faiths. Education of all grades is highly developed and entirely under state control and support. Attendance is compulsory and religious instruction is required. No country in the world has so small a percentage of illiteracy. Every university, of which there are many, has a theological faculty supported by the state. Besides these there are seminaries for the training of ministers in the denominational tenets and in practical knowledge necessary to the conduct of the affairs of a parish.

The Germans have shown wonderful intellectual productiveness during the last period. They have been the leaders in every department of theological learning — in exegesis, systematic and biblical theology, in church history, in liturgics, etc. In the field of learning the whole world has gone to school to Germany.

On the other hand in practical service they have not kept pace with English and American Christians. In foreign mission work they have been far behind these two countries, though they have about twenty-five missionary societies and at the outbreak of the war were giving nearly two million dollars annually to support work in many parts of the world.

In social service and various forms of relief work at home the German church has been quite active. In particular the organization of deaconesses, founded by Pastor Fliedner at Kaiserswerth in 1836, was a notable event which has had important effects on woman's work in all other Protestant communions throughout the world. Trained in the Bible and other religious subjects, these women serve in hospitals, poorhouses, orphanages, schools and many other institutions where religious convictions and training add greatly to the value of the service rendered. Many thousand of these Protestant sisters are now engaged in this blessed work.

There are other Protestants in Germany. Baptists numbered about fifty thousand at the outbreak of the war. The Baptist work was instituted by the baptism of J. G. Oncken at Hamburg in 1834 by Dr. Barnas Sears, an American Baptist who was then studying in Germany. They have grown steadily, though long harassed by numerous governmental restrictions and losing considerable numbers by emigrations. They are now well organized and have a very good seminary at Hamburg for the training of ministers. They have for several years been engaged in active and successful mission work in the African colonies of Germany. Besides the Baptists there are Methodists, Mennonites, Independent Lutherans, and a few others numbering in all

about two hundred thousand who are not connected with
any of the state churches.

§ 126

THE SCANDINAVIAN COUNTRIES

Denmark, Sweden, and Norway are the most solidly Lutheran countries in the world. No other form of Protestantism made any impression on these lands during the Reformation era and very little since that time; moreover all
attempts at the reëstablishment of Catholicism have been
completely fruitless. Consequently they are almost unani-
mously Lutheran still. The Lutheran church is established
by law in all of them, but others are tolerated. The Lutheran churches of these three lands have bishops at their
heads. The school systems are all well developed and there
is little illiteracy.

In Denmark the clergy are appointed by the king and
supported by the state. They are educated in the University of Copenhagen and have considerable control over the
public schools, all of which must provide religious instruction. At the last reports available there were between four
and five thousand Baptists, a few thousand Methodists, and
some other evangelical Christians in the country.

In Norway all the clergy are appointed by the king and
have important relations with the school system. All members of the state church are required to have their children
baptized and instructed in its confession. Jesuits are not
tolerated in this country. Six thousand Baptists and ten
thousand Methodists and a very few other evangelical
Christians are found in Norway.

Sweden is the largest and most influential of these countries. The Lutheran church is very firmly established,
though others are tolerated under restrictions. The Swed-
ish church has shown considerable scholarship during the
nineteenth century, producing many men of importance.

The Baptists have been active since 1848 and now number more than fifty thousand, having been more successful in Sweden than in any other European country. Methodists have some fifteen thousand members and there are small bodies of other sects.

All these countries have been engaged in home and foreign missions with zeal and success.

§ 127

LUTHERANS AND EVANGELICALS IN AMERICA

German and Scandinavian immigrants brought their Lutheranism to the United States, and in 1915 together counted 2,434,184, being surpassed in numbers by the Methodists and Baptists only among Protestants. During the last twenty-five years the percentage of increase has been larger than that of any other Protestant group. Diversities of race, language, and doctrinal view-point have caused much controversy, division and strife. At present their membership is gathered into sixty-five synods, all but fifteen of which are organized into five larger bodies known as " General Synod," " United Synod, South," " General Council," " Synodical Conference " and " United Norwegian Church." Of these the first two use the English language exclusively, while the " Synodical Conference " is the most decidedly German and rigidly Lutheran. They are found in largest numbers in the North and the Middle West. An early union of most of these bodies is likely.

They have twenty-eight theological seminaries and forty-one colleges, none of them very well known, however. They are well equipped with hospitals, homes for the aged and orphans, deaconess mother houses and similar institutions; they issue many religious and theological periodicals in various languages.

The Lutherans are active in all forms of service such as home and foreign missions, Sunday school work, social reforms, etc. Together they form one of the vigorous moral and religious forces of our country.

The " German Evangelical " churches are the descendants of immigrants from Prussia and other German states where a union of the Lutherans and Reformed was accomplished after 1817. These united churches dropped both former names and called themselves the " Evangelical Church." When they reached this country they called themselves " German Evangelical " in distinction from a German body very similar to the Methodists which was founded by Jacob Albright a little earlier who had called themselves " Evangelical."

The German Evangelicals have about three hundred thousand communicants, living mainly in the Middle West. Most of them belong to the German Evangelical Synod, organized in 1877. They are engaged in all forms of Christian service, and compose a considerable element of the German population of this country.

(B) REFORMED OR PRESBYTERIAN CHURCHES

§ 128

The Reformed churches have not preserved their unity and solidarity as the Lutheran. They have shown much greater tendency to grant religious freedom and withdraw state aid and hence have been more affected by the introduction of other communions and by schisms in their own body. They have been behind the German Lutherans in the prosecution of scholarly pursuits, but have surpassed the latter in practical service. In particular they have been much more active in foreign missions.

SWITZERLAND

In Switzerland there is absolute liberty of conscience and of creed, and in the canton of Geneva religion has been

disestablished.   In the other cantons one is not compelled
to pay taxes to the support of any confession in which one
does not believe.   A little more than one-third of the population is Roman Catholic, the others are Reformed, with a
very small number of Baptists, Methodists and others.

The Protestants are found in the more intelligent and
progressive city cantons.   They have produced a number of
scholars of note and have made notable contributions to the
theory and practice of education.   They have also taken
deep interest in missions and other benevolent and Christian service.   The Catholics are found in the French and
the mountainous cantons.   The Swiss are brave, free and
honest people.

§ 129

THE KINGDOM OF HOLLAND

About three-fifths of the population of Holland are Protestants, with the proportion gradually increasing.   The
great majority of these belong to the Reformed or Presbyterian confession.   At the beginning of the period the Reformed church was established by law, with toleration of
others.   After the Napoleonic wars the same general conditions as before were restored, Holland and Belgium being
united into one kingdom.   In 1830 friction between the two
parts was so great that they were separated.   Friction
among the Protestants of Holland led to a secession from
the state church in 1834 and the organization of a free
church known as "The Christian Reformed Church."
This body has been evangelical, active and zealous and has
exerted a good influence on the state church.

Finally complete religious freedom has been established
with the state contributing to all religious parties — Protestants, Catholics, Jews — who will accept state aid.   Several parties like the Mennonites, Baptists, etc., decline to
accept such help.

Religion has been banished from the public schools, which

are now entirely secular. Some Protestants as well as Catholics have established Christian schools for the training of their children under Christian influences. Holland has produced a good many scholars of first rate ability, but they have been radicals for the most part, especially in Old Testament criticism.

The Dutch Reformed church has shown some interest in missions, and has sent a good many emigrants to the United States, South Africa and other British colonies. They themselves have several important colonies in the East.

§ 130

SCOTLAND

Scotland is the only other country where Presbyterianism became the established religion. Christianity in this country has had an interesting history during the last period. Scotland had suffered from the prevalent skepticism and coldness of the eighteenth century as much as England, but it did not benefit as much from the Evangelical Revival. Doubtless this failure was due to the reaction of the rigorous Calvinistic theology of the Scotch against the Arminianism of Wesley and his colaborers. At any rate the end of the century found the Scottish church unrevived. However, early in the nineteenth century a real though less striking revival breathed through the entire Scottish people and has continued its blessings to the present time, the leading figures in the early stages being the Haldanes.

The new life soon developed friction within the church, especially over the right of patronage — the king and nobles claimed the right to appoint the ministers, while the congregations demanded the privilege of election or at least of veto on the appointment of an unsatisfactory candidate. Friction over this question had already caused two schisms in the eighteenth century, one in 1733, when the Seceder Church was formed, and another in 1760, when another secession was organized into what was known as the Relief Church. These two churches united in 1847, forming the United Presbyterian Church.

In the meantime the friction had developed to such a point of intensity that Thomas Chalmers, Scotland's greatest preacher at that time, led in 1843 in a schism which carried away nearly half of the nation, who set up an independent church known as the "Free Church of Scotland." The manner in which the Scottish people responded to this effort for freedom is one of the heroic chapters in Christian history. Renouncing every dollar of state aid and endowments they started from nothing and in the course of a very few years were the most influential religious body in Scotland with beautiful and commodious church buildings, excellent educational institutions and well manned and supported missions in many parts of the world. And this too by a people who had hitherto looked to the state and endowments for the support of religious work.

In 1900 the "Free Church" and the "United Church" united to form the "United Free Church of Scotland." It now has nearly as large a membership as the state church and is far more active and effective in its various forms of service. Besides these two large churches there are several smaller Presbyterian churches consisting for the most part of remnants that were left from the various bodies at the unions that have taken place. There are also Episcopalians, Congregationalists and Baptists, all of whom contribute more or less to the religious life of this interesting country.

The various Scottish churches have shown remarkable activity in all forms of Christian service, especially in foreign missions. Many of the most notable missionaries of the nineteenth century have been the gift of Scotland. Names that will instantly occur to every one even superficially acquainted with the history of missions are Duff, Moffat, Livingstone, Paton and others scarcely less famous. Scotland has also produced many scholars of the highest ability and widest influence. They have been particularly notable in biblical studies of a more popular nature.

§ 131

PRESBYTERIANISM IN ENGLAND AND THE BRITISH COLONIES

Presbyterianism as a visible organization and force disappeared from England in the seventeenth century. During the latter part of the eighteenth century a few congregations of Scotch Presbyterians were formed at various points in the country, but continued in more or less intimate relations with the Scottish churches. During the earlier part of the nineteenth century these bodies increased in numbers and size and also incorporated considerable English elements by an active evangelism. Finally all these diverse elements were organized in 1876 as the " Presbyterian Church of England." It now has 350 congregations, 12 Presbyteries and nearly one hundred thousand communicants.

Presbyterians began to emigrate from Scotland to Ireland about 1610 and settle in the north around Ulster. They were at first favored and then persecuted by the English government, many of them being massacred by the Irish Catholics in 1641. After the accession of William and Mary they were not only protected, but received a small donation from the state treasury till 1869. Amidst great difficulties and many losses by emigration they have continued to exist and to grow. In 1840 they organized the General Assembly of the Presbyterian Church in Ireland and now number more than one hundred thousand, forming the most progressive, prosperous and contented portion of the Irish people.

The Scotch have emigrated in large numbers to all the British colonies and have everywhere carried their Presbyterianism with them, organizing flourishing and aggressive churches and forming one of the sturdiest, most moral and religious elements in these new lands.

§ 132

PRESBYTERIANISM IN THE UNITED STATES

The Presbyterians of the United States are chiefly of Scotch descent and continue to form one of the important elements of our religious and national life. They have flourished during the last period, now numbering more than two million communicants organized into several separate churches. The most important of these are the Presbyterian Church in U. S. (Southern) with a membership of three hundred thousand, the Presbyterian Church in U. S. A. (Northern) with a membership of a million and a half, and the United Presbyterian with a membership of a hundred and fifty thousand. Presbyterians have had many divisions during the period, but have also had a number of notable unions, the last being the union of the Cumberland with the Northern Presbyterians in 1906. They have emphasized education especially for the ministry, have maintained until recently a rather rigid type of Calvinistic theology and have exhibited a high standard of Christian living. Their worship is still simple, non-liturgical with the emphasis on the sermon; they maintain the scripturalness of infant baptism but in practice baptize more adults than infants; many of them oppose immersion as unscriptural, thus separating themselves from the conclusions of the scholarship of the world. Some of their more important educational institutions are Auburn, Lane, Louisville, McCormick, Princeton and Western theological seminaries; Princeton, Central, Cumberland, Davidson, Hampden-Sidney universities and colleges.

All forms of Presbyterianism are aggressively and successfully engaged in missionary work. All the principal pagan fields are occupied, educational and benevolent institutions are well established and numerous, education as a missionary agency is largely employed.

Presbyterians have contributed largely to the Christian scholarship and literature of our country and have also played an important part in our political and public life, furnishing several presidents, many distinguished jurists, legislators, governors, etc. Their culture and high character have given them large influence in all walks of life.

(C) THE PROTESTANT EPISCOPAL CHURCHES

I

THE CHURCH OF ENGLAND

§ 133

The Christianity of all the English-speaking lands has been marked by a wonderful lack of organized governmental unity. Old churches have been split into fragments, new churches have been formed and strange religious forms calling themselves Christian have risen to plague the churches and give anxious hours to all lovers of unity, harmony and truth. And yet it is true that English speaking Christianity has been the most active and practically effective in the world, and it is probable that there has been as much actual spiritual unity as in lands where the outward marks of unity were far more apparent. In these respects the mother country has shared the experiences of the United States and the colonies.

HISTORY OF THE ENGLISH CHURCH IN THE LAST PERIOD

The general tendency of the period was toward the liberalizing of the church and the loosening of its hold upon the life of the nation. It was shorn of many of its privileges and has become the religion of a minority of the nation.

Many forces have operated in this direction. For example soon after the death of John Wesley in 1791 his followers began to withdraw themselves from the state church and in the course of the next few years carried a great number of the most earnest and pious people into independent organizations. Then the Baptists and Congregationalists have grown largely at the expense of the state church. Again in 1833 there began a movement variously called the "Tractarian" or "Oxford Movement" which carried a great many people into the Catholic church. Still further in a free country like Britain many people have lost all connection with any church through negligence or skepticism. So far had this gone that in 1915 the state church had fewer sittings in its church buildings than the dissenters and claimed but a few thousand more communicants, those of the state church numbering 2,445,114 and the combined dissenters 2,136,782.

The Anglican church has three well defined parties — the Low Church or evangelical party composed in part of remnants of the Methodist movement, the High Church or Catholic party who are ritualistic and sacerdotal, and the Broad Church or Liberal party who represent the German religious attitude. Among these parties controversies have been frequent and bitter, more than once reaching settlement only in the civil courts. The net result of these years of controversy has been the recognition by the state of the right of all these parties to a permanent place in the Church of England. Undoubtedly the High Church party have forged ahead in recent years until they are now dominant. But the official and upper classes generally are still loyal to this church while the great middle classes have adopted Free Church principles in large measure.

§ 134

CHURCH AND STATE

The Anglican church is still established by law but it has during the nineteenth century lost many of its privileges and prerogatives.   It has rich endowments for many of its parishes, but no one is now required to pay taxes for its support if he is a member of any other church.   The king who must be a member of the state church is its " supreme governor."   He appoints the archbishops and the bishops and some of the lower officials and has the patronage of many of its parishes.   The archbishops and some of the bishops have seats in the House of Lords and the other bishops (with one exception), may be appointed to seats. Parliament is the law-making body of the church.

There is, however, complete religious toleration and the church was disestablished in Ireland in 1871 and in Wales in 1914 to go into effect after the war.   The universities of Oxford and Cambridge were opened to the students of all denominations in the course of the nineteenth century, and the new universities are free to all.   The congregations have no voice in the choice of their rectors, their appointment being in the hands of " Patrons," individuals who for one reason or another have the legal right to " present " men to the livings.   The consent of the bishop is necessary to the induction of the incumbent into office, but once in charge he can be dispossessed only by a process at law.

§ 135

EDUCATION IN ENGLAND

As yet England has no national system of education. The system is a patchwork infinitely complex and only moderately efficient.   There is provision for religious instruction but the state church does not control it, and it is not imposed upon those who do not desire it. Up to the beginning of the nineteenth century higher education was wholly committed to the two old universities of Oxford and Cambridge which were under the dominance of the state church. During the century four new universities were founded — Durham in 1831, London in 1836, Victoria at Manchester in 1880 and Birmingham in 1900. Already in the twentieth century four more have been added — Liverpool in 1903, Leeds in 1904, Sheffield in 1905 and Bristol in 1909. These municipal institutions have no connection with the state church but are democratic in the full sense of the word. As this paragraph is written a great agitation is in progress for the complete recasting of the educational system of the country and it is probable that the close of the war will see a great reform in this direction. The outstanding fact of the century is the loss by the state church of the control over education and the growth of dissent.

§ 136

THEOLOGICAL SCIENCE

The state church has produced many great scholars and preachers during this period. English scholars have been a check on the investigations and the wild speculations of the Germans. They have devoted themselves assiduously to the exegesis of the Scriptures and here have made notable contributions. Lightfoot, Ellicott, Westcott, Hort are names known to all acquainted with the triumphs of biblical scholarship in the nineteenth century. English scholarship, led by the great scholars of the established church, assisted by the scholars of other English and American denominations, gave us the best revision of the Bible made up to that time and only surpassed to the present by the American edition. It has also contributed great hymn-writers and defenders and expounders of Christianity as a whole.

MISSIONS IN THE STATE CHURCH

§ 137

The Anglican church has been very active in its mission work in many parts of the non-Christian world. It has two great missionary societies, the Society for the Propagation of the Gospel organized in 1701 and the Church Missionary Society organized in 1799. The amount of voluntary gifts for all purposes in 1903 was upwards of forty million dollars of which about six millions were for Home and Foreign Missions. Its missions are well equipped in a material way and manned by well trained staffs in all departments of work. It has laid special emphasis on education as a means of missionary work. Many of the most famous and efficient missionaries of the nineteenth century have been members of the English church. In the state church the Sunday school movement was originated by Robert Raikes in 1780, the British and Foreign Bible Society in 1804 and the Young Men's Christian Association by George Williams in 1844.

II

§ 138

THE PROTESTANT EPISCOPAL CHURCH IN THE UNITED STATES

After the Revolutionary War the Episcopal church was organized in entire independence of the English church, with its own bishops, service and methods. It was much depressed for several years on account of the sympathy of its clergy with the mother country during the long and grilling struggle of the Revolution. About 1810 it began to grow and has had a rather remarkable history of prosperity since that time. It has not been torn by controversy quite so much as the Church of England, but it has the same parties — High, Low and Broad — with the High Church forging ahead as in England. This party sympathizes with the Catholics and does not desire to be known as Protestant. The communicants in 1915 numbered a little more than one million, and the number of infant baptisms that year were 53,289 while the faith baptisms numbered 14,537.

On account of its connection with the nobility and governing classes in England it has appealed to the wealthy and socially ambitious in this country, not infrequently luring such members away from other Christian bodies on these grounds. Its orderly and beautiful services, its artistic church buildings, its freedom from revival excitements and methods have attracted others so that its growth has been in no small measure at the expense of other denominations. It has produced a few scholars and preachers of note, but in these regards has not kept pace with the Church of England. But it exerts an influence on our public and social life out of all proportion to its numbers, especially in the federal government and in the army and navy. In general it is sacerdotal and sacramental, refusing to coöperate with other denominations in any sort of religious work; this is especially true of the High Church party. Its worship is liturgical, preaching being little stressed.

In missions it has been quite active and effective. In 1915 the church received from all sources for missions about one and three quarter million dollars, more than twenty millions being given for all purposes. The majority of its work could be described as Home Missions, but it also has work in Africa, China, Japan, Cuba and Mexico. Much of its effort is devoted to school work, hospital work and similar forms of service.

The church is organized into parishes, dioceses, provinces and a General Convention which meets every three years. The last is the legislative, executive and judicial body of the church. Its head is the bishop oldest in length of service known as the " Presiding Bishop "; it is composed of two houses — a House of Bishops and a House of Clerical and Lay Delegates consisting of four clergymen and four laymen from each diocese. Any action to be legal must have the concurrence of both houses and in the lower house the concurrence of both orders sitting separately.

THE EPISCOPAL CHURCH IN THE BRITISH COLONIES

Naturally the Episcopal church is strong in all the British colonies though it is entirely independent of the Church of England. In Canada it has more than a million members, standing third among the denominations in numerical strength; in New Zealand it is first with about forty per cent. of the population; in the various states of Australia from one-fourth to one-half the population is Episcopalian.

The church in the colonies and in America has not produced the high type of intellectual life which is seen in England, but it has been effective in the practical tasks of the Christian life.

(D) THE BAPTISTS IN THE LAST PERIOD

§ 139

IN GENERAL

One of the most striking features of the history of the nineteenth century has been the relative decline of infant baptism among evangelical Christians and the corresponding growth of faith-baptism. Most of the latter movement has been incorporated in the Baptist denomination. Considering the prejudices held against them, the meagerness of their resources and the smallness of their numbers at the beginning of the period they have made remarkable progress. At the beginning of the period they numbered scarcely more than one hundred thousand and were almost

confined to English speaking peoples. They were not unified by any one great leader, were not equipped with educational or religious institutions, were feared because of
their radical democratic views in religion and the state,
were despised because of their meager culture and were
opposed by the biblical learning of the world. They were
without any organization larger than the district association and possessed small means of intercommunication.

In the century and a quarter of the last period they have
increased to nearly eight million communicants who have
voluntarily accepted membership in the regular Baptist
churches, representing a population of not less than twenty
millions. They are still found chiefly among English speaking peoples but have taken root and are growing rapidly in
many other lands. In addition to Baptists other closely
related bodies which reject pedobaptism and practice only
faith-baptism number at least two millions more with a
population of six millions. One further point must be considered in estimating the progress of faith-baptism and
that is the fact that many of the Pedobaptist bodies especially in America administer more faith- than infant-bap-
tisms. Summing all these considerations, the total progress
in this direction can be seen.

During the period Baptists have been able to provide
themselves with educational and missionary equipment, they
have produced a literature of interest and importance, their
fundamental positions and peculiarities are generally recognized by the world's scholarship as scriptural, and they
are now sharing largely in the Christian work of missions
and reforms throughout the world. There is now little disposition to despise them or minimize their significance.

§ 140

BRITISH BAPTISTS

The two greatest groups of Baptists are in Great Britain
and America. The British Baptists have been compelled

to meet the difficulties due to the presence of a state church possessed of traditional social prestige and power, a nation permeated with the sacramental and sacerdotal conceptions of Christianity. But they have made progress. In 1792 they organized the " Baptist Missionary Society," the first society to be organized by Protestant Christians exclusively for the propagation of the gospel among the heathen. It became the model for all other societies. The first missionary was William Carey who became one of the most notable missionaries in the history of Christianity. Gradually most of the denomination became interested in this greatest modern Christian undertaking and throughout the century they have been doing a notable work in many parts of the world, as in India, Ceylon, China, the Belgian Congo, the West Indies, and at various points on continental Europe.

In 1812 the Calvinistic Baptists formed the Baptist Union, which however did not become effective till about 1832. The General or Arminian Baptists held apart till 1891 when they entered the Union and divisive names were dropped.

English Baptists had from the start left the question of open or close communion to the judgment of the individual churches. In the earlier part of the nineteenth century a vigorous agitation in favor of open communion arose and eventually led most of the English churches to adopt that practice and with it " open membership," that is the acceptance from other communions of members who had not received immersion or had even been baptized in infancy. On the other hand the Welsh churches held to the stricter practice which has characterized American Baptists, but they seem to be relaxing their views somewhat in recent years.

In 1915 there were about four hundred thousand Baptists in England and Wales, something over twenty thousand in Scotland and three thousand in Ireland.

British Baptists have produced several men of note during this last period — Robert Robinson, Robert Hall, C. H.

Spurgeon and Alexander Maclaren were among the most notable preachers of the nineteenth century. William Carey was one of the greatest missionaries of all time and Andrew Fuller was a great missionary secretary and theologian. David Lloyd-George is to-day Prime Minister and perhaps the most powerful statesman of the world.

§ 141

BAPTISTS IN THE UNITED STATES

The Baptists have had their greatest success in the United States, doubtless owing to religious freedom and the democratic ideals that have been dominant here. At the beginning of the period they numbered less than one hundred thousand. They have had very few accessions by immigration and yet they now number more than six million communicants in the regular Baptist body besides more than a hundred thousand in smaller bodies.

The conversion of Adoniram Judson and Luther Rice, two young Congregational missionaries, to Baptist views led to the first general missionary organization in 1814 for the prosecution of mission work in foreign lands, Judson and his wife becoming the first missionaries of American Baptists. Rice returned from India to assist in arousing and organizing the denomination, a task to which he devoted the remainder of his life.

Unfortunately the lack of culture and the rigid Calvinistic theology of many Baptists especially in the South led them to oppose the missionary enterprise, causing a serious schism in the body. It began about 1826 and has not yet been entirely healed. Naturally it greatly retarded the growth, that part of the denomination which opposed missions stagnating completely and gradually dying. They were known as " Hardshells," " Anti-effort " or Primitive Baptists.

About the same time another schism was precipitated by

Alexander Campbell, a Scotch Presbyterian, who had adopted Baptist views at least in part, had been baptized by a Baptist preacher and had organized an independent church which had been accepted as a member of a Baptist Association. He was a man of considerable ability, of great skill in debate and of tireless energy. He gradually developed the view that remission of sin is granted under ordinary circumstances only in baptism and that the Holy Spirit operates only through the word. These views with some other peculiarities led to a separation in which he took away a large section of the Baptist body, especially along the Ohio River.

The slavery agitation led to the withdrawal of the churches of the South from the general Baptist body and the organization of the Southern Baptist Convention in 1845. The American Baptist Publication Society had been organized in 1824 and the Baptist Home Mission Society in 1832. Southern Baptists had coöperated in all the national societies, but now organized upon a new plan, viz., one convention with two Boards. They continued to coöperate with the Publication Society till 1891 when the Sunday School Board was added. The northern societies were finally unified on the same plan by the organization of the Northern Baptist Convention in 1907.

Both Northern and Southern Baptists have been busily and successfully engaged in foreign mission work, the principal being in Italy, Africa, India, China, Japan, Mexico, South America and other countries. Baptists have been peculiarly successful in winning numbers, but they are not so well equipped with educational and similar institutions as could be wished. This is especially true of the Southern Baptists. According to the statistics of 1915 there are in South America 14,299, in Africa 17,899, in Asia 216,180 communicants, nearly all the direct and exclusive fruits of American and English Baptist mission work.

During the nineteenth century American Baptists have organized State Conventions throughout the entire country ;

they have founded many colleges and academies of a high order, while Brown University and the University of Chicago are among the leading institutions of higher learning in the world. Baptists have produced several preachers and scholars of note and have exerted considerable influence upon the public life of the country, though their influence is hardly commensurate with their numbers. They have fourteen theological seminaries some of which are among the leading institutions of this kind in the country. Some of the more notable of these are Newton, Rochester, Colgate, Crozer, Southern and Southwestern. On the foreign field they have seminaries at Canton, Shanghai, Rome and Rio Janeiro. Interest in higher education is constantly increasing.

All the British colonies have considerable bodies of Baptists. Those of Canada number about 120,000 communicants and constitute one of the noblest and most efficient groups of Baptists in the world. Australia, New Zealand and South Africa all have small but aggressive and successful bodies of Baptists.

(E) THE CONGREGATIONALISTS

§ 142

BRITISH CONGREGATIONALISTS

The Congregationalists have prospered during the last period. In England there are nearly half a million with a few thousand in Scotland and Ireland. They are flourishing in all the British colonies, and are found in most of the countries of continental Europe, particularly in Sweden where there are more than 100,000.

The Congregationalists of England and Wales have prospered since the beginning of the nineteenth century. They hold firmly to their church independence and are frequently called the Independents. But they also appreciate the importance of coöperation and in 1831 organized the " Congregational Union of England and Wales " for purposes of deliberation and advice, at the same time carefully guarding the independence of the churches. Within the last fifty years associations and local councils have been organized, and quite recently they have formed a national " Council."

English Congregationalists have been active in missions and other forms of service. The " London Missionary Society," organized in 1795 by several denominations, is now Congregational and is one of the most important missionary organizations in the world. It carries on extensive work in South Africa, Madagascar, India, China, the South Sea Islands and the West Indies. They have also been leaders in all forms of home missions and domestic reforms. They have produced many scholars, preachers, statesmen and authors of note, and in general have contributed largely to the intellectual as well as to the practical Christian life of England.

§ 143

AMERICAN CONGREGATIONALISTS

American Congregationalists have been behind their English brethren in no respect. During the last period they have grown rapidly notwithstanding the fact that an arrangement, made in 1801 with the Presbyterians as to coöperation, has cost them, they assert, not less than 2,000 churches as they have spread westward. Early in the nineteenth century a large section of the denomination in eastern Massachusetts, especially in and around Boston, went over to Unitarianism taking with them Harvard, the most important educational institution of the country. This was a serious defection, but did not stop Congregational growth.

American Congregationalists have led all other denominations in their emphasis on education and the effectiveness of their service in that direction. The mere mention of some of the more important of their institutions will serve to indicate the great contribution of this denomination in this direction: Yale, Harvard (originally, but now Unitarian), Amherst, Bowdoin, Dartmouth, Williams, Oberlin, and for women Mt. Holyoke, Smith and Wellesley and for the Negroes, Fisk and Atlanta universities. On the mission field they have Robert College at Constantinople and Doshisha in Japan. Andover, Chicago, Hartford, Oberlin and Yale are some of their theological seminaries. In addition to these institutions of higher learning they have many academies and colleges of lower grade doing the highest quality of work. This educational work has been carried on in a broad nonsectarian spirit almost uniformly. It is probable that the Congregationalists have laid less emphasis on denominationalism than any other similar body in America.

They have produced many scholars, literary men and preachers of note, among the latter Henry Ward Beecher, perhaps America's most famous preacher. A great stream of literature has continually poured from the Congregational presses.

They are now organized into local " conferences," State " Associations " which meet annually, and since 1871 a " Congregational Council " meeting triennially (since 1913 biennially), and covering the entire country. These bodies have only advisory and deliberative powers, the local churches being entirely independent and self-governing. Their fundamental principles of government as stated by themselves are " freedom and fellowship, a freedom which leaves each local church free in its separate affairs, a fellowship which unites all the churches for mutual care and coöperant action." The Congregationalists practice infant- as well as faith-baptism and employ any mode, not regarding this as important, but church membership begins only at conversion. Their worship is simple with emphasis on preaching. In recent years they have shown decided tendencies toward liberal theology.

The Congregationalists were the first Christian body in

this country to feel the foreign missionary impulse and organize for that work. The initial impulse was given by a group of students at Williams College and later at Andover Theological Seminary. As a result of their urgent activity the " American Board of Commissioners for Foreign Missions " was organized in 1810 and sent out its first missionaries in 1812. During the century this Board has been one of the most active and efficient in the world. It now has missionaries in Mexico, Spain, Austria, Turkey, the Balkans, Ceylon, India, China, Japan, Central Africa, the South Sea Islands and elsewhere. Emphasis has been laid on schools, hospitals and the other Christian institutions and as a consequence their missions are now unusually well equipped and ready for a greater work in the new era that is opening.

(F) THE METHODISTS

§ 144

INTRODUCTION

The Methodist church in American began its independent existence in the year 1784. But in England it remained a party in the Anglican church until after the death of John Wesley in 1791. He had opposed separate existence very strenuously and had died in the communion of the state church notwithstanding much friction and bitterness before his death. After his death the sentiment for separation which had long been restrained by his personal influence quickly had its way and separate organization was effected in 1795.

In general the Methodists have prospered greatly especially among English speaking peoples. They are now actively engaged in foreign missionary work though they were rather later than other Christian bodies in beginning. They have been a great popular denomination, accomplishing their service by evangelism at home rather than by education. Consequently they have not produced the schools, literature and scholars which some of the other denominations can show.

Their theology, which has not been much emphasized, has been Arminianism of a rather radical type gradually developing towards Pelagianism which is now the official teaching of the Southern Methodist church in the United States. They have been emotional, given to noisy evangelism in the local church and in camp meetings, the source of most of the so-called " holiness " parties. They have been afflicted by many serious schisms due to questions of method more than to doctrine. In recent years a strong tendency to friendliness among the various Methodist parties has resulted in several important unions both in England and America.

§ 145

METHODISM IN ENGLAND

The death of Wesley was quickly followed by complete separation from the state church. Already the movement had been divided into Calvinistic and Wesleyan Methodists. The former have never been very powerful, but the latter have been the parent church of English Methodism. The Wesleyan Methodist Church was rigidly ecclesiastical, permitting no representation to the laity and exercising an oversight as strict as that of the Jesuits. As the body grew and expanded this feature of its life led to many schisms. The first was in 1797 when the Methodist New Connection was organized with lay representation in its conferences. In 1810 a party who insisted on employing the camp-meeting methods which were at that time so popular and effective in America, were expelled and formed the Primitive Methodist Connection. In 1815 Wm. O'Bryan, who had been expelled for overzealous evangelism, organized the Bible Christians, and in 1828 when an organ was forced on a church in Leeds they withdrew and organized the Wesleyan

Protestant Methodists. And so the disposition to divide has continued. But in 1857 several groups united to form the United Free Churches and in 1907 another union took place by which the United Methodist Church was formed.

Notwithstanding this unfortunate tendency to division Methodists have been an important factor in English religious life and have made some real progress. They have suffered all the difficulties which meet a free church in a country like England, but they have carried their work into the colonies and into many of the great mission fields occupied by modern Protestants. The Wesleyan Methodists are by far the largest body, numbering in Great Britain and Ireland over half a million. The next largest body is the Primitive Methodist Church which has about two hundred thousand. All told the British Methodists of all kinds at home, in the colonies and on the mission fields have nearly a million and a half members. British Methodists have "superintendents" rather than bishops, and do not call themselves episcopal.

§ 146

AMERICAN METHODISM

It is in the United States that Methodism has had its greatest triumphs. Its schisms have been fewer, while its theology, methods, type of Christian life and form of church government have admirably fitted it to deal with the pioneer and fluid social conditions which have obtained in America during this period. Its itinerant ministry have reached every nook and corner of the country with a "free, full and present salvation," full of emotion and vocal expression. It has used all its resources of power in men and women to a remarkable degree, and as a consequence has grown more rapidly than any other Protestant body. It has been and is one of the great popular religious bodies of the country. Beginning late in the eighteenth century it now claims about seven and a half million communicants in the United States

alone.   Of these nearly one and a half millions belong to the
various Negro Methodist churches.   The two greatest
bodies are the " Methodist Episcopal Church " (northern)
with three and a half millions and the " Methodist Episcopal Church, South," with two million members.   The
only other considerable body of white Methodists is the
Methodist Protestant Church.   There are in all sixteen
Methodist churches in the United States each entirely independent of the others.

Methodists are fairly well equipped with educational and
other benevolent institutions.   They are actively engaged
in missionary work at home and abroad and are among the
foremost in all efforts at moral and religious reforms.   The
educational standards of their ministry are not so high as
some others and the fervor and effectiveness of their evangelism seems to be on the wane.   They have two great publishing houses and are pouring a stream of literature of
various kinds from their presses.   They have produced several men of note for scholarship and ability as preachers.
The bishops are without dioceses, but act as superintendents of the entire church.   They have great power over
the so-called " traveling preachers," especially in the Southern church, appointing them to positions annually and sending them where they will.   The General Conference of each
church is the legislative and governing body for the whole
of that church and meets every four years.   The Southern Methodist Church was organized in Louisville, Ky., in
1845 as a result of the agitation over slavery.   At the General Conference of the northern church in 1900 women were
admitted to membership and the lay and clerical membership were equalized.   At the same Conference all limitations
as to the length of the pastorates were abolished and the
matter was left to the judgment of the bishops in each
case.   The time limit in the Southern church is still four
years.

The Methodists carry on mission work in Africa, India,
China, Japan, South America, Korea, the South Sea Islands

and many of the European countries. These missions are usually well equipped with schools, hospitals and other adjuncts of the most effective missionary service.

(G) AMERICAN CHRISTIANITY

§ 147

IN GENERAL

American Christianity is the most diverse and complex in the world. Old world forms have been transplanted to this country and many new types have been developed on our soil. The voluntary system has given opportunity for innumerable schisms and has left a larger part of the people outside all church relations than is found in any other country. But notwithstanding these facts, perhaps because of them, there is, it is believed, less bitterness of religious feeling, more religious activity and a stronger and more vigorous humane sentiment than in any other country in the world. And this is true notwithstanding the fact that recent years have seen such an enormous influx of foreigners that the country has not as yet been able to absorb and digest them thoroughly. Our public school system is the melting pot. The second generation of immigrants usually speak English only and have thoroughly imbibed the peculiar American view of life.

The larger Christian bodies have already been dealt with at some length. Of these bodies the Roman and Greek Catholic still have much of the characteristics of a foreign institution. A large part of the membership and a still larger proportion of the priesthood are of foreign birth. The Greek Catholic, Armenian, Syrian and other oriental churches are almost wholly foreign. Among the Protestant churches the Lutherans and "Reformed" are the only bodies that continue much of their foreign characteristics. All others have been thoroughly Americanized. In recent

years a distinct effort has been made by Germany to prevent the assimilation of German immigrants to American
ideals and institutions; the success of this German propaganda would perpetuate a very alien element in the life
of our nation.

§ 148

OTHER CHRISTIAN AND QUASI-CHRISTIAN BODIES

It is impossible for lack of space to notice the multitude
of smaller bodies of Christians in the United States, each
of them more or less important for the life of our country
and the progress of the kingdom of God, each expressing
the religious convictions of some group of people. Only
the more important of those which have had their birth on
American soil and in some way seem to demand some attention will be noticed here.

1. *The " Disciples" or " Christians."* The work of Mr.
Alexander Campbell in connection with the Baptists has already been touched upon. Soon after he and his followers
separated from the Baptists they succeeded in uniting with
similar movements started by Barton W. Stone, and others
who had called themselves Christians. This explains the
confusion as to name. The chief article in their program
is the union of all Christians on the basis of the New Testament Scriptures. This in their view involves the rejection
of creeds, hierarchies, elaborate ecclesiastical machinery and
ritual, denominational names and whatever else is not scriptural, and conversely the adoption of a scriptural name,
baptism on the basis of repentance and faith and for the
remission of sins, democratic church government, etc.

In their earlier history they were excessively polemical
and belligerent, but more recently many of them have
dropped this characteristic in a measure and are living in
peace with their neighbors. They have been wonderfully
vigorous and active and have grown very rapidly. They
are Arminian in theology in so far as they can be said to

have a theology, and practice "open communion," celebrating the supper every Lord's day. To put their object in their own words, "We plead for the restoration of primitive Christianity — its name, its faith, its ordinances and its life." In 1915 they reported a membership of 1,142,206 in the United States and Canada. They are conducting missions in Africa, Australasia, India, China, Japan, Russia and other countries and claim in their foreign fields nearly seventy-five thousand communicants.

They make no distinction between clergy and laity and are congregational in church government. They are organized with district, state and national organizations for the promotion of their general missionary and benevolent work. Most of this is done through "The American Christian Missionary Society" with headquarters in Cincinnati.

2. The "Church of Jesus Christ of Latter Day Saints" or "Mormons," was founded by Joseph Smith, Jr., at Fayette, N. Y., in the year 1830. Smith was born and reared in Vermont in the midst of poverty, ignorance and superstition. He early began to see visions, finally alleging that the so-called Book of Mormon had been revealed to him written on gold plates in reformed Egyptian characters; with the plates were two crystals by means of which he had been able to make a translation. The Book which is regarded as the foundation of Mormonism was published and the church organized in 1830. In 1831 the church moved to Kirtland, O., thence to Jackson County, Mo., then back to Nauvoo, Ill., and finally in 1847 to Utah, where the majority still reside. Everywhere they were mobbed and roughly handled, Smith and his brother Hyram being killed in the jail at Carthage, Ill., in 1844. The reasons for this persecution were partly religious, partly political and social and partly economic.

The Mormons have prospered at Salt Lake City which they founded. They have transformed the entire region into a fertile and productive agricultural section. They now number 330,000 communicants while the "Reorganized" branch reports 67,000. Mormons reside chiefly in Utah but are also found in surrounding states and have colonies in Mexico and Canada. They early began foreign mission work and have brought many converts from European countries.

In organization they are a great hierarchy in which practically every man holds some office. They claim a continuous gift of prophecy through their president, regarding his revelations, together with the Bible ("when properly translated") and the Book of Mormon, as the revealed will of God. Their view of God is more heathen than Christian; they believe in Jesus Christ and forgiveness through him; repentance, faith and baptism by immersion for the remission of sins.

In 1843 Smith had a revelation not only approving but recommending polygamy, which was practiced till 1890 when under pressure from the United States Government it was suspended but not repudiated. Smith also taught that marriages were sealed in heaven and were an eternal relation. In mission work they go in pairs and do most of their proselyting in conversations. They have at Salt Lake City a "tabernacle" which is open to the public and a "temple" to which none but approved Mormons are admitted.

As a social, political and economic system Mormonism has had a remarkable history, though its political history now seems to be at an end. Religiously and morally its influence has been bad and it has contributed nothing to the intellectual or spiritual riches of our country.

3. *The Church of Christ Scientist,* was founded by Mary Baker G. Eddy, who claimed to have discovered its principles in 1866, published the foundation book "Science and Health with Key to the Scriptures" in 1875 and founded the First Church now known as the "Mother Church" in Boston in 1879. After a time the sect grew rapidly, and while its exact numbers are not known it claims in 1907,

the last date for which figures are given, 85,096 in the United States with members in many other countries. They are confined to the cities and are most numerous in the large cities in the northern part of the United States and in England. They come almost exclusively from the comfortable middle classes. Great numbers have been neurotics and believe themselves to have been healed of some disease.

Mrs. Eddy was a prolific writer, as well as lecturer, teacher and healer. She amassed a fortune in a comparatively short time through the enormous charges made for all her services to suffering humanity. Her early life was a fight with disease, her temper remained uncertain, her will imperious, her personality and life unattractive. Her education was meager and her writings are full of crudities, crass contradictions, and statements which to others than Christian Scientists are blasphemies. At times she talks as if she regarded herself as the third person in the Trinity. She claimed to have received the principles of Christian Science by direct revelation from God, saying of " Science and Health " that God was its author while she was " only a scribe, echoing the harmonies of heaven in divine metaphysics."

The central tenet of the system is the " Allness of God," the unreality and nothingness of matter, evil, sin and suffering. All is God and God is good, therefore all is good. Evil and suffering are the figments of mortal mind and have no existence outside man's mind. All causes are mental, " every effect a mental phenomenon." As Mrs. Eddy never seemed settled as to her convictions concerning her own position in the divine order, so she never seemed certain as to what position she ought to ascribe to Jesus Christ. Often she employs with regard to him the language of orthodox Christianity; again she denies to him all significance beyond that of a teacher; sometimes she distinguishes between Jesus and the Christ after the fashion of the Gnostics of early Christian history.

The system is essentially pantheistic, though this is denied by its devotees. It may be regarded as crude philosophy, a system of mental therapeutics or a new religion. It claims to be based on the Bible, but all rational interpretation is made impossible by her "Key to the Scriptures," which may lock but never opens the Scriptures. The system destroys the Christian conception of God, the historical character and atoning work of Jesus Christ, makes all Christian history and thought a lie, obscures the distinction between good and evil thereby weakening the ethical sense, renders all efforts for the relief of human want and suffering absurd, denies the resurrection of the dead and clouds belief in personal immortality. Some of its writings seem to have originated in the bedlam of a mad house. And yet it has power. Why?

Mainly because of its resolute assertion of the spirituality of the universe against the materialism of the age in which we live; its invincible optimism in the midst of the pessimism which has afflicted the world for half a century; its healing power in certain classes of functional diseases, which is perhaps its greatest attraction as shown by the testimony of its members; its elimination of all ecclesiasticism, laying all responsibility for its propagation on laymen and women; the democratic nature of its public services; and finally the strange personality of Mrs. Eddy who dominated people as if they were hypnotized.

The "Mother Church" at Boston is the controlling body, but the branch churches and societies have their own individual government. There are no pastors in the ordinary sense of the term, no ordinations, no ordinances. There are "readers," men and women, who must be approved by the "Mother Church" and are elected for three years. These use lessons that are prepared and sent out from Boston. For the general propaganda "lecturers" are employed and sent out from Boston to every church at least once a year. Much use is made of tracts and other publications. All together it is one of the strangest phenomena that has appeared in Christian history, the only religion founded by a woman.

4. *The Salvation Army* was founded by William Booth, an English preacher of the Methodist New Connection. In prosecuting his evangelistic work he formed plans and adopted methods that were too unconventional and radical to be acceptable to his church. Accordingly in 1865 he began independent open air preaching in the worst section of east London. Four years later his work was enlarged and extended and given the name of the Christian Mission. In 1878 he reorganized it on a military basis and gave the new organization the name of " Salvation Army."

Its organization and nomenclature are thoroughly military. Booth was the general until his death in 1912 when he was succeeded by his son Bramwell. " International Headquarters " are located in London; the Army is divided into " Territories " under " commissioners," these into " Provinces," these again into " Divisions " and finally these into local stations called " Corps." In this vast organization all the various grades of officers of an ordinary army are found. The organization has a uniform, a flag, and in general the paraphernalia of an army, and is equally as autocratic in government.

Men and women have exactly the same opportunities and responsibilities, the only distinction being based on ability, piety and faithfulness. In doctrine it is thoroughly orthodox and evangelistic. Its preaching is simple, direct and brief, an effort to impress upon the hearers the fact and the ruin of sin, the possibility of immediate and triumphant salvation through Jesus Christ, the urgency of the call. Much of the preaching consists of testimonies to the power of God as experienced in the life of the individual. The purpose of the organization is to reach the religiously, morally and materially destitute which the churches do not and apparently cannot reach. It is confined to the cities, and is now doing work in nearly all the countries of the world.

Its work is of two kinds — religious and relief. It is not a church, has no ordinances or ordination. Its converts are not counted as members except as they become " soldiers," that is " workers," in the cause. Many of its converts unite with the churches. It obeys the Master's command to " go " by preaching on the streets where there are teeming multitudes that never enter the churches, and in rented halls, theaters and other buildings as they can be gotten, in those sections of the city that are deserted by the churches.

Their relief work has attained enormous proportions and a great variety of forms, such as industrial homes for men and women, maternity homes, cheap hotels, rescue homes for fallen women and drunkards, employment agencies, Christmas dinners for the poor, day nurseries for the children of working mothers, and others too numerous to mention.

In its methods the Salvation Army discards all the usual conventions which surround religious efforts and resorts to every possible means of attracting and holding attention — brass bands, drums, popular songs, flags, etc. For this and other reasons even the church people at first looked askance or even opposed it, but long since it has conquered its enemies and is now generally recognized as one of the most beneficent institutions of our day.

5. Other bodies which can only be named are Adventists (six bodies), with 106,347 communicants; Brethren Dunkards, (4 bodies), 123,844; Eastern Orthodox (7 bodies), 467,500; Christians, 113,887; Churches of God (Winebrennarian), 28,650; Evangelical (2 bodies), 205,255; Friends (Quakers, 4 bodies), 120,712; German Evangelical Protestant, 34,704; German Evangelical Synod, 264,097; Scandinavian Evangelical (3 bodies), 72,900; Mennonites (12 bodies), 61,331; Pentecostal (2 bodies), 33,409; Reformed (4 bodies), 502,602; Spiritualists, 200,000; Unitarians, 70,-542; United Brethren (2 bodies), 360,387; Universalists, 55,000; Independent Congregations 48,673. In addition to

these, each of which counts more than twenty-five thousand communicants, there are many smaller bodies numbering less than this. All together the statistics of the last Year Book of the Federal Council gives the number of Christian communicants as 38,380,670.

There are more than two and a half million Jews in the United States of whom nearly half live in New York City. Moreover they exercise an influence on our social, economic and political life out of all proportion to their numbers.

§ 149

SOME OTHER ORGANIZATIONS

1. *The Young Men's Christian Association* was organized in London in 1844 by George Williams among dry goods clerks. It was intended to care for the moral, religious and social welfare of young men who are without homes in the city. This original purpose has been enlarged as the organization has spread and developed until its scope now includes the general welfare of young men of every class everywhere. It provides for clean and healthy bodies by facilities for exercise and bathing under competent supervision, and at places for cheap rooms under the most sanitary and morally sound conditions; it also seeks to elevate the social and amusement life of young men, believing that these are matters of the highest importance.

It provides a common meeting place for evangelical Christian forces, assists in evangelistic efforts and occasionally attempts campaigns of its own, seeks to train young men for more effective work in all lines of Christian endeavor. It has afforded a great opportunity for the layman who wished to give himself to Christian service. It now has many distinct departments such as boys' work, railroad work, student work, army and navy work, Negro work, county work, etc. It has become an educational institution of considerable importance, not only along religious lines but in many other directions. All the leading countries of the world now have organizations which have become one of the chief means of recommending the practical truths and ideals of Christianity to public attention. In 1914 there were in all the world 8,906 associations with more than a million members, more than five thousand officers and 1,608 buildings valued at $90,385,728. The local associations, whose active members must be members of evangelical churches and whose associate members must be young men of good moral character, are entirely independent and autonomous, owning their property, electing their officers and managing all their affairs. The International Committee with headquarters at New York provides literature, text-books, etc., whose use, however, is not obligatory. There is also a World's Conference with a Central International Committee at Geneva, Switzerland. Catholics have a somewhat similar organization under strict ecclesiastical control called Young Men's Institutes.

The Young Women's Christian Association also originated in England when two separate organizations were formed in 1855 for the benefit of homeless young women. These organizations were later united to form the Young Women's Christian Association. In organization, aims and methods it is closely conformed to the men's organization. Moreover its history has been very similar. Its work has now spread over the world and is growing rapidly in all its departments.

2. *Young People's Societies* in the churches are a marked feature of present day Christian life especially in America. They arose as the result of a feeling that the young people of a church should be trained in the doctrines and practices of the body with which they are to render their Christian service. Most of them are strictly denominational under church or denominational control. They seek to train their members in the knowledge of the Bible, Christian history, missions, social service and practical efficiency. The most notable of these organizations are the following: " Young

People's Society of Christian Endeavor," founded in 1881 by Francis E. Clark, a young Congregational pastor at Portland, Me.; it is interdenominational and a model for all similar societies: "Epworth League," formed at Cleveland, O., in 1885, by the union of a number of preëxisting Methodist societies and is exclusively Methodist: "Baptist Young People's Union of America," organized at Chicago in 1891; it now has a special southern section and is exclusively Baptist: "Luther League of America," organized at Pittsburg in 1895, is exclusively Lutheran; and several others of less importance in other denominations.

3. The Federal Council of the Churches of Christ in America, organized in 1908 at Philadelphia, is the outcome of several earlier efforts at the creation of some body which would serve as an agency for common council and other common interests of evangelical Christians in America. As organized it is the coöperation of the various denominations for service rather than an attempt at union or definitions on theology, polity or worship. It has no authority over its constituent bodies, its function being limited to the expression of advice and council as to courses of action, promoting "the spirit of fellowship, service and coöperation."

The Council meets every four years, being represented between meetings by an Executive Committee with headquarters in New York. Thirty of the denominations and churches of the country are now represented. Its work is accomplished through Commissions which consider such subjects as Foreign Missions, Home Missions, Christian Education, Social Service, etc. It also publishes annually a Year Book setting forth the most important facts concerning all the Christian bodies of the United States. The organization is hardly old enough to have demonstrated its usefulness.

§ 150

THE WORLD'S RELIGIOUS FORCES TO-DAY

It is probable that the world was never more profoundly interested in religion than at present, nor ever recognized more clearly the value of religion for the life of man in this world not to speak of the next. It is of interest, therefore, to set out according to the best available statistics and estimates the religious complexion of the world in 1915. The figures are for population not communicants since for many of the religions there is nothing corresponding in the least to Christian church membership. As given by Whittaker's Almanac, London, the race is divided as follows:

Christians	564,510,000
Confucianists and Taoists	300,830,000
Mohammedans	221,825,000
Hindus	210,540,000
Animists (Pagans)	158,270,000
Buddhists	138,031,000
Shintoists	25,000,000
Jews	13,052,846
Unclassified	15,280,000

According to these figures the so-called Christian population constitutes nearly one-third of the human race, more than any other two religions. Only Christians are vigorously missionary. The pure pagans have now dwindled to a comparatively small part of the race consisting of the native populations of Africa, Australia, South America and some of the islands of the Pacific.

The three great groups of Christians are given as follows: Roman Catholics, 272,860,000; Eastern Orthodox, 120,000,000; Protestants, 171,650,000.

QUESTIONS AND SUGGESTIONS FOR FURTHER STUDY

INTRODUCTION

§ 1

Questions: What is the history of Christianity? What is meant by its external history? Its internal history? To what Old Testament figures may it be compared? What power has Christianity to-day?

Topics for further Study: Age of the human race at the birth of Christianity. Relation of Christian history to other forms of history. Are there any breaks in Christian history? Forces that have made Christianity victorious. Forces that have caused the variations in its history.

§ 2

Questions: What civilizations had risen and decayed before the birth of Christianity? What were the two great civilized peoples of the Mediterranean? What was the dominant political power? What was the condition of the peoples living around the empire? Tell of the condition and character of the Romans. The Greeks. The Jews. What was the Jewish expectation about the Messiah?

Topics: What is meant by civilization? The effect of civilization on religion. The effect of Roman domination on subject peoples. Differences between Roman and Greek civilizations and religions. Character of the Jews who lived among the heathen.

§ 3

Questions: What of poverty and wealth? Character and importance of slaves? Greek, Latin and Jewish literature and writers? Culture of the masses? Books and schools? Character of the Jewish education?

Topics: Number and character of slaves in Roman empire. Effect of slavery on the moral and economic conditions. Causes of the decline of literary production. The exhaustion of the Greek genius.

§ 4

Questions: What were the moral conditions within the Roman empire? Causes of these conditions? Character and effects of Roman amusements? What was the current view as to the number and character of the gods? Of immorality? Were the various peoples generally religious? How did they worship? Religious instruction and sacred books?

Topics: Origin of religion. Significance of the universality of religion. Relation between morals and religion. Effects of idolatry on morals. Comparative effects of polytheism and monotheism on morals and life.

§ 5

Questions: What people produced the leading philosophy of the ancient world? What was its relation to the religion of the masses? Of the cultured? Who was the most spiritual of the philosophers? What did philosophy strive to do? What was its relation to Christianity?

Topics: Relation of Philosophy to Religion. Relation of Philosophy to practical life. Why was the Greek the philosopher of the ancient world? Why did philosophy decay?

PLANTING CHRISTIANITY

§ 6

Questions: What great change took place in the Roman government? How did this affect the people? Character of the emperors in the first century? Fortunes of the Jews in this century? Did conditions help or hinder the spread of Christianity?

Topics: Relation of government to the religion and morals of the people. Forces that operated to transform the Roman republic into a monarchy. Jewish political helplessness in all ages. Relation of the city of Jerusalem to Jewish national life.

§ 7

Questions: Sketch the life of Jesus to the beginning of his public ministry. Give a sketch of John's life. Give the contents of John's teachings and show the relation of these to common Jewish beliefs. How did Jesus ally himself with John and his teachings? Give a summary of Jesus' teachings and works. Causes of opposition to him? Evidences of his resurrection? The extent of his own ministry and the reasons for its limitations? His final command to his disciples?

Topics: Relation of Jesus to the working people. Relation of Jesus to Jewish social and religious life and beliefs. How far did Jesus fulfill Jewish expectations concerning the Messiah? How far were Jewish expectations a perversion of Old Testament teachings? How far did John's views agree and how far disagree with current Jewish expectations?

§ 8

Questions: What is Christianity as a historic force? How much is new and how much is inherited from Judaism? What are the distinctive elements of the Christian type of life? What is the distinctive Christian faith? What is the distinctive Christian hope? How far are these peculiarities found among others than Christians?

Topics: Consider how much of the content of Christianity is found in the hearts of mankind and how much is a direct revelation through Jesus and others. Do missionaries have to create religion in a heathen land? If not, what is the relation of Christianity to existing religions?

§ 9

Questions: How far did Jesus spread the gospel by his own preaching? What did Pentecost do for the spread of the gospel? When and why did persecution break out? What effect did it have on the spread of the gospel? Show the steps by which the Christian missionaries began to preach among the Gentiles. Why did the Christians hesitate to preach to the heathen?

Topics: Religious prejudice. The benefits that had come to the world through Jewish exclusiveness. Points of

superiority in the Jewish religion and life over those of the
Gentiles. Sources of this superiority. Significance of Pentecost for the history of Christianity.

§ 10

Questions: Give an account of the early life of Paul.
Of his conversion. Of his entrance upon Christian work.
Trace on the map the journeys of Paul in the pursuit of his
missionary labors. What was the substance of his preaching to Jews? To Gentiles? What do we know about the
later work of the Twelve? How far had Christianity
spread by end of the first century?

Topics: How to explain a great man like Paul. Elements of greatness in Paul. Paul's adaptability to various
conditions, races and occasions. Paul's chief contributions
to the history of Christianity.

§ 11

Questions: How early did the Christians begin to organize? What was the basis of their organization? In
what sense were the churches democracies? What were the
qualifications for membership? Size of the churches?
What were the officers of the churches? Their duties?
What were apostles, prophets and evangelists? Describe
Christian worship. Meaning of baptism and the Lord's
supper?

Topics: Relation of organization to the success of any
movement like Christianity. Points of strength and of
weakness in a democracy. Difficulties in obtaining satisfactory officials in the early churches. Financial support
of the early churches. Purpose of worship. Relative value
of free and of liturgical worship. Relation of the ordinances to the spiritual content of Christianity.

§ 12

Questions: What was the first great danger that Christianity encountered? How did the Jewish Christians believe
that the Gentiles could be saved? How did the work of
Paul and Barnabas raise the question in acute form? What
was the practice of these missionaries? Why did they
carry the question up to Jerusalem? What was the decision

of this first Christian council? How important was the
question involved? Was the decision of the council accepted and acted upon? What other dangerous forms of
error existed in these early days of Christianity? What was
the general content of faith which most Christians accepted?

Topics: Relation between the inner spiritual contents of
Christianity and the outward expressions of that faith. The
effect of ceremonialism on spirituality. The motives of the
Judaizers. Paul's emancipation from current Jewish no-
tions. Various sources of error in Christian doctrine.

§ 13

Questions: How did the moral life of the early churches
compare with the moral life of the churches of to-day?
By what sins were the early churches afflicted? How did
the churches deal with these sins? How well did the Christians bear up under persecution? How did the Christians
relate themselves to heathen society? Was there any of the
asceticism or monasticism which characterized so much of
later Christianity?

From what stratum of society did the early Christians
chiefly come? From what races? What languages were
used in missionary work?

Topics: The moral tonic of Christianity. The degree
in which Christianity has been successful in fighting and
eradicating the evils of society. Points in which there have
been marked improvements. Less improvement. Causes
of asceticism.

Reasons why one class of society accepts Christianity
more readily than another. Same as to race. Is it easier
for a poor man to be a Christian than for a rich man? A
Gentile than a Jew? An ignorant than a learned man?

SECOND PERIOD 100–323

§ 14

Questions: Were conditions favorable for Christian
progress in this period? What were Rome's chief external
enemies? Where did she extend her territory? From
what internal disorders did she suffer in the third century?
What of her material prosperity? When was citizenship

extended to all free men? What signs of decay can we observe? What was the relation of Christianity to the empire during this period?

Topics: Causes of national decay. Causes of the decay of Rome. Relation of war and conquest to national decay. Relation of poverty and wealth to national strength and national decay. Did the imperial government help or hinder Christianity in this period?

§ 15

Questions: How widely was education diffused? What sort of education was it? Was it helpful or hurtful to life of the people? What of the old idolatrous Roman religion? What was emperor worship? Its origin and significance? What new religions were coming in from the East? How did they compare with the old Roman religion? What was the general attitude toward new religions? Was this feeling hurtful or helpful to the spread of Christianity?

Topics: Causes of skepticism. Cures of skepticism. Relation of education to moral and religious welfare. Why one religion is preferred above another. Why Christianity is always ultimately accepted when fairly presented.

§ 16

Questions: What success did Christian missions have in this period? What advantages enjoyed by modern missions, were wanting in this period? What do we know about the details of missionary work? What nationalities were active in this period? What new versions of the Scriptures were made? What notable men were converted? Tell of the conversion of Constantine. What great benefit did he confer on the Christians?

Topics: Explain the rapid progress of Christianity in this period. Elements in it which appealed to that world. Effects of the Latin translation of the Bible. Effects of governmental favor on the history of Christianity and its character. Visions and their reality.

§ 17

Questions: State the main causes of the persecution of the Christians. Number of Christians who perished?

What is meant by sporadic persecution? How many general persecutions? When? Kinds of punishments? Literary attacks on Christianity? Arguments against Christianity? Work of Celsus. How did the Christians defend themselves? When and how did they finally obtain peace?

Topics: The moral element in the opposition to Christianity. Effects of persecution upon Christianity, good and bad. Elements in Christianity that made it able to resist all the might of the Roman empire. Behavior of the Christians under persecution. The continuity of opposition to Christianity through the ages. Why?

§ 18

Questions: What is meant by saying that Christianity had been changing as it spread? How had the conception of the church changed as to membership, government, function, unity, infallibility?

Topics: Causes of the changes in the inner life of Christianity. Preëxisting religious and social beliefs, practices and institutions as factors in the changes. Unholy ambitions of men as factors.

§ 19

Questions: What officials of early Christianity disappear in this period? Show how the two officers of the local church change into three. Trace the steps by which the bishop of one church grows into the bishop of a diocese. How archbishops or metropolitans develop. How Patriarchs. Show how the laity lost influence and the bishops grew in importance. What functions did the bishops come to perform? What lower officers were developed?

Topics: Influence of civil government on church government. Forces that tended to centralize the government of the church under the bishop and eliminate the layman. Essentials of democratic government.

§ 20

Questions: What is meant by sacraments? When was something else accepted in place of immersion for baptism? What preparation was made for baptism? What ceremonies immediately preceded and followed baptism? What significance was now attached to baptism? Who administered baptism? When and why did infant baptism originate? Who administered the Lord's supper? Who partook of the supper? What later Catholic ideas are already growing up in connection with the supper?

Topics: Forces that gradually transformed the ordinances of baptism and the supper. What it is in human nature that leads people to rely on external ceremonies for salvation. The relation between ceremonies and the spiritual life. Reasons that moved Jesus to approve these ceremonies when he must have known how they would be abused.

§ 21

Questions: What is meant by liturgical worship? Causes that led to its development? Time of worship? Character of worship? What annual festivals were developed? With what meaning? Places of worship? Arrangement of the house? Contents of the worship? Preaching and instruction? Origin of the term " mass "?

Topics: Advantages and disadvantages in annual religious festivals. Relation between religious instruction and religious efficiency. Preaching as a factor in Christian civilization. Relation between church buildings and church efficiency.

§ 22

Questions: What was the general tendency of Christian life in this period? How did the church discipline its members? What forms of evil did it attack in this period? And with what success? When and why did monasticism arise? Who was the first prominent representative of the monastic life? In what country? Who produced the first rule and when? How did Christians begin to regard the married and unmarried states? What was the general attitude of Christians toward public life in the army? The state? How did Christians dispose of their dead? What were the catacombs? What did Christians do for schools and education?

Topics: Value of church discipline as a moral agency. Value of asceticism as a protest against worldliness. The monastic ideal of life. Moral effects of the emphasis on the celibate life. Relation of the Christian man to public life.

§ 23

Questions: Show how our New Testament books were produced, selected from among others and gathered into a canon. What does " canon " mean? How did the so-called Apostles' Creed originate? Give its contents. What did most Christians believe about Christ.

Topics: Christianity as a literary force. Superiority of the New Testament writings over other Christian writings of the same period. Tests for determining the canonical character of a writing. Value of creeds. Dangers of creeds. The intellectual necessity for systematized Christian doctrine. The relative strength of Unitarianism and Trinitarianism in Christian history.

§ 24

Questions: What were some of the causes of schisms? Why were the great body of Christians called Catholics? Why were they drifting away from the apostolic moorings? Give the origin, teachings and history of the Montanists. The Novatians. The Donatists. What did these schisms have in common? Give an account of Gnosticism. Of Manichæism. What did they have in common? How serious were these various schisms and heresies? What was the tendency in heathen literature? In Christian literature? What forms did Christian literature take?

Topics: Causes of Christian divisions. The psychology of sectarianism. The psychology of Catholicism. Advantages and disadvantages of Christian unity and uniformity. Relation of Christian to non-Christian thought. Relation of knowledge and faith. Causes of the decline of heathen and rise of Christian literature. Relation of " polite " to distinctively religious literature.

THIRD PERIOD 323 TO 600

§ 25

Questions: What great European upheaval in this period? What was the character and condition of the Germans at this time? Why were they able to break into the empire at this time? How was the Roman government divided after the death of Constantine? Where was the new capital? Effect of the German invasion on the empire? What sort of governments did the Germans set up? How did the subject peoples conquer their conquerors? What were the immediate and what the more remote effects of the German invasion?

Topics: Motives actuating the Germans in their attack on the Roman empire. Causes of the increasing weakness of the empire. Comparative advantages and disadvantages of consolidated imperial and smaller national governments. Did the German invasion destroy or save Europe?

§ 26

Questions: Success of missions in this period? What was the attitude of the Roman government toward Christianity after Constantine? Efforts of Julian? When was Christianity made the established religion of the empire? What was then done with the old heathenism? When did the heathen culture come to an end? How thorough was the work of Christianizing in this period? Was governmental favor an advantage? What was the religious condition of the Germans when they poured into the empire? To what two forms of Christianity were they converted? Which form finally triumphed among them?

Topics: Tell of the conversion of Ireland. Of Scotland. Show how far Christianity spread eastward in this period. Tell of the work of Ulfilas among the Visigoths. Political and social ferment as a Christian opportunity. The effect of powerful patronage on the progress and purity of Christianity. Effect of the union between church and state on Christianity. On the State. Character of "mass conversions." Effects of the German invasion and the fall of the Roman empire on the history of Christianity. Character of the Christianity of Ireland and Scotland. Character of the Christianity that went eastward into Armenia, Persia, etc. Character of early German Christianity. Effects of national character on Christian types.

§ 27

Questions: What was the general tendency in the development of church government in this period? Growing

power of the clergy? Church courts and law, their origin
and jurisdiction? Church property? Relation of the State
to the appointment of church officials? Trace the rise of
the bishop of Rome into a world power. Origin and various grades of councils? Importance of Ecumenical councils? Dates and work of two very important councils.

Topics: Increase of ecclesiastical organization as related to increase of Christian service. Forces operative for
the elimination of the laity and the elevation of the clergy.
Social conditions operating for the creation of church courts
and church law. Historical, political and social conditions
that worked for the elevation of the bishop of Rome. Religious and cultural effects of the church's claim of infallibility.

§ 28

Questions: Interest of the world in theology in this
period? Character of the theological controversy of the
period? What part did the government play in these controversies? What was the question involved in the Arian
controversy? How serious was the controversy? What
was the decision of the Council of Nicea? How far has
that decision held the assent of the Christian world to the
present?

Topics: Relation of the Greek mind to theological spec-
ulation and controversy. Moral effects of making orthodoxy the supreme test of Christianity. Theology as a divisive force in the Christian body. Causes of the comparative
ineffectiveness of Unitarianism in Christian history.

§ 29

Questions: General tendencies in the development of
the doctrines of baptism and the supper? What as to the
form or mode of baptism? Infant baptism? Effects of
baptism? Administrator of baptism? Postponement of
Baptism? Views as to Christ's presence in the supper?
The mass as a sacrifice?

Topics: Absorption of heathen ideas in connection with
baptism and the supper. Effects of these changes upon the
religious and moral life. Baptism and the supper as means
for preserving the purity of Christian doctrine and life.

§ 30

Questions: The preaching of this period compared with that of earlier periods? Extent of Christian instruction preceding baptism? Christian culture and schools? Church building in this period? Help of princes and the wealthy in this work? Character of worship in the great churches by the end of this period? What were the three cycles of the Christian year? What was the purpose of these festivals?

Topics: The character of preaching as related to the general culture of the age. The effect of culture on the character of Christian worship. Church buildings as related to wealth and culture. Relative value of simplicity and ornateness in worship. Origin and effects of a special clerical dress. Origin and effects of lights, censers and pictures in worship.

§ 31

Questions: Considerations moving Christians to retire into monastic life? Magnitude of the movement? Necessity for organization? Where, when and by whom was the first order organized? What services did the monks and nuns render? What were some of the effects good and bad of monasticism? What effect was Christianity having upon public life? What evils of the ancient world were being abolished?

Topics: The appeal of the monastic life to the men and the women of the Middle Ages. The effects of the monastic movement upon the religious, moral and cultural life of the Middle Ages. Effects of different types of Christianity on the private and the public life of the people.

FOURTH PERIOD 600–1050

§ 32

Questions: What was the general tendency in the earlier part of this period? When did the light begin to break? Why is the period called the "Dark Ages"?

Give the main facts of Mohammed's life. Sources of his doctrines? Year from which the Mohammedans

date their era? What world conditions favored the spread
of the new religion? What motives actuated the Mohammedans in their conquests? Trace the course of their
expansion in the West and the East. The effects of
their conquests upon Christianity? What are the principal beliefs of the Mohammedans? How do they worship? What is the origin and character of their bible?
Some of their social ideas and practices? General effects
of their fatalistic views? Effects on the heathen whom
they conquered?

Topics: Relation of the fall of the Roman empire to the
" Dark Ages." Relation of the German invasion to the
same.

Origin of religion. Origins of religions. Character and
history of Mohammed. Religion as an element in racial
unity and efficiency. Elements of power in Mohammedanism. Religion as a hindrance to progress. Force as a
means of spreading a religion.

§ 33

Questions: Effect of Mohammedanism on the missionary activities of the Christians who were subjected to Mohammedan rule? Name the leading groups of Slavs.
Where did they settle? When and by whom were they first
evangelized? What type of Christianity did they receive?
How did they receive Christianity? Are they religious or
indifferent?

Topics: The paralyzing effects of Mohammedanism on
all moral and philanthropic activities. The character and
history of the Slavs. The type of Christianity which they
received. Relation between the Greek Catholic religion and
the history of the Slavs.

§ 34

Questions: What became of the Christianity of North
Africa? Effect of the Mohammedans on Christianity in
Italy and Spain? What had been the effect of the German
invasion on the Christianity of Britain? When and how
did the Christianizing of these Germans in Britain begin?
Give an account of the work of the missionaries from Rome.

Of the Scotch. When and where did the Anglo-Saxons decide to accept the Roman type? What changes did those of the Scotch type have to make? How soon did the remainder of the British Isles accept the Roman type? When were they thoroughly Romanized? Give an account of Scotch missions on the continent. What of the missionary zeal and energy of the Anglo-Saxons? Give an account of the Christianizing of the Dutch (Frisians). Give an account of the work of Boniface the " Apostle of Germany." The efforts of Charlemagne in the interest of Christian missions? Christianizing the Scandinavian countries? Work of the English in that direction?

Topics: Missionary energy as related to national character. Missionary energy of the Roman and the Greek Catholic churches compared. The failure of the Scotch type of Christianity in competition with the Roman. Advantages and disadvantages accruing to the British Isles by the adoption of the Roman type. The Catholic church as the bearer of culture as well as religion to the Germanic peoples.

§ 35

Questions: What differences led to estrangement between the East and the West? What religious differences developed in the course of time? What ecclesiastical rivalries accentuated these differences? When did strained relations begin to develop? When did the final break come and how? What efforts at reconciliation have been made?

Topics: Effects of the Greek and Latin languages on the history of Christianity. Striking mental and spiritual differences between the Greeks and the Latins. How far the Slavs have modified the Greek Catholic church. Racial differences as a factor in Christian history. Forces that work to perpetuate religious schisms when they once occur. Forces that tend to bring about reunion.

§ 36

Questions: Attitude of early Christianity toward worship of images? When and how did they get into Christian worship? Who opposed them? Who supported them? How do you explain this? Effort of Leo III to eliminate them?

When and how were they restored? What distinction was made by the Council in 787? On what grounds do the Catholics deny that they are idolators? What difference between the usage of the Greek and the Roman Catholic churches? The second attempt to remove them and its failure? What was the attitude of the pope and the Western church? What great change in the political allegiance of the pope was brought about by the controversy? What was the attitude of Charlemagne? What were the total results of the controversy?

Topics: The psychology of image worship. Its power in the history of Christianity. Is there any legitimate use of pictures or statues in Christian worship? When and wherein are they objectionable? Difficulties in attaining a purely spiritual worship entirely devoid of symbolism.

§ 37

Questions: How did the pope come to be a land owner? How was ownership gradually transformed into political control? How did the Frankish kings assist in the establishment of the papal states? How long did these papal states stand? What brought them to an end?

Topics: Historic consequences of the alliance of the popes and the Frankish kings. Effects of temporal rule upon the fortunes of the pope. Effects on the history of Italy. On the German empire. Effects on the spiritual influence of the pope.

§ 38

Questions: End of the western part of the empire? Eastern part? Which German tribe reunited the fragments in the West? Work of Charlemagne as King? Made emperor? Two empires? Importance of Charlemagne's act? Decay of imperial power? Restored by whom? Emperors and popes? Effect of imperial dominance?

Topics: Persistence of the imperial idea. Its effects on the world. Effectiveness of the empire as a form of government. Influence of the German empire upon the papacy.

§ 39

Questions: What five events or movements contributed

to the rise of the Pope in this period? What was the " Donation of Constantine"? What effect did it have on the fortunes of the papacy? What was the papal ambition from
this time onward? How did missions extend the Pope's
power? What peculiar dignity and power was conferred
on the bishops in Germany? What did this lead the State
to do?

Topics: Contents of the Pseudo-Isidorian decretals and
the Donation of Constantine. The Pope's use of these documents through the centuries.

§ 40

Questions: Spread of monasticism into mission fields?
Relation of the monks and nuns to the mission work? Service to schools? To education and literature? Power of
monasticism in the Catholic church from this time on.

General tendencies in Christian life? Causes of decline
in morals? Character of the higher clergy? Lower clergy?
Effects of the use of Latin in the church services as this
language died? Translation of the Scriptures into the living languages of Europe? Process of endowing the
churches? What was the tithe? What is private confession? When was the organ introduced into the services in
the West? How did the *indulgence* originate?

Topics: Service of monasticism in the conservation of
culture. Peculiarities of the monastic mind. Service of
the monks in building a Christian civilization for the Germanic peoples.

Absorptions from Germanic heathenism found in the
Catholic church. Effect of political activities on the character and efficiency of the clergy. The retention of Latin
in worship as Christianity spread into non-Latin lands.
Decline in the use of the Bible and the relation of this fact
to the moral and religious decline. Motives appealed to
by the church to secure gifts. The psychology of confession. Of private confession.

§ 41

Questions: How far did all Christianity become Catholic? What non-Catholic Christianity continues in the East?
Give an account of the history and doctrines of the Pauli-

cians. Of the Bogomiles. How did the Catholic church treat these parties?

Topics: Sources of the anti-Catholic parties. Importance of the differences.

FIFTH PERIOD 1050 TO 1305

§ 42

Questions: Where did the Turks originate? What sort of people were they? When did they accept Mohammedanism? Their conquest of Persia? Their attack on the Christian empire and the Mohammedan Arabs? Extent of their conquests in this period? When was Jerusalem captured by them?

What are the Crusades? What caused them? From what part of Europe did the crusaders go? What did the first Crusade accomplish? What form of Christianity did it set up in the East? How long did the Crusades last? What effect did the Crusades have on the Turkish invasion of Western Asia? What effect did they have on Constantinople? What was the condition of the eastern empire and the Turkish empire at the close of the period?

Topics: Interior Asia as the cradle of nations and the source of religions. Character and ability of the Turks. Mohammedan Turks compared with Mohammedan Arabs. The Turks as the scourge of Western Asia.

Complex of motives that actuated the Crusaders. Religion as a cause of wars. The psychology of pilgrimages. Veneration for holy places. General effects of the Crusades on the fortunes of Christianity and Mohammedanism in the East.

§ 43

Questions: General tendencies in the West? Moorish culture in Spain? Revival along the northern shores of the Mediterranean? Inroads of the Northmen on their southern neighbors? Immediate and ultimate effects of these invasions? Normans in France? Union of England and France by William the Conqueror? Normans in the Mediterranean and Italy?

Topics: Motives actuating the movements of the North-men. Forces that are making for improvement in the West in this period.

§ 44

Questions: Successful mission work of this period? Type of Christianity received by Northern and Western Europe? A religious revival in the West? Church schools and their work? Origin of the oldest European universities? Literature produced in the West? Distinctive Catholic doctrines worked out?

Topics: Causes of the great intellectual and religious revival. Relation between intellectual vigor and religious earnestness and activity. Character of scholasticism. Its permanent value. Its failure and the causes. Relation between Catholic doctrines and the Mediæval mind. Catholic doctrines and the modern mind.

§ 45

Question: When did the papacy reach the zenith of its power? Work of Hildebrand? Changes in papal elections in this period? What other factors contributed to the rise and power of the papacy?

Topics: The papacy as a political power in the Middle Ages. Relation of clerical celibacy to papal control of the church. Was the papacy a beneficent power in the Middle Ages?

§ 46

Questions: How did the church and the state come into conflict? Why did the state wish to appoint ecclesiastical officials? How had the state abused this power? What did the princes do? Three notable victories of the Pope over princes? What was the papal theory as to the relation between church and state? What was the effect of the long struggle on the two powers? Which seemed to have the better of the fight at the end of the period?

Topics: Causes of conflict between church and state. Causes peculiar to the Catholic church. Relation of church property to the conflict. Should the state limit the amount of property to be held by the church? Has the state any religious duties? Has the church any political duties?

§ 47

Questions: What was the older monastic ideal? What was the newer ideal? Why were they called friars? Why mendicants? Give an account of Francis and his order. Of Dominic and his order. What position did they attain in the Catholic church? What was their influence on the church's life? How were they organized? How did they differ from each other?

Topics: The spirit of service breaking through monastic limitations. The mendicant orders as missionary agencies in subsequent Catholic history. Revival of preaching in these orders. The neglect of preaching in the Middle Ages. Why does the Catholic church in general lay so little emphasis on preaching?

§ 48

Questions: What were the two great periods of theological formulation to this point in Christian history? How did they differ from each other? Name some of the great theologians and writers of this period. What Catholic doctrines were discussed to a finish in this period?

Topics: Origin of the new intellectual atmosphere and ability of this period. The nations which led in productive scholarship. The subjects with which scholars occupied themselves. Nature and methods of their work. Influence of Aristotle on the intellectual work of this period.

§ 49

Questions: What is the Mass? In what sense is it regarded as a sacrifice? Why is the wafer worshiped? Why was the cup withdrawn from the laity? When and why was infant communion discontinued? What are the bread and the wine supposed to become in the process of consecration? How is the wafer administered? What movements brought about a revival of preaching? What new annual festivals were created in this period? How large a place did annual festivals fill in the life of the church? What of church architecture in this period? Name some of the great cathedrals and tell something of such buildings in general.

Topics: Human nature's demand for sacrifice in religion. Forces that created the sacrifice of the Mass. The faith that accepts the doctrine of transubstantiation. The moral and religious effects of worshiping the wafer. Sacramental salvation inimical to preaching. Building as an act of worship. Time, talent and money expended on church and monastic buildings. The effect of Christian art and architecture on faith and morals of the masses.

§ 50

Questions: When did evangelical sects appear in western Europe? How much did they differ from the Catholic church? How far were they agreed among themselves? What were the principal evangelical parties? Give an account of the Waldenses, their origin, beliefs and later history.

Topics: Renewed circulation of the Bible as related to the evangelical revival. Moral and religious effects of Bible reading as seen in history.

§ 51

Questions: When did Christians begin to persecute heretics? What motives actuated them? Did the church itself ever execute heretics? Did the State always execute the church's sentences? Upon whom rested the duty of apprehending and convicting heretics in the earlier period? How well was it done? What new tribunal was created for this purpose? When was it committed to the Dominicans? Its character? Punishments inflicted? Number who perished? How far was the Catholic church responsible for these deaths?

Topics: The psychology of persecution. The Inquisition as an agency of ecclesiastical and political tyranny. Effects of the Inquisition on the intellectual and moral life of Spain and France. Relation between individual freedom and social progress.

SIXTH PERIOD — 1305 to 1517

§ 52

Questions: Original home of the Mongols? Their condition when they first appeared? Trace their conquest of China. Hindoostan. Trace the history of the branch that entered Russia. Their treatment of the Mohammedans of Persia and Syria? The religion of the various branches of Mongols? Tamerlane's invasion? The end of the western Mongols?

Topics: History of the Mongols. Effects of the Mongol domination on the history of Russia. Successes and failures of the peoples of central Asia. Points of weakness and of strength in these peoples. The character of their native religions.

§ 53

Questions: What completed the dissolution of the first Turkish power? Who began the organization of another Turkish empire? Describe the expansion of this government to the capture of Constantinople. Show the extent of the Turkish empire at the close of this period. Give an account of the treatment of the Christians by the Turks. When and how did the Sultan of Turkey become the *spiritual* head of the Mohammedans?

Topics: Conditions that favored the expansion of Turkey. The character of the Turk as a man, a ruler and a soldier. General effects of Turkish domination on the moral and social welfare of the subject peoples.

§ 54

Questions: What of the existence of Christianity in central Asia in this period? Prester John? What induced the Pope to send missionaries to eastern Asia? What great traveler visited the East? What of the religious conditions found in this region? How were the missionaries received? What success did the missionaries have? What brought their efforts to an end?

Topics: War and conquest as occasions for the spread of Christianity. Marco Polo's travels. Influence of Christianity on Buddhism in southern Asia. Christianity and Buddhism compared.

§ 55

Questions: What missionary expansion in Russia in this period? What beneficent change in the government of the Russian church? What rôle did monasticism play in the Christianizing and civilizing of Russia? How did this monasticism differ from that of the West? Monastic buildings? Union with the Roman Catholic church? Relation of Russian religion and culture to Constantinople? National symbols of that relation?

Topics: Constantinople as an influence over Slav peoples. Relative effectiveness of eastern and western monasticism. The influence of the crown over the life of the Russian people. The sentimental power of Constantinople. Things that have retarded the progress of the Russian people.

§ 56

Questions: Stability of life in the West in this period compared with that of the East? The two great movements of the peoples of this period? Give the history of the struggle between the Mohammedans and Christians in the Spanish peninsula. What Christian kingdoms were formed? How did France and England become involved in the Hundred Years War? The fortunes of the struggle in the earlier years? How was the tide turned against the English? How much of French territory did they hold at the end of the period? How do you explain Joan of Arc?

Topics: Decay of Mohammedan power in Spain. Effects of the long struggle with Mohammedanism on the character of Spanish Christianity. The feudal idea of the relation between the prince and his people. The effect of the Hundred Years War on the subsequent relations of the French and English peoples. Explain the power of Joan of Arc. Psychology as a factor in war.

§ 57

Questions: What of the importance of the nobility in the Middle Ages? What influences now contributed to their downfall? What forces created the cities? What forces contributed to the rise of the kings? How did the cities organize for self-defense. What beginnings of democracy are seen? How did all these changes affect religion?

Topics: Feudalism as a social, political and economic system. Its effects on religion. Forces operating for its ruin. The king as a democratic institution. The influence of social and economic organization on religious life.

§ 58

Questions: How did the popes become subservient to France? What do papal historians call these seventy years? Where was the papal court during this time? What caused the Great Schism? How was it finally closed? What of the character of later popes of this period? What was the general effect of all these things on the power and influence of the papacy?

Topics: Papal power as a world menace. Seeds of decay within the papacy itself. History of the Council of Constance. Growing nationalism as a menace to papal power. The character of the popes as a menace to Christianity. Conflicting ideas as to the relative authority of the Pope and the Council.

§ 59

Questions: What four causes of the decline of missions in the Catholic church? What success had the church in its efforts to win over the Greek church to union? What efforts were made for the conversion of the Mohammedans? Why?

Topics: Contact with the heathen as a missionary motive. Methods of bringing American Christians into contact with missionary needs. Reciprocal effects of home Christianity and mission fields upon each other.

§ 60

Questions: Spread of the Jewish people? Persecution by the Christians? Causes of these persecutions? How were the Jews compelled to live? How did the Jews become the great money lenders of Europe? How far was the religious motive operative? How much mission work was attempted among the Jews? Give an account of the work of Ferrer.

Topics: Comparative failure of mission work among the Jews. Christianity's want of success among the followers of other forms of Monotheism. Jewish race characteristics and Jewish religion as factors in their resistance to Christianity. Racial feeling as a factor.

§ 61

Questions: What is meant by the Renaissance? By Humanism? What was the essence of the new spirit in the world? In how many striking ways did this new individualism manifest itself? What was the new education? What part did the Greek language and literature and the classic Latin language and literature have in the revival? What effect did this education have upon the mind of Europe? How was the Greek revived? What is meant by the critical spirit? Was it helpful or hurtful to Christianity? In what sense were the Middle Ages an "Age of Faith"? What effect did the critical spirit have on the accumulated superstitions of the Catholic church? What part had the Bible played in the life of the Middle Ages? Attitude of the Catholic church toward the circulation of the Bible? Why? When were the two Testaments printed in the original languages? When and where was the Bible again translated into the language of the people? Importance of this service? Who did this work? Introduction of the Bible into the class-rooms of the universities? Great inventions and their effects — Printing? Mariner's compass? Gunpowder? Discovery of America, of a sea-route to India? Circumnavigation of the globe? Effects of these discoveries? When did a vernacular literature begin? Significance of this movement? How did this prepare for the Reformation? Name some of the great authors who wrote in their vernacular. Attitude of this literature toward the church? Development of Christian painting and its service to the Catholic religion? Some of the great Italian painters of the period? Why was all this movement sometimes called Humanism?

Topics: The new spirit abroad in the world after the middle of the fifteenth century. The new education as contrasted with the earlier. Italy as the leader of the great intellectual revival. Relation of intellectual activity and freedom to religious reform. Services and injuries that have flowed from the critical spirit. Causes of Catholic opposition to the circulation of the Bible among the people. Bible circulation as an element in social, moral and intellectual progress. Influence of geographical discoveries on the world's thinking. Relation of printing and a vernacular literature to general progress. Christian art as an expression of Christian faith.

§ 62

Questions: Whence came the demands for reform of the church? Why was England in the lead in making these demands? Give an account of the life of Wycliffe. His doctrines? His efforts at the spreading of his views? Treatment of him and his followers? Origin of the reformatory movement in Bohemia? Who were the leaders? Give an account of Hus' life. Subsequent treatment of his followers. Where else did reformers appear in this period? Tell of the work of Savonarola.

Did the popes help or hinder the new intellectual movement? Did they foster or oppose the movements for religious reform? How do you explain the difference? Condition of the church on the eve of the Reformation?

Topics: Religious, moral, political and intellectual factors in the stimulation of reform. Source of Wycliffe's teachings. History and character of the Bohemians. Condemnation and execution of Hus. Failure of all the reformers of this period. Weakness of Savonarola as a reformer.

How and why the popes helped the Renaissance and hindered the Reformation. Immediate effect of the Renaissance on moral conditions. Permanent effect of the Renaissance on educational methods and cultural materials. The Renaissance and the modern mind.

SEVENTH PERIOD 1517 TO 1648

§ 63

Questions: What of the importance of the Reformation? What were the main divisions of the Christian world at the outbreak of the Reformation. Describe briefly the location and condition of the Greek church. Roman Catholic church. The evangelical sects. The non-Catholic eastern churches.

Topics: Why the Eastern churches were not affected by the Revival of Learning. The number, character and beliefs of the principal evangelical sects at the beginning of the Reformation. The part they were prepared to play in the coming reform.

§ 64

Questions: Which of the great churches was the only one affected by the Reformation? What was the Catholic church as a system of government? What was its plan of salvation? Name the seven sacraments in logical order. What is their relation to the work of salvation? State clearly the Catholic view of the significance of Baptism. Of Confirmation. Of the Eucharist. Of Penance. Of Marriage. Of Ordination. Of Extreme Unction. Doctrine of Good Works. Place and benefits of the Mass in the Catholic system? Character of Catholic worship? Main elements of Catholic theology? Catholic view of the future life? Significance of the confessional? Explain the nature and the use of the *indulgence*. The scandal of its sale. What of the wealth of the church?

Topics: Moral and religious effects of the theory of sacramental salvation. How this theory binds the human soul. Papal government as an essential part of the Catholic system. Infant baptism as a basal factor in the existence and character of the Catholic church. How the sacraments put the church in control of every important crisis in life. How belief in Purgatory helps the church to control the life. The power and the dangers of the confessional. The place of the indulgence in the every day religious life of the Catholics. The wealth of the church as a source of corruption.

§ 65

Questions: What five forms did the Reformation take as it developed differences?

Topics: Causes that developed divisions in the ranks of the reformers. Effects of personal peculiarities of leaders. Effects of national character. Of political and other conditions.

§ 66

Questions: Where and when did the Reformation begin? Give an account of Luther's family and education. His entrance into a monastery? How did he become professor at Wittenberg? Effects of the visit to Rome? Effect of his teaching on himself? Sale of indulgences on the border of Saxony?

Topics: Luther's environment. His education as a factor in his future history. Rome as a factor. Bible study as a factor.

§ 67

Questions: What did Luther propose in his theses? Effect of the theses on Germany? Attitude of the ecclesiastical authorities? Why was his prince able to protect him? How did the Pope seek to suppress him? What did the Emperor do? Luther's courage? Why kept at the Wartburg?

Topics: Political conditions in Germany as affecting the success of the Reformation in that country. Luther's ability as a source of his safety. The new spirit of freedom as a protection to Luther.

§ 68

Questions: When did Luther renounce his monastic vows and marry? When was the reform introduced into Saxony? How was the reform introduced? What was the new relation between church and state? What part did the state play in the movement? How rapidly were the reforms introduced into other German states and how widely? Where did the movement fail?

Topics: Difference in attitude of Catholics and Protestants toward the marriage of the clergy. Difference in attitude toward monasticism. New relation between church and state in Germany and its influence on subsequent history.

§ 69

Questions: What was the first effect of the reform on the life of the people? How do you explain this? What doctrines held by the Catholic church did Luther retain? What was his view of the plan of salvation? What was the relation of Lutheran baptism and ordination to that of the Catholics? His view of the Lord's supper? What distinctive Catholic doctrines did he reject?

Topics: Catholic elements carried over into Lutheranism. Comparative power of the moral appeal in Catholicism and in Lutheranism. Justification by faith as a religious principle. Effects of the abolition of monasticism. Religious and moral effects of the marriage of the clergy. The moral value of the Protestant view of the future life as compared with the Catholic view.

§ 70

Questions: Success of Lutheranism in the Scandinavian countries? Form of government of the church in these lands? Impressions made on the eastern border of Germany? Permanency of the effect in these lands? Impression made on south Germany and the Austrian lands? Impression made in Italy? In Spain? In Portugal?

Topics: Lutheranism as the Teutonic type of Christianity. Reasons for its failure among the Poles and the Bohemians. Reasons for its failure among the Latin peoples. Catholic governments as a hindrance to the progress of reform.

§ 71

Questions: The character of Switzerland and its people? Family and education of Zwingli? How did he reach his reformatory convictions? Where and when did he begin his reformatory work? His principle of reform as compared with Luther's?

What cantons were reformed? What cantons remained Catholic? First "war of religion"? Fate of Zwingli?

Topics: Zwingli's personality compared with Luther's.

History of Switzerland in relation to the German empire and the Catholic church. Biblical nature of Zwingli's views.

Relation between topography and religion. Conservatism of country and mountain people.

§ 72

Questions: How far did Zwingli agree with Luther? How did he differ from Luther on baptism? On the Lord's supper? Seriousness of the latter difference? How did Luther view Zwingli's position?

How widely did Zwingli's views spread? What limited their influence? What became of the movement finally?

Topics: Moral and religious value of Zwingli's views as compared with those of Luther. Zwingli's greater emancipation from Catholicism than Luther's. The Bible in the two systems.

National boundaries as limitations of religious influence. Nationalism and internationalism in their effects on religion.

§ 73

Questions: Nationality, family and education of Calvin? His record as a student? His conversion? Subsequent life in France? Settlement in Geneva?

Calvin's difficulties in Geneva? His exile and triumphal return? His influence in the city and canton? His influence in the Protestant world? Upon what was this influence based?

Topics: Mental and spiritual characteristics of the French seen in Calvinism. Influence of the study of law on theology as seen in history. Great theologians who were educated for the law. Calvin's position as related to those of Luther and Zwingli. Forces that led Calvin to renounce the Catholic church.

§ 74

Questions: Give the characteristics of Calvin's theology. Its influence in the great struggle against the Catholic church? Describe the Calvinistic system of church government. How does it compare with other forms of democracy? What three officers has this system? What was the Calvinistic type of Christian life? What was the attitude of Calvinists toward Anabaptists and other dissenters from their national churches? What was Calvin's view of baptism and the supper? What was his view of the future life?

Topics: How far Calvin's personal peculiarities enter into his system. How far theology should be controlled by logic. Theoretical religious freedom with actual persecution by Calvinists. Effects of Calvinism on the moral earnestness of the people. Effectiveness of the Calvinistic type of democracy in church government.

§ 75

Questions: Difficulties encountered by the reform in France? Progress made? When was the Calvinistic church of France organized? How did Protestantism become a political party? How many civil wars in France? What was the night of St. Bartholomew? When did the Protestants obtain the first enduring peace? What were the provisions of this Edict of Nantes? Progress of the Protestants under the protection of this Edict? Condition of the Protestants after the revocation of the Edict. Effect of this persecution on the religion and history of France? How were the Netherlands affected by the reform? Attitude of their ruler Charles V? Why were they detached from the empire and transferred to the crown of Spain? Effect of this transfer on their religious condition? Causes of the revolt under William of Orange? Its results? When was Calvinism introduced? Why a Calvinistic state church? The struggle for religious and political liberty and its effects on the rest of the world?

Condition of Scotland at the outbreak of the Reformation? Attitude of the Scotch government? John Knox and his conversion? Education and character of Mary? Knox's early reformatory efforts? Legal reformation of the country in 1560? Return of Mary from France and struggle with Knox? Character of the state church? Presbyterianism under James?

Give an account of the influence of Calvinism in Germany. In Switzerland. In Hungary. In England.

Topics: Calvinism as an international type of Christianity. The elements of Calvinism which have most affected the world. The aggressive character of Calvinism. Permanent marks of Calvinism made on English character. Calvinism as a political force. As a social and moral force.

§ 76

Questions: Relation of the Anabaptists to earlier sects? To the Catholic church? To Luther and Zwingli? Why did they break with the reformers? What was their view of infant-baptism? Source of their faith-baptism? Why called Anabaptists? What did they call themselves? Why and how were they opposed? Their later history? What are their most important doctrines and practices? What was their view of the state? Of the constitution of the church? What radical social views did they hold?

Topics: The sect life of the Middle Ages. Its relation to the Reformation and the later freedom and progress of Europe. Relation of Mediæval Christianity to infant baptism. The hold of infant baptism on the Christian world. The political and social views of the Anabaptists as compared with those of the modern world.

§ 77

Questions: Condition of England at the outbreak of the Reformation? Character of Henry? Attitude toward reform? Demand for a divorce? Pope's embarrassment? His policy? Henry's method of securing the divorce? When was he declared head of the church?

Topics: The English Reformation as an expression of English character. Governmental domination of the reform in England. The divorce as a factor. The Catholic church and the dissolution of marriage. Subjection of the church by the English government.

§ 78

Questions: Give an account of Tyndale's work. Coverdale's Bible? Matthew's Bible? The Great Bible? Dissolution of the monasteries and the confiscation of their property? How far was England reformed at Henry's death?

Topics: Bible translation as a means of reform. Monasticism as a hindrance to reform. Use made by Protestants of the confiscated Catholic property. Effects of state control of religion in England.

§ 79

Questions: Character of Edward VI? What advance was made under him in the way of reform? Origin and character of the " Book of Common Prayer "? The Protestant creed? Elimination of Catholic priests and the introduction of Protestant ministers? What was the Act of Uniformity? Its effects?

Topics: Relation between the official reform of the church and the actual reform of the people. Advantages and disadvantages of a uniform service. Advantages and disadvantages of a written service. Wisdom of imposing one service on a entire nation? The English as compared with other Protestant service books.

§ 80

Questions: Character and purposes of Mary? Her view of Protestantism? How did she reëstablish Catholicism? What two things was she unable to restore? Effect of her marriage to Philip? Her treatment of the Protestant leaders? Give an account of Cranmer's weakness.

Elizabeth's character and religious convictions? Her religious life to the beginning of her reign? How did she abolish the Catholic church and restore Protestantism? In what sense was her reign a " glorious era "? Basis of the English church?

Topics: England's religious vacillation at this period. Permanent effects of Mary's bloody reign on English character. Sinister influence of Philip on European history. Protestant martyrs.

Impress of Elizabeth's character on the English church. Relation of religious reform to the outburst of intellectual activity in the Elizabethan era. To England's political and military power. Permanent contribution of Elizabeth to England's history.

§ 81

Questions: Closeness of the English church to the Catholic church? Organization? Ordinations and baptism? Catholic doctrines and practices abolished? Doctrine of the supper? Appointment of bishops? Transaction of former papal business? Character of the worship? Subjection of the church to the state? Attitude of the state toward dissenters?

Topics: The English church as a distinct type of Prottestantism. Explain the conservatism of the English reform. Catholic elements finally retained in the church.

§ 82

Questions: What was Puritanism? How was it introduced into the English church? Character, influence and origin of the Geneva version of the Bible? What were the chief demands of Puritanism? Its relation to the Civil War? What became of Puritanism?

Topics: Fundamental contentions of Puritanism. Why did it fail? Its permanent impress on English character. Comparative religious value of Puritanism and Anglicanism.

§ 83

Questions: How did Puritanism break up? Life of Robert Browne? Sources of his views? The principal elements of his position? The founding of the first independent church? Treatment and subsequent history of Browne? Congregation at London? Congregations at Gainsborough and Scrooby? Flight into Holland? Reestablishment of Congregationalism in England? Growth and influence in that country? Establishment of Congregationalism in America? Growth and influence in New England? Relation of English Baptists to continental Anabaptists? Founding of the first English Anabaptist church in Holland by Smyth? His efforts to unite with the Anabaptists or Mennonites? First Confession of Faith and the return to England? Their main contentions? Their sufferings and growth? Origin of the Calvinistic English Bap-

286 THE COURSE OF CHRISTIAN HISTORY

tists? Their reception and growth? First and second confessions? Relation to the Arminian Baptists? How both
differed from the continental Anabaptists? Establishment
of the two parties of Baptists in America? Difficulties and
growth? Relations with each other? Other parties developed in America? Their contribution to religious freedom in America?

Origin of the Quakers? Fox's experience? Principal
doctrines of the Quakers? Treatment by the English and
colonial governments? Woman's work among them?
Their relation to Pennsylvania? Their ultimate influence?

Topics: Influence of the Anabaaptists in the struggle for
religious freedom. Relation of infant baptism to religious
persecution. Relation of faith-baptism to religious freedom. Browne's democracy compared with that of Calvin.
Relation of the English Baptists to the English Congregationalists. Infant baptism in the Congregational system.
Moral and religious significance of faith-baptism. Fundamental contentions of Quakerism. Its efficiency as a form
of Christian faith?

§ 84

Questions: Early effects of the Reformation on the
Catholic church? Action of Catholic princes? The emperor's efforts? What seems to be the main cause of failure
in the reform movement?

§ 85

Questions: History of Ignatius Loyola? Formation of
the Society of Jesus? What was his purpose? How are
members admitted? How educated? Character of the organization? Its methods? Influence of the Jesuits? Their
efforts to stop the Reformation? Their relation to the
Thirty Years War?

Topics: The Jesuits as an expression of Spanish Christianity. Effects of Jesuit training on the intellectual and
moral life of the individual. On the Catholic church as a
whole. The moral precepts of the Jesuits. Jesuit support
of papal pretensions. Jesuit influence on the subsequent
history of the Catholic church. Their missionary methods
and history. Loyola's " Spiritual Exercises."

§ 86

Questions: Why had the Protestants wanted a Council? Why had the emperor desired one? Why were the popes unwilling? What finally induced the pope to hold one? Size, date and character of the Council of Trent? What two lines of subjects did it consider? What did it accomplish?

Topics: History of church councils. Constitution, control and methods of the Council of Trent. How far church councils express the convictions of their entire constituency. The history of councils as affecting the validity of their conclusions.

§ 87

Questions: When did the Catholics bring the Reformation to an end? Where did they stamp the movement out entirely? Results in France? Ireland and Belgium? What success in other Protestant lands? What gains did they make through colonization? What gains through missions in America? In eastern lands? What finally became of these promising missions?

Topics: Motives that led Protestants to join the Catholic church. Missionary zeal of the Catholics as compared with the inactivity and opposition of the Protestants. Rapidity of conversion in Catholic missions. Instability of the convert and the work generally. Catholic missionary methods as compared with those of Protestants. Life of Loyola. Of Xavier. Jesuit missionaries in America.

§ 88

Questions: Catholic reforms concerning *Indulgences, Education of the clergy, Preaching and Instruction, Bible Translation, the Popes.*

Topics: Public criticism as a stimulus to church reform. Protestant opposition a means of uplift to the Catholics. Effect of Catholicism on the moral and spiritual life of Protestants. How far the popes are a moral and religious influence in the Catholic church.

§ 89

Questions: Why did the Reformation become a political question? Name the various religious wars with their results in Switzerland, Germany, France, the Netherlands. Give an account of the Thirty Years War. The Peace of Westphalia. Attitude of the pope to this treaty and his subsequent influence on international relations.

Topics: Religious differences as incitements to war. Were the results of these wars favorable to Catholics or Protestants? The pope as an instigator of war. Social economic and religious effects of the Thirty Years War.

§ 90

Questions: How much of the world's territory was Christian at the beginning of this period? Why had Christianity not spread for some centuries? What now opened the way for further expansion? Where did the Spanish and Portuguese settle and what religion did they carry with them? Where did Protestants settle? What types were represented and what eventually became of them? Expansion of Russia and the Greek church?

Topics: Relation of discovery and colonization to the expansion of Christianity.. Compare those portions of the new world settled by Catholics with those settled by Protestants as to political and social progress, intellectual, moral and religious attainments. Causes of the differences discovered.

EIGHTH PERIOD 1648 TO 1789

§ 91

Questions: What difficulties in the presentation of our materials from this point onward? What of Christian divisions and strifes as compared with the past? Special causes of divisions in English Christianity?

§ 92

Questions: The principle of authority in the Reformation? Right of private interpretation of the Bible? Authority of creeds? Effect on religious freedom? Religious strife as a cause of skepticism? Rejection of the principle of authority? What is Rationalism? What did its advocates expect of it? Forms of skepticism? Countries affected? What effect did this rationalism have upon religious beliefs and practices? What effect even on those who remained orthodox? What effect on morals?

Topics: The Principle of Authority in Religion. The Principle of Freedom in Religion. The function of reason in life. In religion. The optimism of Rationalism. Its bitterness toward the Christian religion. Moral effects of the various forms of skepticism.

§ 93

Questions: Decline of the individual churches and denominations? Two tendencies? Condition of the state churches? Of the free churches of England and America —Baptists, Congregationalists and Quakers? Tendencies on the continent? Beginnings of improvement toward the end of the period?

§ 94

Questions: Effect of Rationalism on the Catholic church? Struggle between France and the papacy? What were the Gallican Liberties? Revival of Augustinianism in France and its effects? Great preachers in this period? Condition at the close of the period? Free thought in Austria? Reforms of Joseph II? Threat of separating German Catholics from the papacy? Why did these reforms not last? What created a demand for the suppression of the Jesuits? What countries banished them and why? When and by whom were they suppressed?

Topics: Comparative effects of Rationalism on the Catholic and Protestant churches. Reasons for the difference. How far is rationalism constructive? Relation between faith and reason in the religious life. Causes of the suppression of the Jesuits.

§ 95

Questions: Dangers of freedom? What is meant by intellectual freedom? Effect of the new freedom on philosophy? Attitude toward the church? Effect on superstitions and errors? Effect on truth? What is meant by political freedom? A new republic? Limitations on kings and princes? How much gain was this? What is meant by religious freedom? Who was the first to establish a government with absolute religious freedom? What effect had religious freedom in the federal constitution upon the religious establishments in the states? Progress of religious freedom in the period since Williams? What was the character of the education of the Middle Ages? What classes were educated? How was education supported? What changes as to the diffusion and the support of education since the Reformation? The freedom and expansion of the press?

Topics: Losses and gains of freedom. Difference between liberty and license. The world's gains and losses in the eighteenth century. Blessings and dangers of intellectual freedom. Of political freedom. Of religious freedom. How are the dangers of freedom to be avoided?

§ 96

Questions: Evangelical truth and light not dead but only hidden? Why is the German revival called Pietism? Life and work of Spener? His views? Attitude of the state church of Germany? Founding of the University of Halle? Halle Orphan House? Weakness of Spener's movement? Causes of final failure? Moral and religious condition of the American colonies? What is meant by the "Great Awakening"? Life and work of Jonathan Edwards? Work of Whitefield in America? Permanent effects of the revival? Moral and religious condition of Britain in the early eighteenth century? Family and education of the Wesleys? Of Whitefield? Their conversion? Their preaching? Opposition of the English church? Why field preaching? Character of their preaching and singing? How did they take care of their converts? Show how the Methodist organization was created. Source of the Methodist type of piety? Organization of independent Methodist churches in America and England? Effects of the evangelical revival on the life of England and America?

Topics: Compare the German and English revivals and explain the differences. Relation between the American and the English revivals. Cultured preachers as revivalists. Religious and moral decay as a background for revivals. Permanent effects of a revival on the life of the people. Characteristics of eras preceding great revivals.

§ 97

Questions: Extent of Catholic missions in this period? Their success in the far East? In Central and South America? When and where were the earliest missionary efforts of Protestants? Who was the first in America? When, where and how did concerted effort among Protestants begin? Describe the Danish-Halle Mission and its work. Describe the organization of the " United Brethren." Tell of their devotion to foreign missions.

Topics: Causes of the long delay of Protestants in entering upon foreign missionary work. Colonies as mission fields. Missionary interest and work of German Protestants. Life of Zinzendorf. History of the *Unitas Fratrum.*

NINTH PERIOD 1789 TO 1917

§ 98

Questions: What of the progress of the world in this last period? What of the increasing complexity of life? Causes of complexity?

What as to the amount of improvement in political conditions? What of the extension of constitutional government and its benefits to the people? What of the extension of the republic as a form of government and its efficiency and blessings? Development of democracy within the various nations? Points of advance in this regard? Colonization by Russia? England? Partition of Africa? Decline of Turkey? Of Spain? Expansion of the United States? Of Russia? Rise of China and Japan? Unification and growth of Germany? Of Italy? Points in which the state expanded its functions in this period?

Topics: Explanation of the tremendous progress of the

last period. Political progress as an index and a help to general progress. Gains and losses in the state's control and support of education and charities. Gains and losses in passing from autocracy to democracy. Gains and losses in national consolidation and unification. The increasing nationalism of the period. Its dangers and promise.

§ 99

Questions: What of general improvement of social conditions? How have living conditions been improved? Effect of crowding into the cities? Decline of the nobility? Disappearance of slavery and serfdom? Improvement in the condition of the laboring classes? Diffusion of education and its effects? Cheapening of books and periodicals? Problems of literacy? Increase in military establishments? Why? Increase in the use of machinery and its effects? Progress in the mastery of the powers of nature? Effects of ease of communication and transportation? Progress of women.

Topics: Relation between living conditions and morals. Between living conditions and religious faith. Advantages and dangers of large leisure. Effects of the great material progress on the spiritual values of life. Moral and religious effects of the diffusion of education and the expansion of the press. Effects of woman's increased activities upon the religious and moral conditions of the world. Upon woman's own character.

§ 100

Questions: Disappearance of slavery and serfdom? Attitude towards alcholic beverages at the beginning of the period? Extent of drinking? Tendency at present? What success? Success in fighting the gambling evil? In the abolition of dueling in America? In other lands? What of vice or the " social evil "?

Topics: Forces operating toward moral reform. Forces in modern life that tend to lower moral standards and living. Moral history of mankind during the last century and a half.

§ 101

Questions: Present status of dissenters in countries which have established churches? What countries have established churches at present? In what countries has complete disestablishment and consequent religious freedom been established? The outlook in other lands?

Protestant missions in the preceding period? Protestant missions in this period? The pioneer in the English speaking world? Date of the organization of the Baptist Missionary Society? Organization of similar societies by other denominations in England and America? What nations have taken the lead in foreign missions? What has been accomplished in the way of equipment? In converts? Reflex influence of foreign missions?

What had the Reformation done for the translation and circulation of the Bible? What was done in the way of the exploration of Bible lands and the consistent study of the Bible? What has been done in this period in the study of Bible lands, peoples and customs? Translations and circulation? Study of the original text, writing of commentaries, etc.? Development of the Sunday school as an agency for Bible study and religious education?

Causes of the forming of extra-ecclesiastical organizations? Name some of the most important of these organizations and describe their work. What of them as a feature of religious life?

The position of the layman in the Mediæval church? Attitude of the reformers toward the layman and his work? What parties gave large place to the layman in the Reformation period? His work in the nineteenth century? Organizations and positions in which he works?

What place did the Mediæval church have for woman's activities? What did the Reformers do for her? What parties at the Reformation granted her some freedom? What position has the nineteenth century opened for her in religious work? How has she prepared for her enlarged opportunities?

What did infant baptism do for the young? Why did not evangelical Christians expect early conversions? What of the average age of conversion in this last period? How has this changed the church organizations, services and general tone? Is this healthy?

What is evangelism? What view of religion does it necessarily antagonize? Extent of evangelism at present? Causes of this evangelistic activity? Why must evangelism specially characterize those bodies that reject infant baptism? Forms of evangelism? What of the future?

Extent of infant baptism during the Middle Ages? Attitude of the Catholic church toward those who rejected it? What did the great reforming parties do with infant baptism? What of the Anabaptists? Progress of faith-baptism before the attainment of religious freedom? Decline of infant baptism in recent years? Its causes? Growth of the bodies who practice only faith-baptism in recent years? Number who now practice only faith-baptism?

Beneficence in the early days of Protestantism? More recent tendencies?

What of skepticism and opposition to Christianity in the Middle Ages? What of this growth in modern times? Various forms? How far have skeptics accepted Christian ethics? Nietzsche?

What of Christian divisions since the Reformation? Why? What is the more recent tendency? Notable cases of union in recent years? Of federation and coöperation where union is not contemplated?

Topics: Progress of toleration and religious freedom in the last period. Causes of this.

Protestant missions as an expression of the fundamental impulse of Christianity. Influence of missions on recent world movements. Reflex influence of missions on home Christianity. Moral and social influence of missions on non-Christian lands.

Reciprocal influence of modern civilization and Bible circulation on each other. Contribution of the last period to better knowledge of the Bible.

Significance of extra-ecclesiastical organizations. Their influence on the life of the churches and on Christianity in general.

The " laicising " of Christianity in the last period. Its significance for the future.

Place and importance of woman's activities in modern Christianity. Its probable effects on the character and aggressiveness of Christianity.

Infant baptism as a support of sacramental Christianity. Place of infant baptism in evangelical Christianity? Causes and effects of its decline in the last period. Total effects of the incorporation of the young into the churches.

Relation between evangelism and the voluntary principle. Effects of religious freedom and faith-baptism on the need of evangelism.

Extent and causes of the growth of opposition to Christianity in modern times. Power of Christian ethics in theory and practice.

Forces of the modern world operating to bring about Christian coöperation and in some cases union. Its promises and its dangers.

§ 102

Questions: Location of the Greek Catholic church? Nationalities which are members? Causes of their backwardness? Their services to the rest of Christendom? What divisions has it? In what sense is it one? In what respects does it agree and in what differ from the Roman church? What languages do the various divisions use? How many are national churches established by law?

Topics: Past services of the Greek Catholic church to the history of the world. What promise is in the church for the future. Its theology compared to that of the Roman church. Its worship thus compared. Its monasticism and views of marriage.

§ 103

Questions: Present number of Orthodox Christians in Turkey? How is the church organized and governed? What is the condition of these Christians? What other churches are subject to the patriarch of Constantinople? The churches of Sinai and Cyprus?

§ 104

Questions: Progress of Russia in the last period? Education in Russia? Organization and government of the

church? Relation to the civil government? Condition of
the church in general? Sects in Russia? Roman Catholics
and Protestants? Other religions? Religious persecution
in Russia?

Topics: The Russian people and the Russian church.
The religious and moral nature of the Russian. The Russian church at present a hindrance or a help to the Russian
people? The sect life of Russia as a promise.

§ 105

Questions: When and how did Greece gain her independence of Turkey? How was her church organized?
What of its membership and efficiency? What other than
Orthodox Christians are found in Greece?

Topics: Grecian struggle for independence. Blight left
behind by Turkey even after her expulsion. The modern
Greek compared with the ancient. Causes of the differences.

§ 106

Questions: Bulgaria's struggle for independence? The
organization of her church? Religious freedom and state
support? Other Christians beside the Orthodox? Work
of Methodists? Struggle of Servia for freedom? How
the church is organized and governed? Backwardness of
the Servians? Religious intolerance? Other religions?
Progress of Roumania since gaining her freedom? Organization and government of the church? Religious freedom? Cultural progress? The other Orthodox churches
mentioned above?

Topics: Race, history and present moral and cultural
status of the Bulgars. Balkan antipathies and hatreds with
their causes. History and sufferings of the Serbs. Probable effects of the present war on their social, political, moral
and religious life. Racial descent and history of the Roumanians. Present cultural status. Probable effects of the
war on this country.

§ 107

Questions: What was the status of the Greek Catholic
church at the beginning of the period? What new king-

doms have arisen during the last period? What progress has Russia made? How does this church stand in relation to the other great divisions of Christendom at present?

Topics: The Greek Catholic or Orthodox church as a factor in the future moral, religious, social and political history of the world. Elements of vitality and power in it. Elements of weakness and backwardness.

§ 108

Question: What has been the general history of this group of churches?

§ 109

Questions: Location of the Armenians? Their sufferings in the past? Their number? Organization of the Armenian Church? View of Christ? Principal ecclesiastical practices? Language of worship? Work of American Congregationalists among them?

§ 110

Questions: Location and number of the Nestorians? Language of worship? Work of American Presbyterians among them? Origin of the Jacobites? Their numbers and faith?

§ 111

Questions: Number and origin of the Copts? Their sufferings? Religious views and practices? Work of the Presbyterians among them? Location, numbers, history and present political condition of the Abyssinians? Government of their church? Beliefs and practices? Language of worship? Attitude toward other Christians?

§ 112

Questions: Meaning of the term Uniats? How do they differ from Greek and Roman Catholics?

Topics: The possibility of reviving all these eastern heretical churches. The obligation of Protestant Christians to them.

§ 113

Questions: Treatment of the Catholic church by the

French Revolution? Its recognition by Napoleon? His subsequent confiscation of the papal state and imprisonment of the pope? Pope transferred to France? Restoration by the Congress of Vienna? Period of reaction and papal gain? Gradual amalgamation of the states of Italy into one country? Capture of Rome and confiscation of the papal state? Pope a sovereign in the Vatican? Present position of the pope as to temporal sovereignty? Evidences of the increase of the pope's power over the Catholic church? What is the doctrine of the Immaculate Conception? When promulgated? What the Syllabus of Errors? When published? In what sense is the pope considered infallible? Effect of this decree on his influence in the church? Number and location of the Catholics? To what race do they mainly belong? What nations are predominately Catholic? Gains of the Catholic church — reëntering Protestant lands? Growth in the United States? New states of Belgium and Latin America? Italy? Missions? Losses in the decline of Spain, Portugal and Austria? Loss of power in Catholic states? Decline of monasticism? Protestant missions in Catholic lands? What is Modernism? How influential is it? How does the church oppose the entrance of all modern ideas into its membership? Probabilities for the future? Contribution of the Catholics to scholarship and learning in the last period? Treatment of its great men? Probabilities for the future?

Topics: Democracy as an enemy of papal sovereignty. The reaction following the French Revolution. Confiscation of the papal state a loss or gain to the papacy? In what sense is the pope the " sovereign pontiff "? The influence which the increasing power of the pope within the Catholic church is having on that body. The place which Mary and the other saints fill in the popular thought and worship of the church. Attitude of the church to the modern world as revealed by the Syllabus of Errors and the fight on Modernism. Infallibility as a dogma and in practice. Value of Catholicism as seen in the present condition of Catholic nations. Causes of the mutual antagonism of the Catholic church and modern scholarship and social effort.

§ 114

Questions: Trace the process of unifying Italy. What was left to the pope? Italy's progress since the unification? Expansion? Number and character of the population? Religious conditions? Atheism of the government? Monasticism? Education and culture? Church buildings and art? Moral and religious conditions in general?

Topics: How far the Catholic church is responsible for the present condition of Italy. Catholicism as a provoker of Atheism. Catholicism as a hindrance to general education and culture. Comparative progress of Catholic and Atheistic Italy. Attitude of cultured Italy toward the Catholic church and religion in general.

§ 115

Questions: The political history of France since the Revolution? Population and birth rate? Religion under Napoleon's arrangement? Separation of church and state and present arrangement? Struggle with the monks and nuns over the schools? Religion and the schools at the present time? Monasticism? Church buildings in France? Number and influence of Protestants? Their religious condition? Present moral and religious condition as a whole in France? The French colonies and their religious condition?

Topics: Religious conditions in France as an outcome of its history. The great struggle over the schools. Struggle with monasticism. Superstitions fostered by the church. Missionary zeal of the French Catholics. Causes of Atheism in France.

§ 116

Questions: Tremendous decline of Spain? Present population? Illiteracy? Religious complexion of the country? Abolition of the Inquisition? Status of Protestants? Monasticism? Free Thinking? Attitude of the cultured classes?

Topics: History of Spain in Nineteenth Century and its lessons. Religious intolerance as a clog on progress. Attitude of the church toward education.

§ 117

Questions: Population of Portugal? Colonies? Educational and religious status? Treatment of the monasteries? Disestablishment? Protestant missions?

§ 118

Questions: Union with and separation from the kingdom of the Netherlands? Her neutrality? Colony? Character of the people? Relation between church and state? Number and status of Protestants? Monasticism? Struggle between liberals and clericals?

§ 119

Questions: Sketch the political history of Austria during the last period. Present status of the sovereign in Austria and Hungary? Relation between these two portions of the empire? Main elements in the mixed population of the country? Religious complexion of the country? Status of the Catholic church? Character of this church in Austria? Presence of Protestants? Work of Baptists? Religious freedom?

Topics: Causes of decline in the standing of Austria. Complexity of racial and religious life. The Catholic religion as a provocation in the present war. Relation between Austria and the Vatican in recent years. History, character and religion of the Hungarians.

§ 120

Questions: Change in the political status of the Latin-American countries in the last period? Racial complexion of these lands? Recent immigration? Present social and political conditions? Position of the Catholic church in these countries? Schools and education? Moral and religious conditions? Monasticism? Religious freedom?

Topics: Moral and social results of racial mixtures in these countries. Causes of the instability of governments. Causes of the violence and incompetence of the people. The moral weakness of the people.

§ 121

Questions: Freedom granted these islands? Educational and economic progress since that date? Recent Protestant work?

§ 122

Questions: Remnants of Catholics left in Germany by the " ecclesiastical reservations act "? Catholics in south Germany? Gains? The Catholics as a force in politics of Germany? Percentage of Catholics in Germany? Their general character? Small percentage of Catholics in the Scandinavian countries? Catholicism never entirely suppressed in Britain and Ireland? Recovery of civil rights? Reorganization of the hierarchy? Increase and present numbers in England and Wales, Scotland and Ireland? Character of the English Catholics? Catholics in the British colonies? Rate of growth in the United States? Reason? Numbers and equipment? Conversions of Protestants? Character of American Catholics?

Topics: Influence of Catholics in Protestant lands. Subservience of public officials. Relation of the Catholics to the minor municipal offices. Catholics as an influence on our moral, spiritual and social life. Are they a political menace?

§ 123

Questions: Catholic activity in mision work? How directed? How supported? Character of the work done? Who furnishes the missionaries? Catholic methods of counting converts?

§ 124

Questions: Progress of Protestants in this period? The three greatest states? Social conditions in Protestant as compared with Catholic countries? Protestant divisions and growing fellowship?

Topics: Social value of Protestant as compared with Catholic principles. Political value. Freedom and contentment as bonds of political union. Significance for the future of growing Protestant fellowship.

§ 125

Questions: Size and location of the Lutheran group? Racial relations and homogeneity? Organization in various lands?

Union of Lutheran and " Reformed " in several of the German states? Relation between church and state? Education and religious instruction? Theological faculties and seminaries? Contribution of the Germans to theological culture? To practical Christian efforts and missions? The deaconess movement and its service? Other Protestants in Germany? Origin and work of the Baptists?

Topics: Religious history of Germany in the last period. Effects of compulsory religious education in the state schools? Effects of an educational system completely controlled by the state? Effects of a non-Christian education. Failure of German Christianity to ameliorate German character as seen in events of the present war.

§ 126

Questions: Scandinavian countries overwhelmingly Lutheran? Attempts to restore Catholicism? Relation of state and church in these countries? Religious freedom? Relation of the clergy to the schools? How does Sweden compare with the others? Baptists and Methodists in each of these countries? Theological scholarship and culture?

Topics: Contribution of the Scandinavian countries to freedom and culture. Character and culture of the people in each country.

§ 127

Questions: Number, origin and recent growth of the Lutherans in America? Organization? Language used in worship? Equipment as to theological education, religious press, orphanages, deaconesses, etc.? Their work in a practical way? Origin and character of the German Evangelicals? Distinguished from the " Evangelicals "?

Topics: The Germans as an element in American life — economic, moral, religious, social? Their relation to the struggle for temperance reform? Significance of their effort to preserve their German language and culture in America.

§ 128

Questions: Unity and progress of the various Reformed churches of the world? Their services as compared to the Lutherans? Religious freedom among them? Religious freedom and disestablishment in Switzerland? Proportion of Reformed, Catholics, Baptists and Methodists? Scholarship and practical service of the Protestants?

Topics: Contribution of Switzerland to the educational theory of the world in the last period. Other contributions. Swiss character and its relation to Swiss religion.

§ 129

Questions: What were the religious and political conditions in the Netherlands at the beginning of the period? Effects of the Napoleonic wars? Separation from Belgium? Formation of the "Christian Reformed Church" in 1834? Progress of religious toleration and freedom? Relation of the state to the various churches? Religion and the public schools? Scholarship among the Dutch? Foundation of private Christian schools?

Topics: Character and achievements of the Dutch. The Dutch in the struggle for religious freedom.

§ 130

Questions: Coldness and skepticism in the Scotch church? Failure of the Evangelical Revival in Scotland? Later revival? Friction over the right of patronage? Independent churches originating in 1733 and 1760? In 1847? The great split in 1843? Success and activities of the "Free Church of Scotland"? Further union in 1900? General character and activity of Scottish Christianity? Missions?

Topics: Contribution of the Scotch to theological scholarship. To missions throughout the world. Scottish character as made by Presbyterianism. Social and moral conditions.

§ 131

Questions: Disappearance of the Presbyterians from England in the seventeenth century? Reëstablishment in the eighteenth and nineteenth? Present condition of Presbyterianism in England?

§ 132

Questions: Origin of American Presbyterians? Present numbers and organizations? Unions? Character of their ministry and worship. Baptism among them? Theological and other schools? Mission work? Contributions to scholarship?

Topics: Presbyterians as a cultural, moral and religious factor in American life.

§ 133

Questions: Lack of unity in English-speaking Christianity? Practical efficiency of same? Spiritual unity as compared with the Christianity of other lands?

General tendency in the English church? Comparison with the Free churches of England? Causes of this relative decline? Effect of the Wesleyan movement? The "Tractarian Movement"? Skepticism and indifference.

Topics: Relative efficiency of the state and the free churches of England. Loss of privileges by the state church. Present advantages of the state church over others? Hardships of dissenters in England.

§ 134

Questions: What of the wealth of the state church? Relation of the king to the church? Appointment of the bishops and the lower clergy? Influence of the bishops on public life? Where has the church been disestablished? Present status of the two older universities?

§ 135

Questions: What of the English educational system? Religious instruction in the schools? Number of new universities? How do they differ from the older ones?

Topics: History and character of the Universities of Oxford and Cambridge. Character of English education as compared with that of other lands. Influence of the state church on education. Influence of religion in English education.

§ 136

Questions: Contribution of the state church to preaching and theological scholarship? In what departments of theological learning have they made greatest contributions? New revision of the Bible?

§ 137

Questions: Activity of the English church in missions? Its societies? Material equipment of its missions? What great organizations of the modern Christian world were created by members of the state church?

Topics: Opportunities for great scholarship in the English church. Stimulus to great preaching. Adaptability of the state church to modern conditions. Influence of the church upon public and private life. Affinity of the English with the Catholic church.

§ 138

Questions: Condition of the Episcopal church in America after the Revolution and its causes? Oragnization of the church? What three parties are in the American as in the English Episcopal church? Which party is leading? What is it in this church which attracts members from other denominations? What gives it disproportionate influence on public life? Its attitude towards other Christians? Extent and success of its mission work? How is the church organized? Methods and powers of the General Convention? Strength of the Episcopal church in the colonies? Its contributions?

Topics: Contribution of the Episcopal church to the life of the United States since the Revolution. Warriors and statesmen who have been members. The extent of democracy in its government. The character of its Christian life. The liberality of its members. Its contribution to scholarship, preaching, etc.

§ 139

Questions: Baptists as an incorporation of those who favor faith-baptism? Rapidity of their growth? Difficul-

ties they have been compelled to overcome? Numbers of
the bodies closely related to the Baptists? Faith-baptism
in Pedobaptist bodies? The equipment they have acquired?
Standing they have attained?

Topics: Significance of fundamental Baptist principles for the progress of the world. Their affinity for and
adaptableness to the modern world. Baptists as the catholic type of Christianity. Elements of the ecclesiastical and
political institutions of the world that are opposed to them.
Their affinity with the social and religious aspirations and
strivings of the modern world. Baptist principles and modern education and culture. Baptist principles and freedom
of thought and investigation. Opportunities of larger service now opening before Baptists.

§ 140

Questions: Difficulties of British Baptists? Their relation to the beginnings of modern missions? Their work on
the foreign field? Organizations? The "Communion
Question" among them? "Open membership"? Their
present numbers and influence? Notable men produced by
them?

§ 141

Questions: Success of the Baptists in the United States
and its causes? Present numbers and influence? Their entrance upon foreign mission work? Causes and effects of
anti-missionism among them? Causes and effects of the
schism led by Mr. Campbell? Organization of the Southern Baptist Convention? Plan of organization as compared
with that in the North? Extent and success of Baptist
missions? Equipment in the foreign field? Organization
of Baptists on the home field? Educational institutions?
Their learning, preaching, etc.? What of the Baptists in the
British colonies?

Topics: Elements in American life that are congenial
and favorable to the Baptists. Contributions of the Baptists to the political and religious life of America. To the
moral reforms. To the missionary spirit and activities.
Differences between Northern and Southern Baptists.

§ 142

Questions: Prosperity of and present numbers of British Congregationalists? Numbers on the continent? Church independency? Organization for coöperative tasks? Their missionary work? Their great society? Their practical work on the home field? Their contributions in scholarship, preaching, statesmanship and other intellectual pursuits?

Topics: The democracy of the Congregationalists. Democracy with coöperation. Their emphasis on culture. Their influence on English life and history. Their close affiliations with the Baptists.

§ 143

Questions: Growth of American Congregationalists? Losses and their causes? Rise of Unitarianism? Contribution to the cause of education in this country? Some of their many great institutions? Scholars and preachers? Their organization? Their work for foreign missions? Its extent and character.

Topics: Why American Congregationalists lead in education. Why they more than others suffered from the Unitarian defection. The type and effectiveness of their democracy. Why they have not spread to the South, nor largely to the West. Why they have led in missionary activities.

§ 144

Questions: Attitude of Wesley toward separation from the state church of England? Why and when did his followers separate? What of the prosperity and general character of the Methodists? Evangelism as compared with education among them? Their theology? Emotion among them? Schisms? Recent unions in England?

Topics: Effectiveness of the Methodist type of Christian life. Classes to which it appeals. Their contribution to the life of the world.

§ 145

Questions: The Calvinistic Methodists? Character of church government in the Wesleyan Methodist Church?

Results? Various Methodist churches of England and their causes? Difficulties met in England? Mission Work? Organization?

§ 146

Questions: Success of the Methodists in America and its causes? Its growth and present size? Various Methodist churches? Equipment with educational and other institutions? Activities in missions and other forms of religious service? Effectiveness of their evangelism? Organization of the Southern Methodist church? How organized in general? Missionary fields?

Topics: The undemocratic nature of Methodist church government. Comparative effectiveness of Methodists in frontier and in settled conditions. Services to temperance reform. The quality of Methodist preaching and why. Methodist emotionalism as the source of extravagant sects like the " Holy Rollers."

§ 147

Questions: Causes of the variety and complexity of American Christianity? Absence of friction and bitter religious feeling? Humane sentiments? Effect of immigration on American Christianity? Character of the Roman and Greek Catholic churches in relation to our national life? Of the Lutheran?

Topics: Complexity of religious life as an aid to religious freedom. Effects of religious freedom on the purity and vitality of church life. Religious freedom as an aid to good feeling. Comparative dangers and advantages of religious uniformity and religious variety. Gains and losses of denominationalism.

§ 148

Questions: Life and work of Mr. Alexander Campbell? Doctrines and practices of his followers? Recent tendencies in the body? Their growth and success? Mission work? Their organization?

Why the smaller bodies are not noticed here? Life and work of Joseph Smith? Subsequent history of Mormonism? Mormons at Salt Lake City? Their growth and extension? Organization? Continued gift of prophecy? Character and contents of the Book of Mormon? Their view of God? Other doctrines? Polygamy? The "temple" and the "tabernacle"? Social, political and religious effects of Mormonism?

Life and work of Mrs. Eddy? When and how was the Christian Science church founded? Number and character of the Christian Scientists? Doctrines of Christian Science? Relation of the system to the Bible? Its real nature? Criticism of the system? Causes of its power? How propagated and organized? Its healing?

Work of William Booth? How the Army is now organized? Position of women? Its preaching and services? Its two kinds of work? Its methods?

Topics: Extent to which Mr. Campbell and his followers have furthered the cause of Christian union. His views of baptism and the work of the Holy Spirit. His opposition to missions and the support of the ministry. To societies.

Religious and cultural conditions out of which Mormonism grew. Compare the Book of Mormon with other religious books of history. Mormonism as an economic organization.

Christian Science as a symptom and a cure. Its healing power? Effect of its nonecclesiastical character. Its effects on Christian morals and service.

Failure of the churches to reach neediest sections of our cities. Success of the Salvation Army. Something for the churches to learn from the Army. Modifications of ideals and methods needed in the churches.

§ 149

Questions: Organization of the Y. M. C. A. Its original purpose? How has it enlarged this purpose? What are some of the benefits of the organization? Some of the departments of its work? Opportunity for the layman? Present extent of its work?

Organization and work of Y. W. C. A.?

Organization of the young people in the churches? Purpose of these organizations? What are the principal bodies?

What is the Federal Council of the Churches? What is its purpose? Its authority? What denominations are now represented? How is its work done? What has it accomplished?

Topics: Religious and moral conditions within and without the churches which occasioned the formation of extra-ecclesiastical organizations such as the Y. M. C. A. Character of the Christianity which they represent. The distinctly religious element in their work.

Value of the young people's organizations as a means of education and training. Probable effects on the future activities of the churches.

§ 150

Questions: Present interest of the world in religion? Main religions of the world with the number of their adherents? Numerical relation of Christians to others? Numerical relations of the three great groups of Christians?

Topics: Christians most numerous though Christianity is next to the youngest of the religions. Power and efficiency of the Christians as compared with the other religionists of the world. Christianity has lifted most of its adherents from barbarism to their present status within the Christian era. Progress thus far as a guarantee of success in the future.

BIBLIOGRAPHY

Suggestions as to Books that may be used with this volume in reference work.

The better encyclopedias are very serviceable. The following are the best: *The New Schaff-Herzog Encyclopedia of Religious Knowledge,* N. Y., 1908–12; *The Catholic Encyclopedia,* N. Y., 1907–12, particularly important for all Catholic questions; *Encyclopedia of Religion and Ethics,* N. Y., 1908–, not complete, very full and scholarly on all matters treated; *The Encyclopedia Britannica,* eleventh edition, N. Y., 1910.

SOURCE BOOKS: J. C. Ayer, *A Source Book of Ancient Church History, from the Apostolic Age to the Close of the Conciliar Period,* N. Y., 1913; Henderson, *Select Historical Documents of the Middle Ages,* London, 1912; Robinson, *Readings in European History,* 2 vols., N. Y., 1904 and 1906; Gee and Hardy, *Documents Illustrative of English Church History,* London, 1896. On Creeds consult Schaff, *Creeds of Christendom,* 4th ed., N. Y., 1905; Walker, *Creeds and Platforms of Congregationalism,* N. Y., 1893; McGlothlin, *Baptist Confessions of Faith,* Philadelphia, 1911.

Manuals of Church History covering the entire history are Walker, *A History of the Christian Church,* N. Y., 1918, latest and probably the best history of moderate length; Zenos, *Compendium of Church History,* Philadelphia, 1903, brief but good; Newman, *A Manual of Church History,* 2 vols., Philadelphia, 1908; Hurst, *A History of the Christian Church,* 2 vols., N. Y.; very full is Schaff, *A History of the Christian Church,* N. Y., extending to the Reformation.

Histories of Doctrine are Fisher, *History of Christian Doctrine,* N. Y., 1896, the best one volume history; smaller works are Workman, *Christian Thought to the Reformation* (N. Y., 1911), McGiffert, *Protestant Thought before Kant*

311

(N. Y., 1911) and Moore, *History of Christian Thought Since Kant,* N. Y., 1912; McGiffert, *The Rise of Modern Religious Ideas,* N. Y., 1915.

The literature of the various periods and phases of Church History is boundless and extended bibliographies may be found in all the larger works. Only a few additional books can be mentioned here. In making up the list the needs of college students have been kept constantly in mind.

On the early period consult Duchesne, *The Early History of the Christian Church from its Foundation to the End of the Fifth Century,* 2 vols., N. Y., 1909, 1912; Gwatkin, *Early Church History to* A. D. 313, 2 vols., London, 1909; very important is Harnack, *The Mission and Expansion of Christianity in the First Three Centuries,* 2 vols., N. Y., 1908; Dobschütz, *Christian Life in the Primitive Church,* N. Y., 1904; Workman, *Persecution in the Early Church,* London, 1906; Glover, *The Conflict of Religions within the Roman Empire,* London, 1909; Harnack, *Constitution and Law of the Church in the First Two Centuries,* N. Y., 1910; Lowrie, *Monuments of the Early Church,* N. Y., 1901.

On the Greek Church consult the following: Hore, *Student's History of the Greek Church,* N. Y., 1902; Adeney, *The Greek and Eastern Churches,* N. Y., 1908.

For the Middle Ages the following will be found valuable: Maclear, *A History of Christian Missions During the Middle Ages,* London, 1863; Taylor, *The Mediæval Mind,* 2 vols., N. Y., 1914; Harnack, *Monasticism; Its Ideals and Its History,* N. Y., 1895; Workman, *The Evolution of the Monastic Ideal,* London, 1913; Hefele, *A History of the Christian Councils,* Edinburgh, 1871–96; *The Cambridge Mediæval History,* vol. II (*Rise of the Saracens and the Foundation of the Western Empire*), N. Y., 1913; Bryce, *The Holy Roman Empire,* London, 1904; Lagarde, *The Latin Church in the Middle Ages,* N. Y., 1915; Krüger, *The Papacy: the Idea and Its Exponents,* N. Y., 1909; Ludlow, *The Age of the Crusades,* N. Y., 1896; Adams, *Civilization During the Middle Ages,* N. Y., 1900; Workman, *The Church of the West in the Middle Ages,* London, 1900, 2 vols.

For the Renaissance and Reformation the student may

consult the following: Workman, *The Dawn of the Reformation,* London, 1901 ; Van Dyke, *Age of Renascence,* N. Y., 1900; Symonds, *Short History of the Renaissance in Italy;* Walker, *The Reformation,* N. Y., 1900; Lindsay, *A History of the Reformation,* N. Y., 1907; Vedder, *The Reformation in Germany,* N. Y., 1914; Baird, *History of the Rise of the Huguenots,* 5 vols., N. Y., 1907.

For the Baptist Movement Newman, *A History of Anti-Pædobaptism,* Philadelphia, 1897; Vedder, *A Short History of the Baptists,* Philadelphia, 1907.

For the Reformation in Great Britain read Frere, *The English Church in the Reigns of Elizabeth and James I,* N. Y., 1904; Pollard, *Henry VIII,* London, 1905; Fleming, *The Scottish Reformation,* London, 1910; Clark, *History of English Non-Conformity,* 2 vols., London, 1913; Barclay, *The Inner Life of the Religious Societies of the Commonwealth,* London, 1879.

The complexity of modern Christian History and the multiplicity of books on it make it impossible to do more than refer to a few books on various phases of the subject.

On Missions consult Warneck, *Outline of the History of Protestant Missions,* Edinburgh, 1906; Faunce, *The Social Aspects of Foreign Missions,* N. Y., 1914; Robinson, *History of Christian Missions,* N. Y., 1915; Carver, *Missions and Modern Thought,* N. Y., 1908.

Townsend (and others), *A New History of Methodism,* 2 vols., London, 1909; Church, *The Oxford Movement,* London, 1891.

Hurst, *History of Rationalism,* etc., N. Y., 1901 ; Lichtenberger, *History of German Theology in the Nineteenth Century,* Edinburgh, 1889; Swing, *The Theology of Albrecht Ritschl,* N. Y., 1901.

For American Christianity the *American Church History,* 13 vols., by various authors, is the best. It is a history by denominations. There is no good comprehensive view of American Christianity as a whole; Dorchester, *Christianity in the United States,* N. Y., 1895, is probably the best.

Biographies of Christian leaders are numberless and the titles can be obtained from encyclopedia articles and from the books referred to above.

INDEX

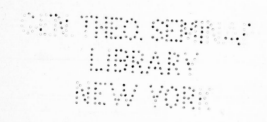

Psychology and Preaching

By CHARLES S. GARDNER

Cloth, 12mo. *Price $2.00*

" Psychology and Preaching " is a thorough study of the more important mental processes involved in preaching, from the standpoint of functional psychology.

After a discussion of the general mental processes — intellectual, emotional and voluntary — as they function in preaching, it takes up first the psychic phenomena of the mass as they appear in assembly and community groups; second, three important occupational types, the minister, the laboring man and the business man; third, the " modern mind " or the peculiar mental attitudes of modern men as contrasted with the characteristic attitudes of more primitive men. The book should be especially helpful to ministers, as well as of service to all who are interested in present day religious problems.

Public speakers generally should find it suggestive.

———

THE MACMILLAN COMPANY
Publishers   64-66 Fifth Avenue   New York

Jewish Theology: Systematically and Historically Considered

By DR. KAUFMANN KOHLER,
President of Hebrew Union College

$2.50

This is the first complete systematic presentation of Jewish Theology to appear in English; the work of a scholar of international reputation, now president of the Hebrew Union College. Its five hundred pages give a detailed yet popular exposition of the belief of Judaism. It will serve both as a text-book for students and as a general source of enlightenment for Jewish and Christian readers.

Dr. Kohler divides his text into three main parts: Part I, God; in which God As He Makes Himself Known to Man, The Idea of God in Judaism and God in Relation to the World, are taken up; Part II, Man; and Part III, Israel and The Kingdom of God.

THE MACMILLAN COMPANY
Publishers   64-66 Fifth Avenue   New York

The Bible at a Single View

With an Appendix on How to Read the Bible

By RICHARD G. MOULTON,

Editor of *The Modern Reader's Bible*

Cloth, 12mo. $1.00

Dr. Moulton's purpose in this book is, as indicated in his title, to present a concise view of the Bible, a view which shall make clear its general character and content and prepare the reader for more detailed study afterward. Dr. Moulton's training and research — he is the author of many books bearing on the Bible and the editor of *The Modern Reader's Bible* — well fit him for the task which he has chosen. This presentation of the broad outlines of the Bible cannot but lead to a more general and clearer appreciation of the content and real spirit of "the greatest book in the world." The appendix offers a course in Bible reading calculated to conserve time and energy and to bring better results than disorganized Bible reading.

THE MACMILLAN COMPANY
Publishers   64–66 Fifth Avenue   New York

DATE DUE

▓▓▓			
▓▓▓			
▓▓			
GAYLORD			PRINTED IN U.S.A.